The Methodology of the Prophets in Calling to Allaah

That is the Way of Wisdom and Intelligence

by
Shaykh Rabee' ibn Haadee al-Madkhalee

Translated by
Aboo Talhah Daawood ibn Ronald Burbank

ISBN 1 898649 17 0

British Library Cataloguing in Publication Data.
A catalogue record for this book is available from the British Library.

First Edition, 1417AH/1997CE

© Copyright 1997 by Al-Hidaayah Publishing and Distribution

All rights reserved. No part of this publication may be reproduced in any language, stored in a retrieval system or transmitted in any form or by any means, electronic, mechanical, photocopying, recording or otherwise without the express permission of the copyright owner.

Printed by: All Trade Printers, Birmingham, U.K.

Typeset by: Al-Hidaayah Publishing and Distribution

Published by: Al-Hidaayah Publishing and Distribution
P.O. Box 3332
Birmingham
United Kingdom
B10 9AW

Tel: 0121 753 1889
Fax: 0121 753 2422
E-Mail: AHPD@Hidaayah.Demon.Co.UK

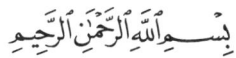

Publishers Note

All praise is due to Allaah, Lord of the worlds. Peace and prayers be upon Muhammad, his family, his Companions and all those who follow in their footsteps until the Last Day.

This is an English translation of the Arabic book, "*Manhajul Ambiyaa fee Da'wah Ilallaah*," by Shaykh Rabee' ibn Haadee al-Madkhalee. The book deals with the extremely important issue of the methodology of giving *da'wah* - it is especially relevant as we live in a time in which there are many Islamic groups, each with its own set of priorities.

Shaykh Rabee' is one of the scholars of Madeenah, who has many books to his credit, and is well known for his strict adherence to the *Sunnah*. He has been recommended and spoken highly of by some of the greatest scholars of our time among them Shaykh 'Abdul-'Azeez bin Baaz who said regarding him and another Shaykh, "Both of these men are from Ahlus-Sunnah and are well known to me for their knowledge, excellence, and correct *'aqeedah*... So I advise that benefit be taken from their books..."

We would like to thank the brothers and sisters who helped in this project particularly the translator for his hard work in translating and in providing an explanatory translation of all the *Aayaat* based on the classical books of *tafseer*. Special thanks are due to Dr. 'Abdullaah al-Farsi for checking the translation and providing some useful points that have been incorporated into the "Introduction to the English Edition."

Al-Hidaayah Publishing and Distribution

Note: All references quoted refer to the Arabic books unless otherwise stated.

Contents

- Introduction to the English Edition — 5
- Preface — 9
- Author's Introduction — 24
- Mankind has been Blessed with Intellect and Natural Inclination to the Truth — 32
- Mankind has been Blessed by the Sending of the Messengers and the Books Which have been Revealed to them — 34
- The Importance of *Tawheed al-Uloohiyyah* (Singling out Allaah with all Worship) — 37
- Examples From the Calls of Some of the Messengers — 41
  - Nooh — 50
  - Ibraaheem — 56
  - Yoosuf — 72
  - Moosaa — 80
  - The Escalation of the Tyranny of the Pharaoh and how Moosaa and his People Faced it with Patient Perseverance and Forbearance — 84
  - Muhammad (ﷺ) — 87
  - The Torture Endured by the Companions Because of their Adherence to *Tawheed* — 94
  - The Great Importance Given to the *'Aqeedah* in the Madinan Period — 96
- A Summary of the *Da'wah* of the Prophets — 135
- The View of the Scholars of Islaam with Regard to the Imaamate and their Proofs of its Obligation — 181
- Conclusion — 227
- Appendix — 228
- Glossary — 244

بِسْمِ اللَّهِ الرَّحْمَنِ الرَّحِيمِ

Introduction to the English Edition

All praise and thanks are for Allaah alone, and may his *salaat* and *salaam* be upon his final Messenger Muhammad.

Anyone who has studied the Qur'aan and the *Sunnah* knows that the loftiest goal which the Muslim aims to implement in himself and amongst the people is the worship of Allaah alone without partner. Every action which the Muslim does within the *Sharee'ah*, then He does them as a means to a higher goal which is the worship of Allaah alone. This is the purpose for which he was created, as Allaah says in his book:

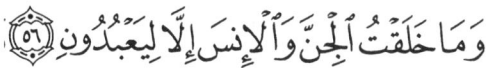

"I have not created the jinn and mankind except to worship me alone."

[Soorah adh-Dhaariyat (51):56]

So the Muslim's prayer, his fasting, and his sacrifices are all a means to establish the *tawheed* of Allaah; that he alone is worshipped. The same applies in his call (*da'wah*) to Allaah: it too is a means to achieve the goal, which is the establishment of *tawheed*. This is the goal which all the Prophets and Messengers worked towards in their call, as Shaykh Rabee' ibn Haadee al-Madkhalee explains in this book of his entitled: "The Methodology of the Prophets in Calling to Allaah - That is the way of Wisdom and Intelliegence." In this book, Shaykh Rabee' emphasises, with proofs, that the call of the prophets was an organised call resting upon strong foundations and firm pillars. One of the most important pillars which their call rested upon was that the Prophets always began their call with that which was of primary importance, then with that which comes next in importance and so on. So all of the Prophets, from the first of them to the last of them, followed a single methodology in their call and began from a single starting point which is the establishment of *tawheed*, the root of all fundamentals, and the removal of *shirk*, the greatest of all oppression. This is the greatest and most important issue which they relentlessly conveyed to all mankind, despite their varying situations, times and conditions. So every Messengser sent to his people began his call by saying:

$$\text{قَالَ يَنقَوْمِ ٱعْبُدُواْ ٱللَّهَ مَا لَكُم مِّنْ إِلَٰهٍ غَيْرُهُۥ}$$

"O my people! Worship Allaah, you have none other worthy of worship but him."

[Soorah al-A'raaf (7):65]

Shaykh Rabee' further strengthens his arguments in the book by discussing in detail the methodology of specific Prophets in their call to Allaah about whom Allaah speaks in his book and whose example he obligates us to follow. He speaks about how all of them proceeded upon a single methodology in their da'*wah* which had as its beginning, goal and end the *tawheed* of Allaah, the Mighty and Majestic. And at the head of them is the Seal of the Prophets and Messengers, Muhammad (ﷺ), whose example and method of giving *da'wah* is the best example and the complete methodology, in that he remained in Makkah for thirteen years, calling the people to *tawheed* and forbidding them from *shirk*, before he ordered them with prayer, *zakaah*, fasting and *hajj* and before he forbade them them from usury, fornication and theft. This is the clear way which the Prophet left us upon. As the Prophet (ﷺ) said: *"I have left you upon the clear and pure white ground, whose night [is as clear] as its day - no one deviates from it except that he is destroyed"*

[*Hasan*, reported by Ahmad, Ibn Maajah and al-Haakim]

So the way is clear, leaving no room for opinion or analogy, and it has as its signposts the Book and the *Sunnah*. It is only by following the Prophetic way that this *ummah* can return to the honour and glory that it once enjoyed. This is because any call which is not adhering to the Prophetic methodology is an imperfect call, either through addition or deletion, and any call which is imperfect causes an obstacle between Islaam and the hearts, since that which is imperfect and deficient does not lead to that which is perfect and complete. So the matter is as Imaam Maalik, *rahimahullaah*, said, "The end of this *ummah* will not be corrected except by that which corrected its first part."

Today we find many enthusiastic youth who want to see the establishmentof Allaah's law on earth and for the Muslims to become uppermost (but) who are confused about the true perception of affairs. So you see them making light of important matters whilst overinflating matters of lesser importance. And turning the means towards the goals into goals in themselves! They have neglected the importance of *'aqeedah* (correct beliefs) and have instead turned all their attitudes to other matters, which, though important, are not the most important matter and are not those things which the Prophets focussed their call on. So some of them call for the correction of rule and politics. Others give primary importance to practising certain *dhikrs* (rememberence of Allaah) and rituals in the manner of the Soofees. Some speak only of uniting the ranks of the Muslims, without caring about their creed and beliefs, and yet others concentrate on touring the land and attracting people to join them. As the esteemed Shaykh, Saalih al Fawzaan points out in his introduction of this book, their example is "like the case of one who seeks to cure a body whose head has been cut off, since the place of 'aqeedah in the Religion is like the head with respect to the body."

Shaykh Rabee' discusses the methodologies of the contemporary *da'wah* movements who are at variance with the methodology of the Prophets in calling to Allaah and contrasts them in order to precisely show the manner in which these groups and movements have deviated from the Prophetic way in their goals and means. He discusses this issue in a clear, frank and scholarly way, every time quoting proofs and witnesses to what he says.

We ask Allaah to bless Shaykh Rabee' al-Madkhalee for his work and to reward him handsomely for his efforts. And may he guide all those who read this book to the correct methodology, which is the methodolgy of the Prophets, make them firm upon it and grant us its fruits and its blessings in this world and the hereafter. *Aameen*.

Our final call is that all praise and thanks are for Allaah, Lord of all the worlds.

Al-Hidaayah Publishing and Distribution
20th Ramadaan 1417
(30/1/1997)

Preface

All praise is for Allaah, Lord of all the Worlds, who ordered us to follow His Messenger (ﷺ) and to call to His Way, and may Allaah send praises and blessings of peace upon our Prophet Muhammad, and upon his family, his Companions, and those who truly follow them until the Day of Judgement. To proceed:

Calling to Allaah (*ad-Daw'ah ilallaah*) is the way of the Messenger (ﷺ) and his followers, as Allaah, the Most High, says:

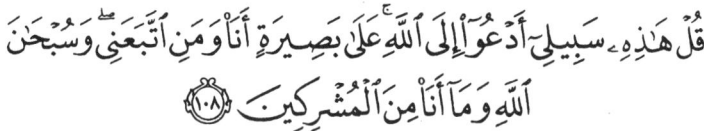

"**Say, O Muhammad (ﷺ): This is my way, I call to Allaah (i.e. to the testification that none has the right to be worshipped except Allaah, alone, with no partner) upon certain knowledge - I, and those who follow me. I declare Allaah free and far removed from all that they associate as partners with Him, and I am free of those who worship anything else along with Him.**"[1]

Indeed calling to Allaah was the mission of all the Messengers and their followers, in order to bring the people out from darkness and into light, from unbelief (*kufr*) to true Faith (*eemaan*), from *shirk*[2] to *tawheed*[3], and from the Fire to Paradise. This call to Allaah rests upon firm pillars, and is established upon foundations which are absolutely essential. If any

---

[1] Soorah Yoosuf (12):108.
[2] Attribution of worship or any of Allaah's Rights to others besides Allaah.
[3] The pure worship of Allaah alone, recognising Him as the sole Lord - the possessor of the most perfect Names and Attributes.

of these are missing the *da'wah* will not be correct and will not produce the desired results - no matter how much effort is expended and time wasted - and this is the reality which we witness with regard to many of the present day calls which are not supported by those pillars and built upon those foundations. These pillars which support the correct *da'wah* are clearly shown in the Book and the *Sunnah*, and can be summarised as follows:

1. Knowledge of that which one calls to:

Since the ignorant person is not suitable to be a caller (*daa'ee*). Allaah, the Most High, said to His Prophet (ﷺ):

$$قُلْ هَٰذِهِۦ سَبِيلِىٓ أَدْعُوٓا۟ إِلَى ٱللَّهِ عَلَىٰ بَصِيرَةٍ أَنَا۠ وَمَنِ ٱتَّبَعَنِى$$

"Say, O Muhammad (ﷺ): This is my way, I call to Allaah (to the testification that none has the right to be worshipped except Allaah, alone, having no partner) upon certain knowledge (*baseerah*). I, and those who follow me."[4]

'*Baseerah*' is knowledge. So the caller is certain to face those who are scholars of misguidance, those who will attack him with doubts and futile arguments in order to rebut the truth. Allaah, the Most High, says,

$$وَجَٰدِلْهُم بِٱلَّتِى هِىَ أَحْسَنُ$$

"And argue with them in a way that is better."[5]

Furthermore the Prophet (ﷺ) said to Mu'aadh, *radiyallaahu 'anhu*, *"You are going to a people from the People of the Book."* So if the caller is not armed with sufficient knowledge for him to face every doubt and

---

[4] Soorah Yoosuf (12):108.
[5] Soorah an-Nahl (16):125.

contend with every opponent, then he will be defeated in the first encounter, and will be halted at the beginning of the way.

2. Acting in accordance with that which he calls to:

So that he will be a good example - his actions attesting to his words, and leaving no excuse for the opponents of the Truth. Allaah, the Most High, said about His Prophet Shu'ayb that he said to his people:

$$\text{وَمَا أُرِيدُ أَنْ أُخَالِفَكُمْ إِلَىٰ مَا أَنْهَاكُمْ عَنْهُ ۚ إِنْ أُرِيدُ إِلَّا ٱلْإِصْلَاحَ مَا ٱسْتَطَعْتُ}$$

"I do not wish to forbid you from something and then do it myself. Rather I only wish to rectify you as far as I am able."[6]

Allaah, the Most High, said to His Prophet Muhammad (ﷺ):

$$\text{قُلْ إِنَّ صَلَاتِي وَنُسُكِي وَمَحْيَايَ وَمَمَاتِي لِلَّهِ رَبِّ ٱلْعَالَمِينَ ۝ لَا شَرِيكَ لَهُ ۖ وَبِذَٰلِكَ أُمِرْتُ وَأَنَا۠ أَوَّلُ ٱلْمُسْلِمِينَ ۝}$$

"Say, O Muhammad (ﷺ): Indeed my Prayer, my sacrifice, my living and my dying are all purely and solely for Allaah, Lord of all the Worlds. There is no share in any of that for other than Him. That is what my Lord ordered me, and I am the first of this nation to submit to Allaah as a Muslim."[7]

---

[6] Soorah Hood (11):88.
[7] Soorah al-An'aam (6):162-163.

Allaah, the Most High, said:

$$\text{وَمَنْ أَحْسَنُ قَوْلًا مِّمَّن دَعَا إِلَى اللَّهِ وَعَمِلَ صَالِحًا وَقَالَ إِنَّنِي مِنَ الْمُسْلِمِينَ ﴿٣٣﴾}$$

"Who is better in speech than one who calls the people to Allaah and does righteous deeds?"[8]

3. Purity of intention (*al-ikhlaas*):

Such that the call is made purely and sincerely to seek the Face of Allaah (and seeking His Reward) - not for show, or repute, or status, or leadership, nor desiring worldly goals - since if any of these goals adulterate it, the call will not be for Allaah, rather it would then be a call for oneself or for the attainment of the worldly goal - as Allaah informs that His Prophets said to their people:

$$\text{لَا أَسْأَلُكُمْ عَلَيْهِ أَجْرًا}$$

"I do not ask you for any reward for conveying this Qur'aan."[9]

$$\text{لَا أَسْأَلُكُمْ عَلَيْهِ مَالًا}$$

"I do not ask you for any wealth for my admonition."[10]

4. Beginning with what is of primary importance, then with that which comes next in importance, and so on:

---

[8] Soorah Fussilat (41):33.
[9] Soorah al-An'aam (6):90.
[10] Soorah Hood (11):29.

So firstly he calls to the correction of *'aqeedah* (belief and creed) - by ordering that all worship is made for Allaah, and *shirk* is forbidden. Then ordering the establishment of the Prayer, and the payment of the *Zakah*, and that the obligatory duties are carried out and that forbidden things are avoided. This was the procedure followed by all of the Messengers, as Allaah, the Most High, says:

$$وَلَقَدْ بَعَثْنَا فِى كُلِّ أُمَّةٍ رَّسُولًا أَنِ ٱعْبُدُوا۟ ٱللَّهَ وَٱجْتَنِبُوا۟ ٱلطَّٰغُوتَ$$

"We sent a Messenger to every nation, ordering them that they should worship Allaah alone, obey Him and make their worship purely for Him, and that they should avoid everything worshipped besides Allaah."[11]

Allaah, the Most High, says:

$$وَمَآ أَرْسَلْنَا مِن قَبْلِكَ مِن رَّسُولٍ إِلَّا نُوحِىٓ إِلَيْهِ أَنَّهُۥ لَآ إِلَٰهَ إِلَّآ أَنَا۠ فَٱعْبُدُونِ ۝$$

"We did not send any Messenger before you, O Muhammad (ﷺ), except that We revealed to Him that none has the right to be worshipped except Allaah - so make all of your worship purely for Allaah."[12]

Furthermore when the Prophet (ﷺ) sent Mu'aadh to Yemen he (ﷺ) said to him, *"Indeed you are going to a people from the People of the*

---

11 Soorah an-Nahl (16):36.
12 Soorah al-Ambiyaa (21):25.

Book - so let the first thing that you call them to be the testification that none has the right to be worshipped except Allaah. So if they accept that then inform them that Allaah has obligated five Prayers upon them in each day and night..."

The best example of giving *da'wah* is to be found in the method of the Prophet (ﷺ) - it is the most perfect and complete methodology - in that he (ﷺ) remained in Makkah for thirteen years, calling the people to *tawheed* and forbidding them from *shirk*, before (he ordered) them with Prayer, *Zakaat*, Fasting and *Hajj*, and before he (ﷺ) forbade them from usury, fornication, theft and murder.

5. Patient perseverance in facing difficulties encountered in calling to Allaah, and in facing harm from the people:

For the path of *da'wah* is not strewn with roses, rather it is covered with hardships and hazards. The best example of this is the case of the Messengers, may Allaah's Praises and Blessings of peace be upon them all, with regard to the harm and the mockery which they suffered from their people. As Allaah, the Most High, said to His Messenger (ﷺ):

وَلَقَدِ ٱسْتُهْزِئَ بِرُسُلٍ مِّن قَبْلِكَ فَحَاقَ بِٱلَّذِينَ سَخِرُوا۟ مِنْهُم مَّا كَانُوا۟ بِهِۦ يَسْتَهْزِءُونَ ۝

"Indeed Messengers were mocked before you, but those who mocked them were overtaken by the punishment which they made light of."[13]

---

[13] Soorah al-An'aam (6):10.

He, the Most High, said:

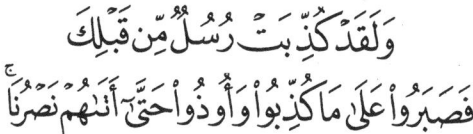

"Indeed Messengers were also denied before you, but they bore these denials with patient perseverance, and they suffered harm until Our help came to them."[14]

Likewise the followers of the Prophets are met with the same harm and hardship in proportion to their effort in calling to Allaah, following the example of those noble Messengers - may Allaah's praises and purest blessings of peace be upon them.

6. The caller must be a person of good manners:

He must use wisdom in his call, since this will be an important reason for the acceptance of his call. Just as Allaah ordered His two noble Prophets, Moosaa and Haaroon, that this was the manner in which they were to face the worst unbeliever upon the earth - Fir'awn (Pharaoh) - who claimed Lordship for himself. Allaah, the One free of all imperfections, said:

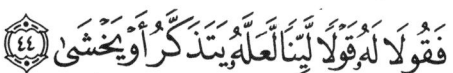

"And speak mildly to him that he might accept admonition or fear and obey Allaah."[15]

Allaah, the Most High, said to Moosaa, *'alayhis-salaatu was-salaam*:

---

[14] Soorah al-An'aam (6):34.
[15] Soorah Taa Haa (20):44.

اذْهَبْ إِلَىٰ فِرْعَوْنَ إِنَّهُ طَغَىٰ ۝

فَقُلْ هَل لَّكَ إِلَىٰ أَن تَزَكَّىٰ ۝ وَأَهْدِيَكَ إِلَىٰ رَبِّكَ فَتَخْشَىٰ ۝

"Go to Fir'awn (Pharaoh) who has transgressed all bounds in his haughtiness, pride and disbelief, and say, 'Will you not purify yourself from the sin of disbelief and be obedient to your Lord, so that you may submit fearfully to Him and obey Him?'"[16]

Allaah, the Most High, said, concerning His Prophet Muhammad (ﷺ):

فَبِمَا رَحْمَةٍ مِّنَ اللَّهِ لِنتَ لَهُمْ ۖ وَلَوْ كُنتَ فَظًّا غَلِيظَ الْقَلْبِ لَانفَضُّوا مِنْ حَوْلِكَ

"By the Mercy of Allaah you behaved with gentleness to them and had you been severe and harsh-hearted they would have left you and departed."[17]

Allaah, the Most High, says:

وَإِنَّكَ لَعَلَىٰ خُلُقٍ عَظِيمٍ ۝

"Indeed you, O Muhammad (ﷺ), are on an exalted standard of character."[18]

He, the Most High, says:

ادْعُ إِلَىٰ سَبِيلِ رَبِّكَ بِالْحِكْمَةِ وَالْمَوْعِظَةِ الْحَسَنَةِ ۖ وَجَادِلْهُم بِالَّتِي هِيَ أَحْسَنُ

---

[16] Soorah an-Naazi'aat (79):17-19.
[17] Soorah Aal-'Imraan (3):159.
[18] Soorah al-Qalam (68): 4.

"O Muhammad (ﷺ), call mankind to the way prescribed by your Lord (i.e. Islaam) with the Revelation sent down to you (the Book and the *Sunnah*), and admonish them with the examples and warnings which Allaah has provided in His Book, and argue with them in a way that is better."[19]

7. The caller must remain firm in his expectation and hope for good:

He should not despair of the effectiveness of his call, or about the guidance of his people. Nor should he despair about the aid and the help of Allaah, even if a long time passes, and again he has the best example in this matter in the Messengers of Allaah. So the Prophet of Allaah, Nooh, *'alayhis-salaatu was-salaam*, remained amongst his people for nine hundred and fifty years, calling them to Allaah.

Also when the harm and the hurt of the unbelievers became severe against the Prophet (ﷺ), and the angel of the mountains came to him (ﷺ) asking if he wanted him to crush them between the two mountains, he (ﷺ) replied, *"No, I wish to have patience with them, hopefully Allaah will produce from their offspring those who will worship Allaah alone, not giving any partner to Him."*[20] If the caller lacks this attribute he will halt at the start of the path and feel discouraged and frustrated.

So whichever call is not built upon these foundations, and whatever methodology is not from the methodology of the Messengers then it will be frustrated and fail, and it will be toil without any benefit. The clearest proofs of this are those present day groups (*jamaa'aat*) which set out a

---

[19] Soorah an-Nahl (16):125.
[20] Reported by Bukhaaree (Eng. trans. 4/300 no.454) and Muslim (Eng. trans. 3/987 no.4425).

methodology and programme for themselves and their *da'wah* which is different to the methodology of the Messengers. These groups have neglected the importance of *'aqeedah* (correct belief and creed) - except for a very few of them - and instead call for the correction of side-issues. So one group calls for the correction of rule and politics, and demands establishment of the prescribed punishments, and that Islamic Law be applied in judging amongst the people, and this is indeed something very important, but it is not what is most important - **since how can one seek to establish and apply Allaah's Judgement upon the thief and the fornicator before seeking to establish and apply Allaah's Judgement upon the *mushrik*, the one who attributes worship to others besides Allaah?! How can we demand that Allaah's Judgement be applied to two men disputing about a sheep or a camel before demanding that Allaah's Judgement be applied to those who worship idols and graves, and those who deny or hold heretical beliefs with regard to Allaah's Names and Attributes, divesting them of their true meanings, or distorting them?!** Are these people not greater criminals than those who fornicate, drink wine and steal?! Those are crimes against mankind, whereas *shirk* and denial of Allaah's Names and Attributes are crimes against the Creator, the One free of all imperfections, and the right of the Creator has precedence over the rights of the creation.

Shaykhul-Islaam Ibn Taymiyyah says in his book, *al-Istiqaamah* (1/466): "So these sins along with correct *tawheed* are better than corrupted *tawheed* in the absence of these sins."[21]

---

[21] The proof for this is the Saying of Allaah, the Most High:

$$\text{إِنَّ ٱللَّهَ لَا يَغْفِرُ أَن يُشْرَكَ بِهِۦ وَيَغْفِرُ مَا دُونَ ذَٰلِكَ لِمَن يَشَآءُ}$$

"Allaah does not forgive that partners should be set up with Him in worship, but He forgives whatever is lesser than that to whom He pleases."

[Soorah an-Nisaa (4):48]

Then another *jamaa'ah* affiliates itself with *da'wah*, except that its methodology is also at variance with the methodology of the Messengers. They give no importance to correct *'aqeedah*, rather they give importance to worshipping and practising some *dhikr* (remembrance of Allaah) in the way of the *Sufis*.[22] *They* concentrate upon going out (*khurooj*) and touring the lands, and what is important to them is that they manage to attract the people to join them, without caring about their beliefs and creed (*'aqeedah*). All of these are innovated ways, taking as their starting point matters which were left until last in the call of the Messengers. This is just like the case of one who seeks to cure a body whose head has been cut off, since the place of *'aqeedah* in the religion is like the head with regard to the body. So it is necessary for these groups to correct their concepts and understanding by referring back to the Book and the *Sunnah* in order to know the methodology of the Messengers in calling to Allaah. For indeed Allaah, the One free of all imperfections, informed that correct rule and sovereignty, which is the central part of the call of the former *Jamaa'ah* whom we mentioned, cannot be achieved except after correcting *'aqeedah* such that all worship is for Allaah alone, and worship of everything else is abandoned. Allaah, the Most High, says:

$$\text{وَعَدَ ٱللَّهُ ٱلَّذِينَ ءَامَنُوا۟ مِنكُمْ وَعَمِلُوا۟ ٱلصَّٰلِحَٰتِ لَيَسْتَخْلِفَنَّهُمْ فِى ٱلْأَرْضِ كَمَا ٱسْتَخْلَفَ ٱلَّذِينَ مِن قَبْلِهِمْ وَلَيُمَكِّنَنَّ لَهُمْ دِينَهُمُ ٱلَّذِى ٱرْتَضَىٰ لَهُمْ وَلَيُبَدِّلَنَّهُم مِّنۢ بَعْدِ خَوْفِهِمْ أَمْنًا يَعْبُدُونَنِى لَا يُشْرِكُونَ بِى شَيْـًٔا وَمَن كَفَرَ بَعْدَ ذَٰلِكَ فَأُو۟لَٰٓئِكَ هُمُ ٱلْفَٰسِقُونَ ۝}$$

---

[22] Publisher's Note: For more information about Sufism refer to "The Reality of Sufism" by Muhammad ibn Rabee' ibn Haadee al-Madkhalee (Al-Hidaayah Publishing and Distribution, U.K., 1995).

> "Allaah has promised those who truly believe (have true *eemaan*) amongst you, and act in obedience to Allaah and His Messenger, that He will grant them rulership upon the earth just as He granted it to those before them, and that He will establish their religion for them, grant them authority to practise the religion which He chose for them and ordered. And He will certainly change their situation to one of security, after their fear, providing that they worship and obey Me, not associating anything else in worship with Me. Then whoever rejects this favour by disobedience to their Lord, then they are the rebellious transgressors."[23]

So these people wish to establish the Islamic State before purifying the lands of idolatrous beliefs which take shape in the worship of the dead, and devotion to tombs, such as is no different to the worship of al-Laat, al-'Uzzaa and the third of them Manaat,[24] rather it is worse. So they are attempting that which is impossible.

Indeed establishment and application of the *Sharee'ah* and the prescribed punishments; establishment of the Islamic State; avoidance of whatever is prohibited; and achievement of whatever is obligatory - all of these things are from the rights of *tawheed*, and matters which perfect it and follow on from it. So how can we give attention to that which is subsidiary whilst neglecting that which is of primary importance?

It is my view that the fact that these groups are at variance with the methodology of the Messengers in calling to Allaah is a result of their igno-

---

[23] Soorah an-Noor (24):55.
[24] Publisher's Note: These were some of the idols that were worshipped by the Quraysh at the time of the Prophet (ﷺ).

rance of this methodology, and the ignorant person is not suitable to be a caller, since one of the most important conditions for *da'wah* is knowledge, as Allaah, the Most High, says about His Prophet:

$$\text{قُلْ هَٰذِهِۦ سَبِيلِىٓ أَدْعُوٓا۟ إِلَى ٱللَّهِ عَلَىٰ بَصِيرَةٍ أَنَا۠ وَمَنِ ٱتَّبَعَنِى وَسُبْحَٰنَ ٱللَّهِ وَمَآ أَنَا۠ مِنَ ٱلْمُشْرِكِينَ ۝}$$

> "Say, O Muhammad (ﷺ): This is my way, I call to Allaah (i.e. to the testification that none has the right to be worshipped except Allaah, alone, with no partner) upon certain knowledge - I, and those who follow me. I declare Allaah free and far removed from all that they associate as partners with Him, and I am free of those who worship anything else along with Him."[25]

So one of the most important qualifications for a caller (*daa'ee*) is knowledge.[26] Then we see that these groups (*Jamaa'aat*) which attribute themselves to *da'wah* are at variance with each other. Each group lays down a programme different to the programme of the others and follows a different methodology to it. This is the inevitable consequence of contradicting the methodology of the Messenger (ﷺ), since the way and methodology of the Messenger (ﷺ) is a single way, containing no division, nor divergence, as Allaah, the Most High, says:

$$\text{قُلْ هَٰذِهِۦ سَبِيلِىٓ أَدْعُوٓا۟ إِلَى ٱللَّهِ عَلَىٰ بَصِيرَةٍ أَنَا۠ وَمَنِ ٱتَّبَعَنِى}$$

---

[25] Soorah Yoosuf (12):108.
[26] But some of those who claim to be callers to Islaam, if you were to ask them, "What is Islaam?" "What are the things which negate Islaam?" Then they would not be able to give a correct answer, so how can it be permissible for such a person to be a caller (*daa'ee*)?!

> "Say, O Muhammad (ﷺ): This is my way, I call to Allaah (i.e. to the testification that none has the right to be worshipped except Allaah, alone, with no partner) upon certain knowledge - I, and those who follow me."[27]

So the followers of the Messenger (ﷺ) are upon this single way and are not divided and split. Rather those who contradict this way are the ones who divide amongst themselves, as Allaah, the Most High, says:

$$\text{وَأَنَّ هَٰذَا صِرَٰطِى مُسْتَقِيمًا فَٱتَّبِعُوهُ وَلَا تَتَّبِعُوا۟ ٱلسُّبُلَ فَتَفَرَّقَ بِكُمْ عَن سَبِيلِهِۦ}$$

> "This is my Straight Path, so follow it, and do not follow any of the other paths, for they will split you and take you away from that way which He prescribed for you."[28]

So because these groups (*Jamaa'aat*) are a threat to Islaam which may obstruct it, or prevent people from entering into it, then this is something which must be properly explained, and it must be made clear that this is something which is not from Islaam at all. Allaah, the Most High, says,

$$\text{إِنَّ ٱلَّذِينَ فَرَّقُوا۟ دِينَهُمْ وَكَانُوا۟ شِيَعًا لَّسْتَ مِنْهُمْ فِى شَىْءٍ}$$

> "Those who divide up the true religion and break up into sects and parties, you, O Muhammad, have nothing to do with them."[29]

---

[27] Soorah Yoosuf (12):108.
[28] Soorah al-An'aam (6):153.
[29] Soorah al-An'aam (6):159.

So since explanation of this is obligatory and it is binding to make it clear, a group of scholars having sincere concern for Islaam and the required level of knowledge and research took on the task of indicating the mistakes of these groups and explaining where they are at variance in *da'wah* with the methodology of the Prophets, so that they may return to what is correct. Indeed the truth is that which the Muslim always seeks, and so that those who do not realise their errors may not be beguiled by them. So from these scholars who took on this great duty of acting upon the saying of the Prophet (ﷺ), *"The religion is sincere advice, the religion is sincere advice, the religion is sincere advice." We said, "To whom, O Messenger of Allaah?" He said, "To Allaah, and to His Book, and to His Messenger, and to the rulers of the Muslims and their common folk,"* - from those who explained this matter and gave sincere advice about it is the noble Shaykh, Dr. Rabee' ibn Haadee al-Madkhalee in his book entitled, 'The Methodology of the Prophets in Calling to Allaah, That is the Way of Wisdom and Intelligence.' For he explains, may Allaah grant him success and reward him with good, the methodology of the Messengers in calling to Allaah, as it is shown in the Book of Allaah and the *Sunnah* of His Messenger (ﷺ). He presents the methodologies of the variant groups in the light of this in order to clearly show the difference between the methodology of the Messengers and these differing and contrasting methodologies which are at variance with it. He discusses these methodologies in the scholarly way and in a just way, whilst quoting examples and witnesses to what he says. So his book, and all praise and thanks are for Allaah, accomplishes the goal, and is fully sufficient for those who desire the truth, and is a proof upon those who are stubborn and obstinate in opposing what is correct.

So we ask Allaah to reward him for his work, and to cause it to be of benefit, and may Allaah send praise and blessings of peace upon Muhammad, his family and true followers, and His Companions.

Written by: Saalih ibn Fawzaan
Teacher in Imaam Muhammad ibn Sa'ud Islamic University.

Author's Introduction

Indeed all praise is for Allaah, we praise Him, we ask for His help, and for His forgiveness. We seek Allaah's refuge from the evils of ourselves and from our evil actions. Whomever Allaah guides, then none can lead him astray, and whomever Allaah misguides, then none can guide him. I testify that none has the right to be worshipped except Allaah, alone, having no partner, and I testify that Muhammad is His Slave and His Messenger. He sent him with guidance and the true religion, that he should make it manifest and victorious over all religions, even though the disbelievers hate that.

A number of matters led me to write about this matter, the most important of them being:

Firstly, the *ummah* of Islaam is in a state of disagreement and divergence in many different areas, both with regard to *'aqeedah* and other matters besides, and they have taken divergent paths. Then a number of calamities have befallen them as a result of this divergence, and due to the fact that in matters of disagreement they do not refer back for their resolution to the Book of their Lord and the *Sunnah* of their Prophet. The true extent and seriousness of these calamities is known only to Allaah - the splits in their ranks, the blazing fires of disputes and arguments between them, then the subjugation of the lands of Islaam by the enemies, and their (the disbelievers) desecration of their abodes, their enslavement and the humiliation of the Muslims.

Secondly, the appearance of ideologies in the Islamic field having their own particular programmes and methodologies to rescue and rectify the condition of the *ummah*. Some are political, some are intellectual, some are spiritual. The followers of each of these ideologies claim that their ideology is the true methodology of Islaam which must be followed and which can alone save the *ummah*.

These two reasons, along with others, prompted me to carry out one of the greatest and most important obligations: explaining the methodology of the Prophets in calling to Allaah, in the light of the Book and the *Sunnah*, and to explain the characteristics which are particular to it, and to make clear the necessity of following it alone, since it is the sole way leading to Allaah, which earns His Pleasure, and it is the sole way to rescue the *ummah* and to attain ascendancy and nobility on this earth and happiness in the Hereafter.

Then, Allaah, the Most High, the Creator, the One who brought everything into existence, the One who formed and fashioned everything, the All-Knowing, the All-Wise, created this tremendous creation and regulated it and ordered it, with His all-encompassing knowledge, His perfect wisdom and comprehensive power, and this was for very great and wise purposes, and lofty and noble goals, far removed from mere amusement, futility or play. Allaah, the Most High, says,

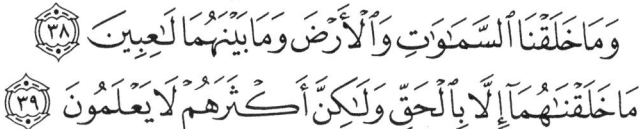

"We did not create the heavens and the earth and all that is between them in play. We did not create them except for a true and wise purpose (to test and examine who are obedient, and to reward them, and who are disobedient and punish them), but most of them do not know."[30]

---

[30] Soorah ad-Dukhaan (44):38-39.

Allaah, the Most High, says,

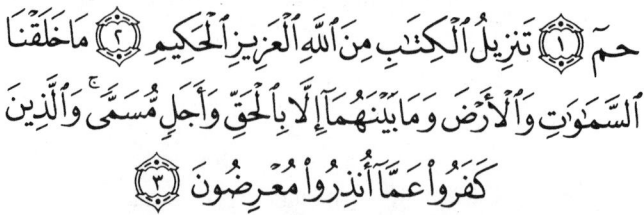

"**Haa Meem.** This Book (the Qur'aan) is sent down by Allaah, the All-Mighty, the All-Wise. We did not create the heavens and the earth and all that is between them except for a true and wise purpose, and for an appointed term. But those who disbelieve turn away heedlessly from the warning given to them."[31]

So He created the *jinn* and mankind and made clear the very great and wise purpose and noble goal for which He created them. He, the Most High, says,

"I did not create *jinn* and mankind except that they should worship Me. I do not seek provision from them, nor do I seek that they should feed themselves or the creation. Verily it is Allaah Who is the sole Provider, the All-Powerful."[32]

---

[31] Soorah al-Ahqaaf (46):1-3.
[32] Soorah adh-Dhaariyaat (51):56-58.

Allaah, the Most High, says,

$$\text{أَفَحَسِبْتُمْ أَنَّمَا خَلَقْنَاكُمْ عَبَثًا وَأَنَّكُمْ إِلَيْنَا لَا تُرْجَعُونَ ۝ فَتَعَالَى اللَّهُ الْمَلِكُ الْحَقُّ لَا إِلَٰهَ إِلَّا هُوَ رَبُّ الْعَرْشِ الْكَرِيمِ ۝}$$

> "Do you think that We created you in play and that you would not be brought back to Us? High and exalted is Allaah, the True King, above what the idolaters associate with Him. None has the right to be worshipped but Him, the Lord of the Glorious Throne."[33]

He, the Most High, says,

$$\text{أَيَحْسَبُ الْإِنسَانُ أَن يُتْرَكَ سُدًى ۝}$$

> "Does the disbeliever think that he will be left unaccountable, without being punished for disobeying the orders and prohibitions of his Lord?"[34]

He, the Most High, says,

$$\text{تَبَارَكَ الَّذِي بِيَدِهِ الْمُلْكُ وَهُوَ عَلَىٰ كُلِّ شَيْءٍ قَدِيرٌ ۝ الَّذِي خَلَقَ الْمَوْتَ وَالْحَيَاةَ لِيَبْلُوَكُمْ أَيُّكُمْ أَحْسَنُ عَمَلًا وَهُوَ الْعَزِيزُ الْغَفُورُ ۝}$$

> "Exalted is He in whose Hand is the dominion of everything, and He is able to do all things. He who created death and life to test who is the best and

---

[33] Soorah al-Mu'minoon (23):115-116.
[34] Soorah al-Qiyaamah (75):36.

most obedient in action, and He is All-Mighty (who severely punishes those who are disobedient), the Oft-Forgiving (who forgives those who turn in repentance to Him)."[35]

So Allaah, the Most High, informs that He created them only to test them, for it to be made clear which of them is best in action, by their submitting and complying to the way of Allaah and following the Messengers of Allaah. And Allaah, the Most High, says,

$$\text{يَـٰٓأَيُّهَا ٱلنَّاسُ ٱعْبُدُوا۟ رَبَّكُمُ ٱلَّذِى خَلَقَكُمْ وَٱلَّذِينَ مِن قَبْلِكُمْ لَعَلَّكُمْ تَتَّقُونَ ۞ ٱلَّذِى جَعَلَ لَكُمُ ٱلْأَرْضَ فِرَٰشًا وَٱلسَّمَآءَ بِنَآءً وَأَنزَلَ مِنَ ٱلسَّمَآءِ مَآءً فَأَخْرَجَ بِهِۦ مِنَ ٱلثَّمَرَٰتِ رِزْقًا لَّكُمْ ۖ فَلَا تَجْعَلُوا۟ لِلَّهِ أَندَادًا وَأَنتُمْ تَعْلَمُونَ ۞}$$

"O mankind, single out your Lord with worship; He who created you and all those who came before you so that you may be of those who seek to avoid Allaah's punishment and Anger, those whom Allaah is pleased with. He Who has made the earth a resting place for you and has made the sky a canopy, and sent down rain from the sky, and brought out with it crops and fruits from the earth as provision for you. So do not set up rivals with Allaah in your worship whilst you know that you have no Lord besides Him."[36]

---

[35] Soorah al-Mulk (67):1-2.
[36] Soorah al-Baqarah (2):21-22.

So He ordered them to fulfil the goal for which they were created. He also explains that He has made available to them every means which will help them to fulfil their great task, and He warned them against deviating from this goal and denying these great blessings:

$$\text{فَلَا تَجْعَلُوا لِلَّهِ أَندَادًا وَأَنتُمْ تَعْلَمُونَ ﴿٢٢﴾}$$

"So do not set up rivals with Allaah in your worship whilst you know that you have no Lord besides Him."[37]

Furthermore, Allaah, the Most High, says:

$$\text{وَلَقَدْ كَرَّمْنَا بَنِي ءَادَمَ وَحَمَلْنَٰهُمْ فِي ٱلْبَرِّ وَٱلْبَحْرِ وَرَزَقْنَٰهُم مِّنَ ٱلطَّيِّبَٰتِ وَفَضَّلْنَٰهُمْ عَلَىٰ كَثِيرٍ مِّمَّنْ خَلَقْنَا تَفْضِيلًا ﴿٧٠﴾}$$

"We have indeed honoured the children of Aadam and have carried them throughout the land (upon riding beasts) and the sea (upon ships), and have provided them with good and pure sustenance, and have given them excellence over many of those whom We created."[38]

Allaah did not give mankind this honour, excellence and high station except due to the importance of the goal for which they were created, which is the worship of Allaah, alone, and to glorify Him and to declare His being exalted and far removed from all defects and from having any part-

---

[37] Soorah al-Baqarah (2):22.
[38] Soorah al-Israa (17):70.

ners or rivals, and High is Allaah and far removed from any such thing. So Allaah often mentions the honour and excellence given to mankind and his standing within the creation, and that other creatures have been subjected to him for his ease and welfare, so that he should fulfil his duty and carry out the purpose for which he was created in the best and most complete manner. Allaah, the Most High, says,

قُل لِّعِبَادِيَ ٱلَّذِينَ ءَامَنُوا۟ يُقِيمُوا۟ ٱلصَّلَوٰةَ وَيُنفِقُوا۟ مِمَّا رَزَقْنَـٰهُمْ سِرًّا وَعَلَانِيَةً مِّن قَبْلِ أَن يَأْتِىَ يَوْمٌ لَّا بَيْعٌ فِيهِ وَلَا خِلَـٰلٌ ۝ ٱللَّهُ ٱلَّذِى خَلَقَ ٱلسَّمَـٰوَٰتِ وَٱلْأَرْضَ وَأَنزَلَ مِنَ ٱلسَّمَآءِ مَآءً فَأَخْرَجَ بِهِۦ مِنَ ٱلثَّمَرَٰتِ رِزْقًا لَّكُمْ ۖ وَسَخَّرَ لَكُمُ ٱلْفُلْكَ لِتَجْرِىَ فِى ٱلْبَحْرِ بِأَمْرِهِۦ ۖ وَسَخَّرَ لَكُمُ ٱلْأَنْهَـٰرَ ۝ وَسَخَّرَ لَكُمُ ٱلشَّمْسَ وَٱلْقَمَرَ دَآئِبَيْنِ ۖ وَسَخَّرَ لَكُمُ ٱلَّيْلَ وَٱلنَّهَارَ ۝ وَءَاتَىٰكُم مِّن كُلِّ مَا سَأَلْتُمُوهُ ۚ وَإِن تَعُدُّوا۟ نِعْمَتَ ٱللَّهِ لَا تُحْصُوهَآ ۗ إِنَّ ٱلْإِنسَـٰنَ لَظَلُومٌ كَفَّارٌ ۝

"Say, O Muhammad, to My slaves who have believed, that they should establish the obligatory prayers perfectly, and spend in charity from the sustenance We have provided for them, secretly and openly, before the coming of the Day of Resurrection when there will be no bargaining and no befriending. Allaah it is Who created the heavens and the earth from nothing, and He sends rain down from the sky and produces fruit and crops with it as a provision for you. He has caused ships to be at your disposal so that you may travel upon the sea (and carry provision from land to land) by His permission and He made the rivers to be of benefit to you. Furthermore, He made the sun and the moon to follow one another, constantly pursuing their courses, to be of benefit to you, and He made the night and the day to be of service to you. And He provided for you from all those things which you require, and if you were to count the blessings of Allaah upon you, then you would not be able to enumerate them (nor to give thanks for them). Indeed those of mankind who deny Allaah's favours, and attribute worship or thanks for the favours to other than Him, are great wrongdoers and extreme in ingratitude."[39]

---

[39] Soorah Ibraaheem (14):31-34.

Mankind has been Blessed with Intellect and Natural Inclination to the Truth

In addition to these great blessings and this great eminence which Allaah has given to mankind, He also gave them the blessing of intellect which raises them to the level of taking on responsibilities given by Allaah, and it also enables them to achieve and comprehend them. He also provided them with natural inclination to the truth which agrees with that which the Messengers of Allaah, *'alayhimus-salaatu was-salaam,* came with: the noble revelation and the true religion which Allaah prescribed, and laid down as the way to be followed for mankind upon the tongues of His noble Messengers, may Allaah's praises and blessings of peace be upon them all. Allaah, the Most High, says,

"So set your face straight upon the true religion, firmly upon His religion and obedience to Him, the true religion of Islamic monotheism (*al-Fitr*) upon which He created mankind.[40] There is to be no

---

[40] *Al-Fitr* means to bring and create, and *al-fitrah* is the condition resulting from it. The meaning is that mankind was born upon a disposition and nature which is ready to accept the true religion. So if he were to be left upon that he would continue upon it, but those who deviate from it do so due to following human weaknesses and blindly following others... (*an-Nihaayah* of Ibnul-Atheer 3/457). Al-Haafidh Ibn Hajr, *rahimahullaah*, said in *al-Fath* (3/248), "The people differ concerning what is meant by *al-Fitrah* and the most famous saying is that what is meant by the *Fitrah* is Islaam." =

change to the religion of Allaah. That is the true religion, yet most people do not know."[41]

Allaah's Messenger (ﷺ) said, *"There is no child born except that it is born upon the fitrah, then its parents cause it to become a Jew, or a Christian or a Magian. Just as an animal gives birth to perfect offspring, do you find them mutilated?"*[42]

'Iyaad ibn Himaar al-Mujaashi'ee, *radiyallaahu 'anhu*, said that the Prophet (ﷺ) gave a *khutbah* one day and said in his *khutbah*, *"Indeed my Lord, the Mighty and Majestic, ordered me to teach you that which you do not know. From that which he taught me this day, 'The wealth which I confer upon My servants is lawful for them, and I created my servants upon the true religion, but the devils came to them and turned them away from their true religion, and forbade for them that which I made lawful for them, and ordered them to associate in worship with Me that for which I sent down no authority..."*[43]

Ibn 'Abdul-Barr said, "That is what was well-known with most of the *salaf* (predecessors), and the scholars of explanation (of the Qur'aan) are agreed that what is meant by the saying of Allaah, the Most High, ...'the true religion of Islamic monotheism upon which He created mankind...' is Islaam."

[41] Soorah Room (30):30.
[42] Reported by Bukhaaree (Eng. trans. 2/247/nos. 440, 441) and Muslim (Eng. trans. 4/1398/no.6423) and in a wording reported by Bukhaaree (Eng. trans. 2/262no.476), Ahmad, Maalik in *al-Muwatta* and at-Tirmidhee, *"Every child is born upon the Fitrah..."*
[43] Reported by Muslim (Eng. trans. 4/1488 no.6853).

Mankind has been Blessed by the Sending of the Messengers and the Books Which have been Revealed to them

Then Allaah did not leave them having to rely upon the intellect and inclination to the correct way which He gave them, rather He also sent Messengers to them as bringers of good tidings and warners. He sent the Books along with them so that they would be a reference for them in those matters where they disagreed, so that no excuse would remain for the people and the proof would be established against them. Then after the sending of the Messengers there would be no remaining excuse for them before Allaah.

Then He obligated upon all the nations obedience to those chosen and excellent Messengers, and that they should follow them and comply with their way. Then He sent down the severest punishment upon those who belied and rejected them in this world, and He will send worse and more terrible punishment upon them, eternal, never-ending torment in the place of just recompense (i.e. Hell). So what was the message which these noble, chosen men, may Allaah's praises and blessings of peace be upon them, brought to their people? Indeed their mission covered everything good and banished every evil. They brought to mankind everything needed for their well-being and happiness in this world and the Hereafter. Indeed there is nothing good except that they informed the people of it, and nothing evil except that they warned the people against it.

From 'Abdullaah ibn 'Amr ibn al-'Aas, *radiyallaahu 'anhu,* who said, "We were on a journey and stopped to alight at a place. Some of us set up tents, others competed with one another in shooting arrows, and others grazed the animals. Then an announcer for Allaah's Messenger (ﷺ) announced that we should gather for the Prayer. So we gathered around Allaah's Messenger (ﷺ) and he said, *'There was never a Prophet before me except that it was a duty upon him that he should guide his nation to every good that he knew and warn them against every evil that he knew. Then as for this nation of yours, its security and well-being is at its beginning and it will be struck in its later part by afflictions, things which you would find disagreeable, and trials will come in succession each one making the previous one seem trifling. So the Believer will say, "This will cause my destruction," then it will be removed, and a further trial will come and the Believer will say, "Rather this is the one." So whoever wishes to be saved from the Fire and to enter Paradise should meet his end whilst having true eemaan in Allaah and the Last Day, and let him treat the people as he himself loves to be treated. Then whoever gives pledge of allegiance to a ruler and gives him his hand and heart sincerely, then let him obey him as far as he is able. Then if another comes to dispute his authority, then strike the neck of the later one.'*"[44] This was the Messengership of the Messengers, that they should guide to every good and warn against every evil. However where did they start, what did they begin with and what did they concentrate upon? There are a number of basic principles upon which their calls were based, and which were the starting point for calling the people to Allaah. These fundamental points and principles are:

1. *Tawheed*.
2. Prophethood.
3. The Hereafter.[45]

These three principles are the point of convergence of their calls, and are their fundamental principles. These are given the greatest importance in the Qur'aan and are fully explained in it. They are also its most important goals upon which it centres and which it continually mentions. It further

---

[44] Reported by Muslim (Eng. trans. 3/1025 no.4546), an-Nasaa'ee and Ibn Maajah.

[45] Imaam ash-Shawkaanee wrote a book in explanation of these three principles, entitled, *Irshaadul-Fuhool ilattifaaqish-Sharaai' 'alat-Tawheed wal-Ma'aad wan-Nubuwwaat,'* in it he quotes proofs from the Qur'aan and the Tawraat and Injeel.

quotes intellectual and physical proofs for them in all the *Soorahs* and in most of its stories and examples. This is known to those who have full understanding, are able to consider carefully and comprehend well. All the Books revealed by Allaah have given great importance to these points and all of the revealed ways are agreed upon them. Then the most important and sublime of these three principles, and the most fundamental of them all is *tawheed* of Allaah, the Blessed and the Most High. This is to be found in most of the *Soorahs* of the Qur'aan, with its three well known categories, indeed it is found actually in every *Soorah* of the Qur'aan. This is because the Qur'aan comprises:

1. Information about Allaah and His Names and Attributes, and this is, the *tawheed* of knowledge (*al-Tawheedul-'Ilmee al-Khabree*).

2. A call to worship Him alone and to attribute no other as a partner to Him in worship, and to reject everything else to which worship is directed besides Him. So this is *tawheed* of intention and requesting/asking (*at-Tawheedul-Iraadee at-Talabee*).

3. Orders and prohibitions and a command to be obedient to Him, and this is from the rights of *tawheed* and is a completion of it.

4. Information concerning the honour which He gives to the people of *tawheed* and the favours which He bestows upon them in this world and the Hereafter. So this is the reward for *tawheed*.

5. Information concerning *shirk,* and the punishment which He sends upon its people in this world, and the severe torment they receive in the Hereafter. So this is the punishment for those who abandon *tawheed*.

So all of the Qur'aan is about *tawheed* and its rights, and its reward; and about the seriousness of *shirk*, its people and the punishment they receive for it.[46]

---

[46] *Sharh at-Tahaawiyyah*, p.88, 1st Edition. 1392 *al-Maktabul-Islaamee*, and the basis if this is taken from the words of Ibn Taymiyyah and his student Ibnul-Qayyim, *rahimahumullaah,* and occurs in *Madaarijus-Saalikeen* of Ibnul-Qayyim (3/450).

The Importance of *Tawheed al-Uloohiyyah* (Singling out Allaah with all Worship)

I will discuss *tawheed* of Allaah with regard to worship (*Tawheed al-Uloohiyyah*) and its importance because of two reasons:

Firstly, that it is the most important part of the call of the Messengers presented to us in the Qur'aan, and because it was the reason for the continual struggle between them and their enemies, the proud and haughty, and the obstinate, in every nation. It has continued as the reason for conflict until this day, and perhaps it will continue as such until the Day of Resurrection, as a trial and test for the inheritors of the Messengers, and in order to raise their station.

Secondly, the most severe and dangerous deviation afflicting the Muslims in the east and the west is with regard to it, and this affects the majority of the ignorant amongst the Muslims and many of those who are educated and those who associate themselves with knowledge. So we will begin by presenting the calls of the Prophets in general, and then present the call of some of them in particular.

Allaah, the Most High, says,

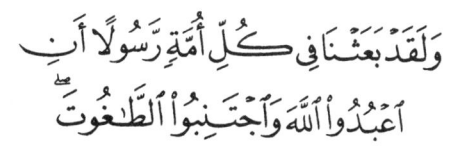

$$\text{وَلَقَدْ بَعَثْنَا فِى كُلِّ أُمَّةٍ رَّسُولًا أَنِ اعْبُدُوا۟ ٱللَّهَ وَٱجْتَنِبُوا۟ ٱلطَّٰغُوتَ}$$

"We sent a Messenger to every nation ordering them that they should worship Allaah alone, obey Him and make their worship purely for Him, and that they should avoid everything worshipped besides Allaah. So from them there were those whom Allaah guided to His religion, and there were those who were un-

believers for whom misguidance was ordained. So travel through the land and see the destruction that befell those who denied the Messengers and disbelieved."[47]

Allaah, the Most High, says,

$$وَمَآ أَرْسَلْنَا مِن قَبْلِكَ مِن رَّسُولٍ إِلَّا نُوحِىٓ إِلَيْهِ أَنَّهُۥ لَآ إِلَٰهَ إِلَّآ أَنَا۠ فَٱعْبُدُونِ ﴿٢٥﴾$$

"We did not send any Messenger before you, O Muhammad (ﷺ), except that We revealed to him that none has the right to be worshipped except Allaah, so make all of your worship purely for Him."[48]

He, the Most High, says after mentioning a number of stories of the Prophets, *'alayhimus-salaatu was-salaam*:

$$إِنَّ هَٰذِهِۦٓ أُمَّتُكُمْ أُمَّةً وَٰحِدَةً وَأَنَا۠ رَبُّكُمْ فَٱعْبُدُونِ ﴿٩٢﴾$$

"This religion of yours is a single religion, and I am your Lord, so worship Me alone."[49]

Allaah, the Most High, says:

$$يَٰٓأَيُّهَا ٱلرُّسُلُ كُلُوا۟ مِنَ ٱلطَّيِّبَٰتِ وَٱعْمَلُوا۟ صَٰلِحًا إِنِّى بِمَا تَعْمَلُونَ عَلِيمٌ ﴿٥١﴾ وَإِنَّ هَٰذِهِۦٓ أُمَّتُكُمْ أُمَّةً وَٰحِدَةً وَأَنَا۠ رَبُّكُمْ فَٱتَّقُونِ ﴿٥٢﴾$$

---

[47] Soorah an-Nahl (16):36.
[48] Soorah al-Ambiyaa (21):25.
[49] Soorah al-Ambiyaa (21):92.

> "O Messengers, eat from the food which Allaah has made lawful, and do correct and righteous deeds. Indeed, I am fully aware of whatever you do. Indeed this religion of yours is a single religion, and I am your Lord so keep yourselves safe from My punishment by obeying Me."[50]

Al-Haafidh Ibn Katheer said, "Mujaahid, Sa'eed ibn Jubayr, Qataadah and 'Abdur-Rahmaan ibn Zayd ibn Aslam said about the saying of Allaah, the Most High, "إِنَّ هَٰذِهِۦٓ أُمَّتُكُمۡ أُمَّةٗ وَٰحِدَةٗ" that it means, 'Your religion is one.'"[51] Then the meaning of these two *Aayaat* occurs in the *Sunnah* in his (ﷺ) saying, *"I am the closest of the people to 'Eesaa ibn Maryam in this world and the Hereafter. The Prophets are brothers, their mothers are different, but their religion is one."*[52]

Also Allaah, the Most High, says about the Messengers who were firmest in determination (*oolul-'adham*), *'alayhimus-salaatu was-salaam*:

$$\text{شَرَعَ لَكُم مِّنَ ٱلدِّينِ مَا وَصَّىٰ بِهِۦ نُوحٗا وَٱلَّذِيٓ أَوۡحَيۡنَآ إِلَيۡكَ وَمَا وَصَّيۡنَا بِهِۦٓ إِبۡرَٰهِيمَ وَمُوسَىٰ وَعِيسَىٰٓ أَنۡ أَقِيمُواْ ٱلدِّينَ وَلَا تَتَفَرَّقُواْ فِيهِۚ كَبُرَ عَلَى ٱلۡمُشۡرِكِينَ مَا تَدۡعُوهُمۡ إِلَيۡهِۚ ٱللَّهُ يَجۡتَبِيٓ إِلَيۡهِ مَن يَشَآءُ وَيَهۡدِيٓ إِلَيۡهِ مَن يُنِيبُ ۝}$$

> "Your Lord prescribed for you O people, the same religion which He prescribed for Nooh, and that

---

[50] Soorah al-Mu'minoon (23):51-52.
[51] Tafseer Ibn Katheer (5/365).
[52] Reported by al-Bukhaaree (Eng. trans. 4/434 no.652) and Muslim (Eng. trans. 4/1260 no.5834).

which We revealed to you O Muhammad (ﷺ), and which He prescribed for Ibraaheem, and Moosaa, and 'Eesaa, that you should establish the religion, acting upon what is prescribed, and not split into sects with regard to it. It is intolerable to the polytheists that you call them to sincerely worship Allaah alone and reject worship of all else besides Him. But Allaah chooses for His religion whomever He pleases and He guides those who turn to Him in repentance and obedience, to act in obedience to Him, and to follow the guidance with which He sent His Messenger."[53]

This was the call of all the Prophets, and at the head of them the Messengers who were firmest in determination. So the Prophets who numbered one hundred and twenty four thousand[54] followed a single methodology in their call, and began from a single starting point which is *tawheed*, the greatest issue and most important principle which they conveyed to all mankind, throughout the ages and despite their varying societies, lands and times. This is a proof that this is the single way which must be followed in calling the people to Allaah, and it is something laid down by Allaah to be followed by all of His Prophets and their true and sincere followers. It is not permissible to change or replace it, nor to turn away from it.

---

[53] Soorah ash-Shooraa (42):13.
[54] As shown by the *hadeeth* of Aboo Dharr, reported by al-Bukhaaree in, *at-Taareekhul-Kabeer* (5/447), and Ahmad in *al-Musnad* (5/178 and 179) by way of al-Mas'oodee, from Aboo 'Umar ad-Dimashqee, from 'Ubayd ibn al-Hashaas, from Aboo Dharr. It is also reported by Ibn Hibbaan as occurs in *al-Mawaarid* (no.94), and Aboo Nu'aym in *al-Hilyah* (1/166-168) and he indicated other chains of narration from Aboo Dharr. It is also reported by Ahmad (5/265), Ibn Abee Haatim in his *Tafseer* (quoted by Ibn Katheer (2/324), and at-Tabaraanee (8/258)). It also has a further chain of narration from Aboo Umaamah quoting the number of the Messengers (*Rusul*) which is three hundred and thirteen, and that is reported by at-Tabaraanee (8/139) and Ibn Hibbaan, as occurs in *al-Mawaarid* (no.2085). Ibn Katheer said, "It is reported by at-Tabaraanee and its narrators are those of the *Saheeh* except Ahmad ibn Khaleed al-Halabee, and he is reliable."

Examples From the Calls of Some of the Messengers

Allaah, the Most High, has informed us about some of the individuals from the greater Prophets, and how they faced their people. We see that all of them proceeded upon the universal way laid down for them by Allaah and they followed the methodology established for all of them by Allaah. Not a single one of them is at variance with it. Allaah, the Most High, says,

﴿وَلَقَدْ أَرْسَلْنَا نُوحًا إِلَىٰ قَوْمِهِ إِنِّى لَكُمْ نَذِيرٌ مُّبِينٌ ۝ أَن لَّا تَعْبُدُوٓا۟ إِلَّا ٱللَّهَ إِنِّىٓ أَخَافُ عَلَيْكُمْ عَذَابَ يَوْمٍ أَلِيمٍ ۝ فَقَالَ ٱلْمَلَأُ ٱلَّذِينَ كَفَرُوا۟ مِن قَوْمِهِۦ مَا نَرَىٰكَ إِلَّا بَشَرًا مِّثْلَنَا وَمَا نَرَىٰكَ ٱتَّبَعَكَ إِلَّا ٱلَّذِينَ هُمْ أَرَاذِلُنَا بَادِىَ ٱلرَّأْىِ وَمَا نَرَىٰ لَكُمْ عَلَيْنَا مِن فَضْلٍ بَلْ نَظُنُّكُمْ كَٰذِبِينَ﴾

"And We sent Nooh to his people saying, 'I am a clear warner sent to you, that you should worship none besides Allaah. Indeed, if you do not make all your worship purely for Him I fear for you the torment of a painful Day.' The chiefs of the disbelievers amongst his people said, 'We see that you are but a man like ourselves and we do not see you followed except by the lowest of the people, in what is apparent to us. Nor do we see that you have any excellence over us, rather we think that you are a liar.'"[55]

---
[55] Soorah Hood (11):25-27.

Allaah, the Most High, says,

وَإِلَىٰ عَادٍ أَخَاهُمْ هُودًا ۚ قَالَ يَـٰقَوْمِ ٱعْبُدُوا۟ ٱللَّهَ مَا لَكُم مِّنْ إِلَـٰهٍ غَيْرُهُۥٓ ۚ أَفَلَا تَتَّقُونَ ۝ قَالَ ٱلْمَلَأُ ٱلَّذِينَ كَفَرُوا۟ مِن قَوْمِهِۦٓ إِنَّا لَنَرَىٰكَ فِى سَفَاهَةٍ وَإِنَّا لَنَظُنُّكَ مِنَ ٱلْكَـٰذِبِينَ ۝ قَالَ يَـٰقَوْمِ لَيْسَ بِى سَفَاهَةٌ وَلَـٰكِنِّى رَسُولٌ مِّن رَّبِّ ٱلْعَـٰلَمِينَ ۝ أُبَلِّغُكُمْ رِسَـٰلَـٰتِ رَبِّى وَأَنَا۠ لَكُمْ نَاصِحٌ أَمِينٌ ۝ أَوَعَجِبْتُمْ أَن جَآءَكُمْ ذِكْرٌ مِّن رَّبِّكُمْ عَلَىٰ رَجُلٍ مِّنكُمْ لِيُنذِرَكُمْ ۚ وَٱذْكُرُوٓا۟ إِذْ جَعَلَكُمْ خُلَفَآءَ مِنۢ بَعْدِ قَوْمِ نُوحٍ وَزَادَكُمْ فِى ٱلْخَلْقِ بَصْۜطَةً ۖ فَٱذْكُرُوٓا۟ ءَالَآءَ ٱللَّهِ لَعَلَّكُمْ تُفْلِحُونَ ۝ قَالُوٓا۟ أَجِئْتَنَا لِنَعْبُدَ ٱللَّهَ وَحْدَهُۥ وَنَذَرَ مَا كَانَ يَعْبُدُ ءَابَآؤُنَا ۖ فَأْتِنَا بِمَا تَعِدُنَآ إِن كُنتَ مِنَ ٱلصَّـٰدِقِينَ ۝ قَالَ قَدْ وَقَعَ عَلَيْكُم مِّن رَّبِّكُمْ رِجْسٌ وَغَضَبٌ ۖ أَتُجَـٰدِلُونَنِى فِىٓ أَسْمَآءٍ سَمَّيْتُمُوهَآ أَنتُمْ وَءَابَآؤُكُم مَّا نَزَّلَ ٱللَّهُ بِهَا مِن سُلْطَـٰنٍ ۚ فَٱنتَظِرُوٓا۟ إِنِّى مَعَكُم مِّنَ ٱلْمُنتَظِرِينَ ۝ فَأَنجَيْنَـٰهُ وَٱلَّذِينَ مَعَهُۥ بِرَحْمَةٍ مِّنَّا وَقَطَعْنَا دَابِرَ ٱلَّذِينَ كَذَّبُوا۟ بِـَٔايَـٰتِنَا ۖ وَمَا كَانُوا۟ مُؤْمِنِينَ

"And to 'Aad We sent Hood, saying, 'O my people worship Allaah, making all of your worship purely for Him, since there is none besides Him having the right to be worshipped by you. Will you not fear your Lord?' The leaders of those who disbelieved amongst his people said, 'We see you upon error (due to your abandonment of our religion and worship of our gods) and we think that you are a liar (in claiming to be a Messenger from the Lord of the Worlds).' He said, 'O my People, I am not upon error, I am indeed a Messenger sent by the Lord of the Worlds. I convey to you the Message of my Lord and am sincere in my advice and faithful to my trust. Do you wonder that Allaah should send admonition for you through a man from amongst you, warning you of Allaah's punishment and to fear Him? And remember the blessings of Allaah upon you in that He made you successors to the people of Nooh (after drowning them for their unbelief and denial of their Messenger), and He increased you in height and size. So remember the favours bestowed upon you by Allaah, so that you may be successful.' They said, 'Do you come to us warning us of punishment from Allaah for that which we practise as religion, so that we should instead worship Allaah alone and forsake what our fathers used to worship? We will not do that, so bring us the punishment which you threaten us with if you are truthful.' He said, 'Allaah's punishment and wrath have become unavoidable for you. Do you dispute with me about mere idols which you and your fathers have given names to, things which can neither bring harm nor benefit, and Allaah has given no proof or excuse for their worship? Then wait for Allaah's judgement between us, I too shall wait.' So We saved Hood and those with him through Our Mercy (due to their *eemaan* and their worship of Allaah alone), and we annihilated those who rejected Our signs and were not Believers."[56]

This was the call of the Messengers, all of them followed this methodology in their *da'wah* to Allaah: they called first to the *tawheed* of Allaah, and that He alone must be singled out with all worship. Then their people opposed them because of this, except those whom Allaah guided, facing them with mockery, charging them with being liars and seeking to ridicule them. As Allaah, the Most High, says:

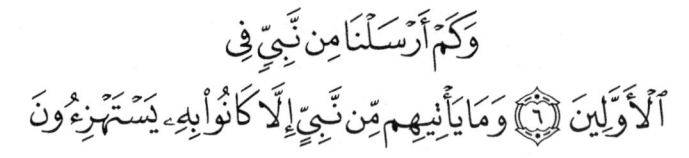

$$وَكَمْ أَرْسَلْنَا مِن نَّبِيٍّ فِي ٱلْأَوَّلِينَ ۝ وَمَا يَأْتِيهِم مِّن نَّبِيٍّ إِلَّا كَانُوا۟ بِهِۦ يَسْتَهْزِءُونَ$$

"Many Prophets were sent to the earlier peoples, and no Prophet came to them except that the people met him with mockery."[57]

There is nothing more severe and hurtful to lofty believing souls than accusations of falsehood, ridicule and mockery. These things are more hurtful to them than being struck with swords, imprisonment and punishment. This fact is mentioned by the Arab poet who said, "Being harmed by close relatives is more painful to the soul than being struck with a sharpened sword."

---

[56] Soorah al-A'raaf (7):65-72.
[57] Soorah az-Zukhruf (43):6-7.

'Aa'ishah, *radiyallaahu 'anhaa*, asked the Prophet (ﷺ), *"Has there been a day more severe upon you than the Day of Uhud?"* So he said, *"Your tribe has troubled me greatly, and the most troublesome thing which I experienced from them was on the day of 'Aqabah when I presented myself to 'Abd Yaaleel ibn 'Abd Kulaal and he didn't respond as I had hoped. So I returned overwhelmed with sorrow and did not recover until I reached Qarnuth-Tha'aalib.*[58] *I raised my head and saw a cloud shading me, then I looked and saw Jibreel in it, and he called me saying, 'Allaah has heard what your people said to you and their reply, and Allaah has sent the Angel of the mountains to you, for you to order him to do whatever you wish.' So the Angel of the mountains called me and greeted me with salaam and then said, 'O Muhammad, Allaah has heard what your people said to you, and I am the Angel of the mountains, and my Lord has sent me to you for you to order me as you wish. So what do you wish?' So Allaah's Messenger* (ﷺ) *said, "No, rather I hope that from their offspring will come those who will worship Allaah alone and not worship anything else besides Him."*[59]

The books of *Seerah*[60] detail some of the answers given by those who mocked him and their scornful stance when he invited them to Islaam. They mention that he went to a number of the nobles and leaders of the tribe of Thaqeef, and they were three brothers, 'Abd Yaleel, Mas'ood and Habeeb and he sat with them and called them to Allaah and asked them

---

[58] A place between Makkah and at-Taa'if also called Qarnul-Manaazil.

[59] Reported by al-Bukhaaree (Eng. trans. 4/300 no.454) and Muslim (Eng. trans. 3/987 no.4425). This *hadeeth* clearly shows the *da'wah* of Allaah's Messenger (ﷺ) and his perseverance in that, and his mildness with his people. See how he was patient with them and asked for them to be spared from destruction which would have wiped them out. He instead hoped for good from Allaah, and hoped that from their offspring would come those who worshipped Allaah alone, not worshipping anything besides Him. Indeed what a noble and lofty goal, which is not realised except by those who taste the blessing of *tawheed* and know its station.

[60] Books about the life of the Prophet (ﷺ).

to support Islaam and stand with him against those of his people who opposed him. So one of them said, "If it is actually true that Allaah has sent you, then He is tearing down the covering of the Ka'bah." The second said, "Could Allaah not find anyone to send but you?" The third said, "By Allaah, I will never speak with you. If you are truly a Messenger from Allaah as you claim, then you are greater than to have me reply to your words, and if you are lying against Allaah then it is not proper that I should ever speak to you." So Allaah's Messenger (ﷺ) left having despaired of good from Thaqeef.[61]

What we see from the *hadeeth* and the story is that mockery and scorn and harm caused by the foolish idolaters was more severe to the Prophets than any other trouble, even more so than the fierce battles in which lives are spent and the blood of their pure companions is shed. Indeed on the Day of Uhud more than seventy Companions of Allaah's Messenger (ﷺ) were martyred.[62] Amongst them: Mus'ab ibn 'Umayr,[63] and

---

[61] *Al-Bidaayah wan-Nihaayah,'* (3/135) and *ad-Durar Fikhtisaaril-Maghaazee was-Siyaar* (p.35) of Ibn 'Abdul-Barr.

[62] Al-Bukhaaree, *rahimahullaah,* said, (Eng. trans. 5/279 ch. 25), "Chapter: The Muslims who were killed on the Day of Uhud... 'Amr ibn 'Alee narrated to us: Mu'aadh ibn Hishaam narrated to us, saying: My father narrated to me from: Qataadah, who said, 'We do not know of any tribe amongst the Arabs who lost more martyrs, and will have superiority on the Day of Resurrection, than the Ansaar.' And Qataadah said: Anas ibn Maalik narrated to us: that seventy of the Ansaar were martyred on the day of Uhud, and seventy on the day of Bir Ma'oonah, and seventy on the day of al-Yamaamah."

[63] From Khabbaab, *radiyallaahu 'anhu,* who said, "We emigrated along with the Prophet (ﷺ) seeking thereby only the Face of Allaah, so our reward became assured with Allaah. Then there were some of us who died not having taken anything from his reward. From them was Mus'ab ibn 'Umayr who was killed on the day of Uhud and did not leave anything behind except a small striped sheet. When we covered his head with it his feet were uncovered, and when we covered his feet with it his head was uncovered. So the Prophet said, *'Cover his head with it, and place idhkhir (a sweet smelling rush) upon his feet.'"* (Reported by al- Bukhaaree (Eng. trans.5/281/no. 408), Muslim (Eng. trans. 2/446/no. 2050), Ahmad and an-Nasaa'ee.

Hamzah ibn 'Abdil-Muttalib[64] the paternal uncle of Allaah's Messenger (ﷺ), and Allaah's Messenger (ﷺ) was injured in the face and his incisor was broken.[65] He also suffered along with his Companions at the hands of the hypocrites, and suffered great harm and hardship before that in Makkah, and at Badr and other battles. Yet despite all of this, the severest trouble which he faced was on the Day of Taa'if because of the mockery and contempt which he faced to such a degree that it is unbearable for pure souls. Furthermore Allaah's Messenger (ﷺ) said, *"Those who suffered the severest trials are the Prophets, then those who are most like them, then those who are most like them after that."*[66]

So those who are most like them, and then those who are next closest are those who proceed upon their methodology in calling to Allaah, and called to what they called to, i.e. to the *tawheed* of Allaah and that He is to be singled out with all worship, and to rejection of all *shirk* (attribution of

---

[64] The story of his martyrdom is to be found in *Saheeh al-Bukhaaree* (Eng. trans. 5/74-277/no. 399) and the *Musnad* of Imaam Ahmad (3/500-501).

[65] From Anas, *radiyallaahu 'anhu*, who said: *"On the day of Uhud the Prophet (ﷺ) was injured in the face and said, 'How can a people who injure the face of the Prophet (ﷺ) be successful?' And so the Aayah, "Not for you is the decision..." (Soorah Aal-'Imraan (3):128) was sent down."* Reported by al-Bukhaaree (Eng. trans. 5/272 ch.20 and Muslim (Eng. trans. 2/985 no.4417), and Muslim also reports (Eng. trans. 2/984/4414) the *hadeeth* of Sahl ibn Sa'd with the wording, *"Allaah's Messenger (ﷺ) was wounded in his face and his incisor was broken and his helmet was crushed upon his head."*

[66] Reported by at-Tirmidhee (4/602 no.2398), Ibn Maajah (2/1334 no. 4023), ad-Daarimee (2/228, no. 2786) and Ahmad (1/172, 174, 180, 185), all of them by way of 'Aasim ibn Abin-Nujood, who is generally acceptable (*sudooq*), but makes mistakes; from Mus'ab ibn Sa'd, at-Tirmidhee declared it to be *hasan saheeh*. But Tirmidhee's declaration of its direct authenticity is debatable, and it as if he took into account other witnesses for it, since there are other supporting narrations for it:

(1) From Aboo Sa'eed al-Khudree, reported by Ibn Maajah (no. 4024), and its chain of narration is declared *saheeh* in *az-Zawaa'id*.

(2) The *hadeeth* of Faatimah bint al-Yamaan reported by Ahmad (6/329).

(3) The *hadeeth* of Aboo Hurayrah indicated by at-Tirmidhee after reporting the original *hadeeth*.

any form or part of worship to anyone besides Allaah). Such people will suffer similar harm and trials as suffered by the Prophets who are their example. It is because of this fact that you see many of the callers departing away from this difficult methodology, and this rugged path, since the caller who follows it will have to face opposition from his mother, his father, his brother, his friends and those whom he loves. He will be opposed by the society which will treat him as an enemy and seek to mock and harm him. So many callers divert their attention to other aspects of Islaam which do have their place, and are not denied by anyone who truly believes in Allaah, except that those aspects do not involve that difficulty and hardship and do not bring about mockery and harm particularly in Islamic societies. This is because the majority of the people of the *ummah* of Islaam are willing to gather around these type of callers, and they throw praise and honour upon them instead of mockery and harm, unless they pose a threat to the rulers and are a danger to their positions, in which case they suppress them brutally. For example political parties which oppose the rulers and threaten to dethrone them. In such a case the rulers will show no love to relatives or friends, Muslims or disbelievers.

Then in any case we say to those callers: no matter how much noise they make, and no matter how high they raise their voices in the name of Islaam, restrain yourselves because you have left the way prescribed by Allaah and His Straight Path, upon which the Prophets and their followers proceeded in calling to *tawheed* of Allaah and to making the religion purely for Him. So no matter how much you speak and raise your voices in the name of Islaam, you are still deviating from the methodology of the Prophets which was laid down by Allaah. No matter how much effort you expend, and how much you manage to extend your *da'wah* and your own methodology, you are still preoccupying yourselves with the means to the exclusion of the goal. Then what use are the means[67] if they merely harm the goal, and they themselves grow at its expense.

Indeed woe to those callers who obstinately persist upon the methodologies which they themselves have innovated, those who fight against the methodology of the Prophets in calling to the *tawheed* of Allaah, beneath dazzling banners and slogans which captivate the simple minded and those ignorant of the methodology and way of the Prophets.

Then to speak comprehensively about the calls of the Messengers to the *tawheed* of Allaah, and the way, and the methodology which they followed, and the terrors and trials and tribulations which they faced in that, is something which cannot be dealt with fully here, so we will suffice with presenting the *da'wah* of five of them, may Allaah send praises and blessings of peace upon them, and this will place us upon clear guidance, whose night is as clear as its day, and is such that no one deviates from it except that he is destroyed.

---

[67] Rule is a means to calling to Allaah as Allaah, the Most High, says:
"Those who, when We establish them in the land, they establish the Prayer, pay the *Zakaat*, call the people to make all of their worship purely for Allaah, and to His obedience and to what is known by the People of *eemaan* to be good: And they warn against attribution of partners in worship to Allaah, and disobedience to Him." [Soorah al-Hajj (22):41].

Nooh

Nooh was the second father of all mankind, and the first of the Messengers (*Rusul*) to the people of the Earth. This great Prophet lived a very long life: he called his people for nine hundred and fifty years to the *tawheed* of Allaah and to making all worship purely for Him. He did not become weary of this, nor lose interest. He called them night and day, in private and in the open. Allaah, the Most High, says,

إِنَّآ أَرْسَلْنَا نُوحًا إِلَىٰ قَوْمِهِۦٓ أَنْ أَنذِرْ قَوْمَكَ مِن قَبْلِ أَن يَأْتِيَهُمْ عَذَابٌ أَلِيمٌ ۝ قَالَ يَٰقَوْمِ إِنِّى لَكُمْ نَذِيرٌ مُّبِينٌ ۝ أَنِ ٱعْبُدُوا۟ ٱللَّهَ وَٱتَّقُوهُ وَأَطِيعُونِ ۝ يَغْفِرْ لَكُم مِّن ذُنُوبِكُمْ وَيُؤَخِّرْكُمْ إِلَىٰٓ أَجَلٍ مُّسَمًّى ۚ إِنَّ أَجَلَ ٱللَّهِ إِذَا جَآءَ لَا يُؤَخَّرُ ۖ لَوْ كُنتُمْ تَعْلَمُونَ ۝ قَالَ رَبِّ إِنِّى دَعَوْتُ قَوْمِى لَيْلًا وَنَهَارًا ۝ فَلَمْ يَزِدْهُمْ دُعَآءِىٓ إِلَّا فِرَارًا ۝ وَإِنِّى كُلَّمَا دَعَوْتُهُمْ لِتَغْفِرَ لَهُمْ جَعَلُوٓا۟ أَصَٰبِعَهُمْ فِىٓ ءَاذَانِهِمْ وَٱسْتَغْشَوْا۟ ثِيَابَهُمْ وَأَصَرُّوا۟ وَٱسْتَكْبَرُوا۟ ٱسْتِكْبَارًا ۝ ثُمَّ إِنِّى دَعَوْتُهُمْ جِهَارًا ۝ ثُمَّ إِنِّىٓ أَعْلَنتُ لَهُمْ وَأَسْرَرْتُ لَهُمْ إِسْرَارًا ۝ فَقُلْتُ ٱسْتَغْفِرُوا۟ رَبَّكُمْ إِنَّهُۥ كَانَ غَفَّارًا ۝ يُرْسِلِ ٱلسَّمَآءَ عَلَيْكُم مِّدْرَارًا ۝ وَيُمْدِدْكُم بِأَمْوَٰلٍ وَبَنِينَ وَيَجْعَل لَّكُمْ جَنَّٰتٍ وَيَجْعَل لَّكُمْ أَنْهَٰرًا ۝ مَّا لَكُمْ لَا تَرْجُونَ لِلَّهِ وَقَارًا ۝ وَقَدْ خَلَقَكُمْ أَطْوَارًا ۝ أَلَمْ تَرَوْا۟ كَيْفَ خَلَقَ ٱللَّهُ سَبْعَ سَمَٰوَٰتٍ طِبَاقًا ۝ وَجَعَلَ ٱلْقَمَرَ فِيهِنَّ نُورًا وَجَعَلَ ٱلشَّمْسَ سِرَاجًا ۝

وَٱللَّهُ أَنۢبَتَكُم مِّنَ ٱلۡأَرۡضِ نَبَاتٗا ۝ ثُمَّ يُعِيدُكُمۡ فِيهَا وَيُخۡرِجُكُمۡ إِخۡرَاجٗا ۝ وَٱللَّهُ جَعَلَ لَكُمُ ٱلۡأَرۡضَ بِسَاطٗا ۝ لِّتَسۡلُكُواْ مِنۡهَا سُبُلٗا فِجَاجٗا ۝ قَالَ نُوحٞ رَّبِّ إِنَّهُمۡ عَصَوۡنِي وَٱتَّبَعُواْ مَن لَّمۡ يَزِدۡهُ مَالُهُۥ وَوَلَدُهُۥٓ إِلَّا خَسَارٗا ۝ وَمَكَرُواْ مَكۡرٗا كُبَّارٗا ۝ وَقَالُواْ لَا تَذَرُنَّ ءَالِهَتَكُمۡ وَلَا تَذَرُنَّ وَدّٗا وَلَا سُوَاعٗا وَلَا يَغُوثَ وَيَعُوقَ وَنَسۡرٗا ۝ وَقَدۡ أَضَلُّواْ كَثِيرٗاۖ وَلَا تَزِدِ ٱلظَّٰلِمِينَ إِلَّا ضَلَٰلٗا ۝ مِّمَّا خَطِيٓـَٰتِهِمۡ أُغۡرِقُواْ فَأُدۡخِلُواْ نَارٗا فَلَمۡ يَجِدُواْ لَهُم مِّن دُونِ ٱللَّهِ أَنصَارٗا ۝

"Indeed We sent Nooh as a Messenger to his people ordering him to warn his people before a painful punishment should come to them. He said, 'O my People, I am a plain and clear warner to you, that you should worship Allaah alone, avoid disobedience to Him and obey me. If you do so He will forgive you your sins and grant you respite until an appointed term. Indeed when the term decreed by Allaah comes it cannot be delayed, and if you knew you would submit to and obey your Lord.' Nooh said, 'O my Lord, I have called my people day and night to worship You alone and warned them of Your punishment but my calling them to the truth only results in them turning away from it.[68] Whenever I call them

---

[68] At-Tabaree reports from Qataadah, "It has reached us that a man would take his son to Nooh and say to his son, 'Beware of this man, don't let him lead you astray, for I remember when I was your age, my father brought me to him and warned me against him just as I am warning you.'"

to worship You alone and to obey You, and to disassociate themselves from the worship of everything but You, so that You may forgive them, they thrust their fingers in their ears and cover themselves up with their garments, so as not to hear. Then they persist in their disbelief and arrogantly and obstinately refuse to follow and submit to the truth. Then I called them loudly and openly, and I called them individually and privately. I said to them, 'Ask your Lord to forgive your sins and repent to your Lord from your unbelief and association of others in worship with Him, and make your worship sincerely and purely for Him, then He will forgive you, indeed He greatly forgives those who turn to Him in repentance and seek His forgiveness. He will then send you rain in abundance, and grant you increase in wealth and children, and provide you with gardens and rivers. What is wrong with you that you do not have awe and fear of Allaah, when it is He that created you in successive stages? Do you not see how Allaah has created the seven heavens one above the other, and has placed the moon therein as a light and has made the sun a lamp? It is Allaah who created you and brought you from the earth, and He it is who will return you to it, and then resurrect you from it. Allaah - it is Who spread out the earth for you, so that you may travel about upon wide roads." Nooh said, 'O my Lord, they have rejected my call and opposed it, and have instead followed the call of those whose wealth and children only increase them in error and take them further away from their Lord. Furthermore the leaders have plotted a mighty plot,

> and they have said, "Do not abandon your gods. Do not abandon *Wadd*, nor *Suwaa*, nor *Yaghooth*, nor *Ya'ooq*, nor *Nasr*." Indeed many have gone astray due to the idols. O Allaah, grant no increase to the transgressors except in error.[69] Due to their sins they were drowned in the Flood and entered into the Fire, and they could find no one to save them from Allaah's punishment."[70]

So what did the *da'wah* of this noble Messenger comprise of, and Allaah has told us the summary of his noble *da'wah* which continued for nine hundred and fifty years?! Indeed it was an earnest and painstaking call to the *tawheed* of Allaah and to make all worship purely for Him. It was a tireless effort and he used every possible means available to him to convince them of his call. He called them privately and individually, and he called them openly. He encouraged them and warned them, informing them of the promise of good for the obedient, and evil for the disobedient. He gave them practical and intellectual proofs, from themselves and their lives, and what they saw before them with regards to the heavens and the earth, and the clear signs and lessons contained in them. All of this failed to benefit them and did not cause them to accept. Rather they persisted in their disbelief and error, and they rejected all this obstinately and arrogantly. They persisted in their adherence to the idols and false and futile objects of worship. So the result of this persistence and obstinacy was destruction and annihilation in this world, and everlasting torment in the Hellfire in the Hereafter.

---

[69] This supplication of Nooh against them came after he was informed by Allaah that they were not going to be Believers, as explained by al-Baghawee.
[70] Soorah Nooh (71):1-24.

At this point we may ask: why did this great Prophet continue for such an extremely long period of time, expending huge efforts, untiringly and without languidness, calling to the starting point of *tawheed*?! Why did Allaah praise him so highly, and cause him to be remembered, and make him one of those Messengers who were the firmest of all in their determination (*oolul-'adhm*)? Does the call to *tawheed* deserve all this esteem? Is this methodology an establishment of this procedure for this noble Prophet in opposition to logic, wisdom and intellect? Or is it pure and certain wisdom, and what is demanded by correct logic and sound and perceptive intellect? Why did Allaah approve of following this methodology in *da'wah* for nine hundred and fifty years, and commend him, and cause his name and his story to endure, and impose it as a duty upon the greatest of the Messengers and the one having the greatest intellect of all the people, that he should take him as an example to follow in his *da'wah* and his perseverance?

The just answer, established upon intellect and wisdom, and upon understanding the status and position of Prophethood, and having the greatest trust in it and giving it its due respect, is that the call to *tawheed* and striving to wipe out *shirk* and to purify the earth from it, does indeed deserve all of this. It is indeed wisdom itself and is demanded by natural inclination and intellect. It is furthermore, a binding obligation upon every caller to Allaah that they understand this methodology, this great and divinely inspired *da'wah* and great goal, and that they devote all their effort and energy to its attainment and its being propagated throughout all of Allaah's earth. Furthermore that they work together, cooperate and unite, and sincerely attest to each others' truthfulness. Just as the Messengers, the callers to *tawheed*, were: the earlier ones telling of the coming of the later ones and the later ones attesting to the truthfulness of the previous ones and promoting their call, and following the same way. It is also binding upon us to believe that if there was any other methodology better and more correct than this methodology, that Allaah would have chosen that for His Messengers and would have favoured them with it. So is it fitting for any Believer to turn away from it and choose a different methodology for himself, and to arrogantly seek to attack this divinely laid down methodology and its callers?!

Ibraaheem

The Father of the Prophets and the Leader of those who worship Allaah alone, upon the true religion, Ibraaheem, the Chosen and Beloved Friend of Allaah (*Khaleelullaah*), who was such that Allaah ordered the best of the Messengers and the final Prophet, and his *ummah*, to emulate him, to take his call as an example, and to follow his way and methodology.[71] Allaah, the Most High, says:

$$\text{وَإِذْ قَالَ إِبْرَاهِيمُ لِأَبِيهِ ءَازَرَ أَتَتَّخِذُ أَصْنَامًا ءَالِهَةً إِنِّي أَرَاكَ وَقَوْمَكَ فِي ضَلَالٍ مُّبِينٍ ۝ وَكَذَٰلِكَ نُرِي إِبْرَاهِيمَ مَلَكُوتَ السَّمَاوَاتِ وَالْأَرْضِ وَلِيَكُونَ مِنَ الْمُوقِنِينَ ۝ فَلَمَّا جَنَّ عَلَيْهِ اللَّيْلُ رَءَا كَوْكَبًا قَالَ هَٰذَا رَبِّي فَلَمَّا أَفَلَ قَالَ لَا أُحِبُّ الْآفِلِينَ ۝ فَلَمَّا رَءَا الْقَمَرَ بَازِغًا قَالَ هَٰذَا رَبِّي فَلَمَّا أَفَلَ قَالَ لَئِن لَّمْ يَهْدِنِي رَبِّي لَأَكُونَنَّ مِنَ الْقَوْمِ الضَّالِّينَ ۝ فَلَمَّا رَءَا الشَّمْسَ بَازِغَةً قَالَ هَٰذَا رَبِّي هَٰذَا أَكْبَرُ فَلَمَّا أَفَلَتْ قَالَ يَٰقَوْمِ إِنِّي بَرِيءٌ مِّمَّا تُشْرِكُونَ ۝}$$

---

[71] As indicated by the saying of Allaah, the Most High:
"Then We revealed to you, O Muhammad (ﷺ), that you should follow the religion of Ibraaheem who was a Muslim upon the true religion and was not one of those who worshipped idols and associated partners with Allaah." [Soorah an-Nahl (16):123].
And the saying of Allaah, the Most High:
"Say, O Muhammad (ﷺ): Allaah has indeed spoken the Truth, so follow the religion of Ibraaheem who was upright, upon the religion of Islaam, and he did not make any share of his worship for any created being." [Soorah Aal-'Imraan (3):95].

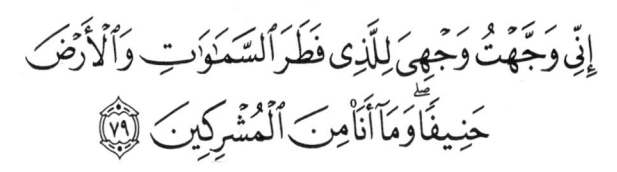

$$\text{إِنِّي وَجَّهْتُ وَجْهِيَ لِلَّذِي فَطَرَ السَّمَاوَاتِ وَالْأَرْضَ حَنِيفًا وَمَا أَنَا مِنَ الْمُشْرِكِينَ ﴿٧٩﴾}$$

"And remember when Ibraaheem said to his father Aazar, 'Will you take idols for worship? Indeed I see that you and those who worship idols along with you are upon clear error.' Likewise We showed Ibraaheem the heavens and the earth (and how they are a proof that the Creator alone should be worshipped), so that he should be one of those who have Faith with certainty. So when the night covered him with darkness he saw a star and said, (as an argument to show his people the error of worshipping anything besides Allaah), 'This is (what you claim to be) my Lord?!' Then when it set, he said, 'I do not love that which passes away.' Then when he saw the moon rising up he said, 'This is (what you claim to be) my Lord?!' Then when it set he said, 'If my Lord did not keep me firm upon the guidance then I would surely be one of the misguided.' Then when he saw the sun, he said, 'This is (what you claim to be) my Lord?! This is greater than the others.' Then when it set he said, 'O my people, I am free from all that you associate as partners in worship with Allaah. Indeed I have turned my face in worship to Him who has created the heavens and the earth, making all worship purely for Him, and I am not from those who worship anything besides Allaah.'"[72]

---

[72] Soorah al-An'aam (6):74-79.

So this was a fervent, vigorous and incessant call to the *tawheed* of Allaah, and to make all of religion purely for Him, and to the elimination and rejection of *shirk*. It begins with the family and extends to the nations, waging war upon *shirk* and the idols and shaking the very foundations of attribution of any worship to the stars. So the chosen and beloved Friend of Allaah proceeded upon the soundest way in debating and arguing in order to establish Allaah's Proof and to refute *shirk* and to show its fallacy and reject the doubts used to support it. So his use of the word 'idols' shows contempt for their phoney and supposed gods, and an exposure of their foolishness. He observed the aforementioned celestial bodies one after the other, each one succeeded the previous one which set and became absent, in order to use their condition as a clear proof of the fallacy of their having any divinity or right to worship as his people claimed. Who was it who protected and guarded them and controlled their affairs and the affairs of the creation when they passed and set?! Therefore they must reject the false divinity and right to worship which they claimed for them and disbelieve in that. It was upon them to wash their hands of them and turn instead to their true God, He Who created and brought into existence the heavens and the earth. He Who does not pass away or depart. He Who knows all about their condition and is fully aware of all their movements and periods of rest. He Who protects and preserves them and controls their affairs. They were strong proofs extracted from the situation they experienced and the visible creation.

Allaah, the Most High, says:

وَاذْكُرْ فِي ٱلْكِتَٰبِ إِبْرَٰهِيمَ إِنَّهُۥ كَانَ صِدِّيقًا نَّبِيًّا ۝ إِذْ قَالَ لِأَبِيهِ يَٰٓأَبَتِ لِمَ تَعْبُدُ مَا لَا يَسْمَعُ وَلَا يُبْصِرُ وَلَا يُغْنِى عَنكَ شَيْـًٔا ۝ يَٰٓأَبَتِ إِنِّى قَدْ جَآءَنِى مِنَ ٱلْعِلْمِ مَا لَمْ يَأْتِكَ فَٱتَّبِعْنِىٓ أَهْدِكَ صِرَٰطًا

سَوِيًّا ۝ يَٰٓأَبَتِ لَا تَعْبُدِ ٱلشَّيْطَٰنَ إِنَّ ٱلشَّيْطَٰنَ كَانَ لِلرَّحْمَٰنِ عَصِيًّا ۝ يَٰٓأَبَتِ إِنِّىٓ أَخَافُ أَن يَمَسَّكَ عَذَابٌ مِّنَ ٱلرَّحْمَٰنِ فَتَكُونَ لِلشَّيْطَٰنِ وَلِيًّا ۝ قَالَ أَرَاغِبٌ أَنتَ عَنْ ءَالِهَتِى يَٰٓإِبْرَٰهِيمُ ۖ لَئِن لَّمْ تَنتَهِ لَأَرْجُمَنَّكَ ۖ وَٱهْجُرْنِى مَلِيًّا ۝ قَالَ سَلَٰمٌ عَلَيْكَ ۖ سَأَسْتَغْفِرُ لَكَ رَبِّىٓ ۖ إِنَّهُۥ كَانَ بِى حَفِيًّا ۝ وَأَعْتَزِلُكُمْ وَمَا تَدْعُونَ مِن دُونِ ٱللَّهِ وَأَدْعُوا۟ رَبِّى عَسَىٰٓ أَلَّآ أَكُونَ بِدُعَآءِ رَبِّى شَقِيًّا ۝ فَلَمَّا ٱعْتَزَلَهُمْ وَمَا يَعْبُدُونَ مِن دُونِ ٱللَّهِ وَهَبْنَا لَهُۥٓ إِسْحَٰقَ وَيَعْقُوبَ ۖ وَكُلًّا جَعَلْنَا نَبِيًّا ۝ وَوَهَبْنَا لَهُم مِّن رَّحْمَتِنَا وَجَعَلْنَا لَهُمْ لِسَانَ صِدْقٍ عَلِيًّا ۝

"And recite to your people from the Book (the Qur'aan), O Muhammad (ﷺ), about Ibraaheem. He was one who was fully truthful and one sent as a Prophet by Allaah. When he said to his father, 'Why do you worship that which cannot hear, nor see, nor benefit you, nor remove any harm from you at all?! O my father, Allaah has given me knowledge which has not come to you, so accept the sincere advice I give you, and I will show you the Straight Way, upon which you will not go astray. O my father, do not worship Satan (by obeying him in his call for you to worship the idols) - indeed Satan is one disobedient to the Most Merciful (Allaah). O my father, I fear for you, knowing that if you die upon attribution of partners to Allaah in worship, and upon worship of Sa-

> tan, that Allaah's punishment and torment will be upon you, and that you will merely be a companion of Satan in the Hell-fire.' He replied, 'Do you reject my gods, O Ibraaheem? If you do not cease abusing and reviling them I will certainly revile you. Go away from me if you wish to remain safe from me.' Ibraaheem said, 'But you are safe from me harming you, I will rather ask my Lord to guide you and forgive your sins. He has always been most Gracious and Kind to me. I shall keep away from you and all that you worship besides Allaah, and I will worship and invoke my Lord, making all of worship purely for Him. I hope that I shall not be one unblest in my worship and supplications.' So when he separated himself from them and all that they worshipped besides Allaah, We gave him a family who were better than them, Ishaaq and Ya'qoob, and we made all of them Prophets, and we bestowed our mercy upon them all, and granted them renown and praise upon the tongues of the people."[73]

So this was a fervent call to *tawheed*, established firmly upon knowledge, reason and intellect, and upon good and sound manners. Guiding the misguided to the Straight Path. It was opposed by blind bigotry and partisanship, based upon desires, ignorance, stubbornness and obstinate pride: otherwise how could anyone worship and humble themselves to those who cannot hear, nor see, nor help them in any way?!

Indeed the knowledge of *tawheed*, O reader, is that knowledge which all the Prophets were honoured with, and with it they assaulted falsehood,

---

[73] Soorah Maryam (19):41-50.

ignorance and *shirk*. So ignorance of this knowledge, the knowledge carried by the Prophets, which guides to the truth and saves from misguidance and *shirk*, ignorance of this is fatal and is a deadly poison which kills the intellect and the ability to think.

$$يَٰٓأَبَتِ إِنِّى قَدْ جَآءَنِى مِنَ ٱلْعِلْمِ مَا لَمْ يَأْتِكَ فَٱتَّبِعْنِىٓ أَهْدِكَ صِرَٰطًا سَوِيًّا ﴿٤٣﴾$$

"O my Father, Allaah has given me knowledge which has not come to you, accept the sincere advice which I give to you, and I will show you the Straight Way, upon which you will not go astray."[74]

Then after these robust efforts in *da'wah* expended by Ibraaheem in calling to Allaah, calling the family and the nation, establishing the irrefutable proofs upon his father and his people, after this he took this great call and confronted that haughty and tyrannical ruler who claimed divinity, he faced him with the full strength and bravery. Allaah, the Most High, says:

$$أَلَمْ تَرَ إِلَى ٱلَّذِى حَآجَّ إِبْرَٰهِـۧمَ فِى رَبِّهِۦٓ أَنْ ءَاتَىٰهُ ٱللَّهُ ٱلْمُلْكَ إِذْ قَالَ إِبْرَٰهِـۧمُ رَبِّىَ ٱلَّذِى يُحْىِۦ وَيُمِيتُ قَالَ أَنَا۠ أُحْىِۦ وَأُمِيتُ ۖ قَالَ إِبْرَٰهِـۧمُ فَإِنَّ ٱللَّهَ يَأْتِى بِٱلشَّمْسِ مِنَ ٱلْمَشْرِقِ فَأْتِ بِهَا مِنَ ٱلْمَغْرِبِ فَبُهِتَ ٱلَّذِى كَفَرَ ۗ وَٱللَّهُ لَا يَهْدِى ٱلْقَوْمَ ٱلظَّٰلِمِينَ ﴿٢٥٨﴾$$

---

[74] Soorah Maryam (19):43.

> "Do you not consider the one (Namrood) who, because Allaah had granted him an extended kingdom disputed with Ibraaheem about his Lord. Ibraaheem said to him, 'It is my Lord (Allaah) Who gives life and death.' He said, 'I give life and cause death.' Ibraaheem said, 'Allaah causes the sun to rise from the east, so if you are truthful then cause it to rise from the west.' So the unbeliever was confounded, and Allaah does not guide the unbelievers to find proof against the people of truth."[75]

So Ibraaheem called this tyrant and claimant to divinity to the *tawheed* of Allaah, and to *eemaan* in His Lordship. But he exceeded all bounds in his arrogance and haughtily refused to accept the *tawheed* of Allaah and to give up on his claims to Lordship. So Ibraaheem debated with him in this brilliant manner whose proof was clear. Ibraaheem said,

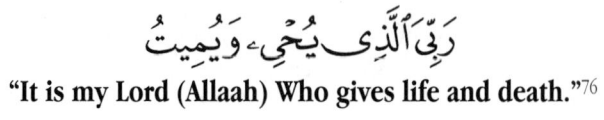

$$رَبِّيَ ٱلَّذِى يُحْىِۦ وَيُمِيتُ$$

"It is my Lord (Allaah) Who gives life and death."[76]

So the stupid tyrant replied that he too could give life and death - meaning that he killed whom he pleased and spared whom he pleased. This answer of his was merely a pretence and a means of fooling the ignorant, and was a way of avoiding the question, since what Ibraaheem referred to was the fact that his Lord created mankind, animals and plants and gave them life, and brought them into existence from nothing. Then He causes them to die with His Power, and that He gives the humans and animals death at the end of their appointed life-spans, due to visible causes which He shows and without visible causes. So when Ibraaheem saw that he

---

[75] Soorah al-Baqarah (2):258.
[76] Soorah al-Baqarah (2):258.

tried to create a pretence to evade the issue, which might fool some of the ignorant and common folk, he then said, as a means of showing the futility of what his saying entailed, that if you are as you claim, then,

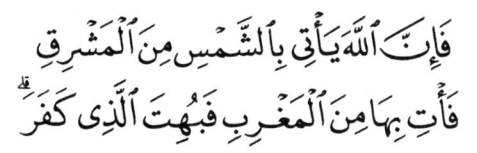

$$\text{فَإِنَّ ٱللَّهَ يَأْتِي بِٱلشَّمْسِ مِنَ ٱلْمَشْرِقِ فَأْتِ بِهَا مِنَ ٱلْمَغْرِبِ فَبُهِتَ ٱلَّذِي كَفَرَ}$$

"'Allaah causes the sun to rise from the east, so if you are truthful then cause it to rise from the west.' So the unbeliever was confounded."[77]

So the unbeliever was left confounded and at a loss for words. His argument was overthrown, he was silenced, struck dumb and falsehood was rendered futile as is always the case. So this contains a lesson for those who listen attentively and witness it, that the call to *tawheed* represents the peak of sincerity, wisdom and intelligence; it proceeds in the due and correct manner, and as Allaah has willed, not merely struggling for kingship, nor seeking to fight for leadership.

If the goal of Ibraaheem had been to attain rulership and authority he would have taken a different methodology to this, and he would have found people who gathered around him and supported him. But Allaah refuses, and His Prophets and the pious callers from the true followers of the Prophets in every time and place, they all refuse except to follow the way of guidance and truth, and to clearly proclaim the truth and to establish the proof against the proud and obstinate.

So Ibraaheem established this great obligation in the best and most complete manner. He established the proof upon his father and his people, upon those who governed them and upon all of his nation. Then when

---

[77] Soorah al-Baqarah (2):258.

he saw that they were persisting in their *shirk* and their unbelief and were established upon falsehood and misguidance, he resorted to censure and correction by means of the hand and use of strength. So where did his change and correction begin, and what was the correct and rightly guided means for correction of the dire situation which had beset his nation? Did he seek to overthrow the state because it was the root of all the evils and corruption and the source of *shirk* and misguidance?! How can that be denied when the ruler claimed lordship for himself and persisted in that claim? So why did Ibraaheem not consider a revolution against this unbelieving government, and at the head of it a tyrant who claimed divinity, and by so doing wipe out all the forms of corruption and *shirk*, and establish in its place the divinely-guided state headed by Ibraaheem, *'alayhis-salaatu was-salaam*?! The answer is the Prophets were far removed from following any such way or even considering it, since this is the way of the oppressors, the ignorant and the foolish, those who seek after this world and strive for authority in it.

Rather the Prophets were callers to *tawheed* and pioneers guiding to the truth, and seeking to save the people from falsehood and *shirk*. So when they applied themselves to correction and changing the state of affairs, and they were the most knowledgeable and intelligent of the people, then they necessarily began with striking at the true sources of *shirk* and misguidance. This is what Ibraaheem, the mild, wise and rightly guided, the heroic and brave, did. Allaah, the Most High, says:

$$\text{وَلَقَدْ ءَاتَيْنَآ إِبْرَٰهِيمَ رُشْدَهُۥ مِن قَبْلُ وَكُنَّا بِهِۦ عَٰلِمِينَ ۝ إِذْ قَالَ لِأَبِيهِ وَقَوْمِهِۦ مَا هَٰذِهِ ٱلتَّمَاثِيلُ ٱلَّتِىٓ أَنتُمْ لَهَا عَٰكِفُونَ ۝ قَالُوا۟ وَجَدْنَآ ءَابَآءَنَا لَهَا عَٰبِدِينَ ۝ قَالَ لَقَدْ كُنتُمْ أَنتُمْ وَءَابَآؤُكُمْ فِى ضَلَٰلٍ مُّبِينٍ ۝ قَالُوٓا۟}$$

أَجِئْتَنَا بِٱلْحَقِّ أَمْ أَنتَ مِنَ ٱللَّٰعِبِينَ ۝ قَالَ بَل رَّبُّكُمْ رَبُّ ٱلسَّمَٰوَٰتِ وَٱلْأَرْضِ ٱلَّذِى فَطَرَهُنَّ وَأَنَا۠ عَلَىٰ ذَٰلِكُم مِّنَ ٱلشَّٰهِدِينَ ۝ وَتَٱللَّهِ لَأَكِيدَنَّ أَصْنَٰمَكُم بَعْدَ أَن تُوَلُّوا۟ مُدْبِرِينَ ۝ فَجَعَلَهُمْ جُذَٰذًا إِلَّا كَبِيرًا لَّهُمْ لَعَلَّهُمْ إِلَيْهِ يَرْجِعُونَ ۝ قَالُوا۟ مَن فَعَلَ هَٰذَا بِـَٔالِهَتِنَا إِنَّهُۥ لَمِنَ ٱلظَّٰلِمِينَ ۝ قَالُوا۟ سَمِعْنَا فَتًى يَذْكُرُهُمْ يُقَالُ لَهُۥٓ إِبْرَٰهِيمُ ۝ قَالُوا۟ فَأْتُوا۟ بِهِۦ عَلَىٰٓ أَعْيُنِ ٱلنَّاسِ لَعَلَّهُمْ يَشْهَدُونَ ۝ قَالُوٓا۟ ءَأَنتَ فَعَلْتَ هَٰذَا بِـَٔالِهَتِنَا يَٰٓإِبْرَٰهِيمُ ۝ قَالَ بَلْ فَعَلَهُۥ كَبِيرُهُمْ هَٰذَا فَسْـَٔلُوهُمْ إِن كَانُوا۟ يَنطِقُونَ ۝ فَرَجَعُوٓا۟ إِلَىٰٓ أَنفُسِهِمْ فَقَالُوٓا۟ إِنَّكُمْ أَنتُمُ ٱلظَّٰلِمُونَ ۝ ثُمَّ نُكِسُوا۟ عَلَىٰ رُءُوسِهِمْ لَقَدْ عَلِمْتَ مَا هَٰٓؤُلَآءِ يَنطِقُونَ ۝ قَالَ أَفَتَعْبُدُونَ مِن دُونِ ٱللَّهِ مَا لَا يَنفَعُكُمْ شَيْـًٔا وَلَا يَضُرُّكُمْ ۝ أُفٍّ لَّكُمْ وَلِمَا تَعْبُدُونَ مِن دُونِ ٱللَّهِ أَفَلَا تَعْقِلُونَ ۝ قَالُوا۟ حَرِّقُوهُ وَٱنصُرُوٓا۟ ءَالِهَتَكُمْ إِن كُنتُمْ فَٰعِلِينَ ۝ قُلْنَا يَٰنَارُ كُونِى بَرْدًا وَسَلَٰمًا عَلَىٰٓ إِبْرَٰهِيمَ ۝ وَأَرَادُوا۟ بِهِۦ كَيْدًا فَجَعَلْنَٰهُمُ ٱلْأَخْسَرِينَ ۝

"We guided Ibraaheem to the truth at a young age before the time of Moosaa and Haaroon, and We knew that he was fitting for that and was a person of true and certain *eemaan* who would worship Allaah alone and not associate any partner with Him. When he said to his father and his people, 'What are these idols which you worship and are devoted to?!' They said, 'We found our fathers worshipping them and have followed them in that.' He said, 'Both you and they in worshipping the idols are in clear error.' They said, 'Are you serious in your saying that you have come with the truth, or are you merely being frivolous?' He said, 'Rather, I bring you the truth. Your Lord, other than Whom none has the right to be worshipped, is the sole Lord and Creator of the heavens and the earth, He Who created you all, not any of the idols to which you are devoted. I am a witness to the fact that none but Him is deserving of your worship.' Ibraaheem said in secret (but was overheard by a single man from his people), 'By Allaah, I intend to destroy their idols when they go off to their festival.' So he broke them to pieces except for the largest of them (upon which he tied the axe with which he had broken the others), so that they might take heed and abandon worship of their idols after witnessing their weakness and futility. The people said, 'Who has done this to our gods?! Whoever has done it is certainly a criminal.' Those who had heard the saying of Ibraaheem said, 'We heard a youth speaking, he is called Ibraaheem.' They said, 'Bring him before the eyes of the people, that they may testify against him.' They said, 'Is it you who did this to our gods, O Ibraaheem?' He said, 'Rather this one, the largest of them did it. Ask the idols who had it done to them, if it is that they can speak.' So they

> turned to themselves and said, 'You know that they are unable to speak.' He said, 'Then will you worship besides Allaah that which cannot benefit you at all, nor harm you. Woe to you and the idols which you worship besides Allaah. Have you no sense to see the futility of your worship of the idols?' They said, 'Burn him and aid your gods, if you do indeed wish to aid them and continue to worship them.' We said, 'O fire, be cool and safe for Ibraaheem.' They wished to cause harm to him, but it was they whom We caused to be the losers."[78]

So Allaah guided Ibraaheem to the truth knowing that he was fitting for that. This wise and rightly-guided Prophet faced corruptions in beliefs (*'aqeedah*) and corruption in rule and authority. A nation whose thinking was degenerate, people whose minds were astray, so that they worshipped idols in the form of pieces of wood, rocks and stars. They were also ruled by a corrupt and evil government lead by a tyrant who claimed divinity, yet the people submitted to his leadership. So where was Ibraaheem to begin his correction? Should he have begun by attacking the ruler, since for certain he had ruled by other than the revealed Law of Allaah and ruled by the laws of ignorance. There is no doubt about that. He also openly claimed Lordship and the right to make and lay down the law. Or should he have begun with correction of beliefs (*'aqeedah*). Correcting the *'aqeedah* of the nation and the *'aqeedah* of the government of ignorance?!

The Qur'aan informs us that this rightly-guided Prophet, the *Imaam* of the Prophets, began with correction of *'aqeedah*, that is the call to the *tawheed* of Allaah, and to make all worship purely and sincerely for Him

---

[78] Soorah al-Ambiyaa (21):51-70.

alone, and fighting and wiping out *shirk*, and demolishing its causes, and tearing it out from the roots. So that is what he did: he called them to the *tawheed* of Allaah, and to renounce the worship of everything besides Him. He argued with them about this matter and they argued with him. But he refuted them with powerful arguments and clear proofs, and he stripped them of everything they sought to use as a proof until they admitted their wrongdoing, misguidance, and their blind-following and stubborn and fatal acceptance of the ways of their forefathers.

$$\text{قَالُوا۟ وَجَدْنَآ ءَابَآءَنَا لَهَا عَٰبِدِينَ ﴿٥٣﴾}$$

"They said, 'We found our fathers worshipping them and have followed them in that.'"[79]

So when Ibraaheem saw obstinate following of desires and intellects as hard as rock, he made a wise and brave plan to destroy their idols. He carried out this plan with full vigour, bravery and courage. Then this heroic act[80] incited the government and the nation against him, and they called him for judgement in public and laid down the charge before him,

$$\text{ءَأَنتَ فَعَلْتَ هَٰذَا بِـَٔالِهَتِنَا يَٰٓإِبْرَٰهِيمُ ﴿٦٢﴾}$$

"Is it you who did this to our gods, O Ibraaheem?"[81]

---

[79] Soorah al-Ambiyaa (21):53.
[80] The great heroic action and the wise call to *tawheed* and to the elimination of *shirk*, is counted by many of the callers to correction these days as being an example of preoccupying oneself with minor and insignificant matters. And there is no action nor power except by the will of Allaah. Indeed it is not the eyes that are blind, but rather the hearts. They think that *da'wah* must begin with a call to the correction and rectification of rulership and government, not correction of *'aqeedah*. In this view Ibraaheem and all the other Prophets were in error with regard to the correct methodology of *da'wah*. (al-Fawzaan).
[81] Soorah al-Ambiyaa (21):62.

So he responded to them in a mocking and sarcastic manner,

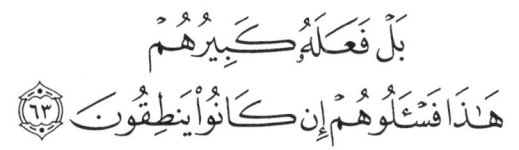

$$بَلْ فَعَلَهُ كَبِيرُهُمْ هَٰذَا فَسْـَٔلُوهُمْ إِن كَانُوا۟ يَنطِقُونَ ۝$$

"Rather this one, the largest of them did it. Ask the idols who had it done to them, if it is that they can speak."[82]

So this mocking reply was like a thunderbolt striking their imbecilic minds.

$$ثُمَّ نُكِسُوا۟ عَلَىٰ رُءُوسِهِمْ لَقَدْ عَلِمْتَ مَا هَٰٓؤُلَآءِ يَنطِقُونَ$$

"Then they relapsed and said, 'You know that they are unable to speak.'"[83]

So when he had divested them of the weapon of argument, they resorted to using force, the weapon used by everyone lacking proof in every time and place,

$$قَالُوا۟ حَرِّقُوهُ وَٱنصُرُوٓا۟ ءَالِهَتَكُمْ إِن كُنتُمْ فَٰعِلِينَ ۝$$

"They said, 'Burn him and aid your gods, if you do indeed wish to aid them and continue to worship them.'"[84]

But Allaah saved His chosen and beloved friend, Ibraaheem, and He threw back the plot of the unbelievers upon them.

$$قُلْنَا يَٰنَارُ كُونِى بَرْدًا وَسَلَٰمًا عَلَىٰٓ إِبْرَٰهِيمَ ۝$$

---

[82] Soorah al-Ambiyaa (21):63.
[83] Soorah al-Ambiyaa (21):65.
[84] Soorah al-Ambiyaa (21):68.

"We said, 'O fire, be cool and safe for Ibraaheem.' They wished to cause harm to him, but it was they whom we caused to be the losers."[85]

So the fact that Ibraaheem was saved from harm in that huge fire, which Allaah caused to become cool and safe for Ibraaheem, was a very great sign, indeed one of the greatest of Allaah's signs proving his Prophethood, his truthfulness, and the correctness of what he came with, i.e., *tawheed* and the declaration of the futility of the *shirk* and misguidance which his people were upon.

Then Allaah rewarded Ibraaheem, *'alayhis-salaam*, for this wise *da'wah*, and this outstanding *jihaad* and sacrifice,

﴿ وَنَجَّيْنَٰهُ وَلُوطًا إِلَى ٱلْأَرْضِ ٱلَّتِي بَٰرَكْنَا فِيهَا لِلْعَٰلَمِينَ ۞ وَوَهَبْنَا لَهُۥٓ إِسْحَٰقَ وَيَعْقُوبَ نَافِلَةً ۖ وَكُلًّا جَعَلْنَا صَٰلِحِينَ ۞ وَجَعَلْنَٰهُمْ أَئِمَّةً يَهْدُونَ بِأَمْرِنَا وَأَوْحَيْنَآ إِلَيْهِمْ فِعْلَ ٱلْخَيْرَٰتِ وَإِقَامَ ٱلصَّلَوٰةِ وَإِيتَآءَ ٱلزَّكَوٰةِ ۖ وَكَانُوا۟ لَنَا عَٰبِدِينَ ۞ ﴾

"We saved Ibraaheem and Loot from their enemies and took them to the land which We have blessed for all the worlds. And We bestowed upon him Ishaaq (his son) and Ya'qoob (his grandson) as an extra favour upon him. And We made all of them those who acted in obedience to Allaah and avoided what He forbade. And We made them leaders to be followed, guiding the people according to Our orders and calling them to worship and obey Allaah. And We in-

---

[85] Soorah al-Ambiyaa (21):70.

spired in them the doing of those deeds which are good, and establishment of the Prayer, and payment of the *Zakaat*. And they were worshippers of Us alone."[86]

---

[86] Soorah al-Ambiyaa (21):71-73.

Yoosuf

The noble one, son of the noble one, son of the noble one.[87] About whom Allaah sent down a long *Soorah* relating his noble life to us, and its stages, from his childhood to his death, and how his circumstances changed, and the difficulties that he faced, and how he faced everything with the Strength of Prophethood and his patient perseverance, wisdom and mildness.

Yoosuf, *'alayhis-salaam*, saw the corrupt outlook of the Pharaohs in Egypt and their oppression, and he knew the beliefs of the nation amongst whom he lived. He knew the corruption of their beliefs and their idolatry, which led them to take idols and cattle as gods to worship besides Allaah. The story of this noble Prophet, *'alayhis-salaam*, is long, and from it, we will examine the story of his imprisonment and his *da'wah* at that time. Allaah, the Most High, says,

---

[87] As indicated in the *hadeeth* of Ibn 'Umar, *radiyallaahu 'anhumaa*, from the Prophet (ﷺ) that he said, *"The noble one, son of the noble one, son of the noble one: Yoosuf the son of Ya'qoob, the son of Ishaaq, the son of Ibraaheem, 'alayhis-salaam."* Reported by al-Bukhaaree (Eng. trans. 4/390/596), and Ahmad in *al-Musnad* (2/96), and also the *hadeeth* of Aboo Hurayrah, *radiyallaahu 'anhu*, that Allaah's Messenger (ﷺ) was asked about the noblest of the people, so he said, *"Those most pious and obedient to Allaah."* They said, *"It is not this that we are asking about."* He said, *"Then the noblest of the people is Yoosuf, the Prophet of Allaah, son of the Prophet of Allaah, son of the Prophet of Allaah, son of the chosen and beloved Friend of Allaah."* They said, *"It is not this that we are asking about."* He said, *"Then is it about the origins of the Arabs that you ask? Then the people are of various origins. The best of them in the times of ignorance are the best of them in Islaam when they attain knowledge and understanding in the religion."* Reported by al-Bukhaaree (Eng. trans. 4/390/597).

وَدَخَلَ مَعَهُ ٱلسِّجْنَ فَتَيَانِ ۖ قَالَ أَحَدُهُمَآ إِنِّىٓ أَرَىٰنِىٓ أَعْصِرُ خَمْرًا ۖ وَقَالَ ٱلْآخَرُ إِنِّىٓ أَرَىٰنِىٓ أَحْمِلُ فَوْقَ رَأْسِى خُبْزًا تَأْكُلُ ٱلطَّيْرُ مِنْهُ ۖ نَبِّئْنَا بِتَأْوِيلِهِۦٓ ۖ إِنَّا نَرَىٰكَ مِنَ ٱلْمُحْسِنِينَ ۝ قَالَ لَا يَأْتِيكُمَا طَعَامٌ تُرْزَقَانِهِۦٓ إِلَّا نَبَّأْتُكُمَا بِتَأْوِيلِهِۦ قَبْلَ أَن يَأْتِيَكُمَا ۚ ذَٰلِكُمَا مِمَّا عَلَّمَنِى رَبِّىٓ ۚ إِنِّى تَرَكْتُ مِلَّةَ قَوْمٍ لَّا يُؤْمِنُونَ بِٱللَّهِ وَهُم بِٱلْآخِرَةِ هُمْ كَٰفِرُونَ ۝ وَٱتَّبَعْتُ مِلَّةَ ءَابَآءِىٓ إِبْرَٰهِيمَ وَإِسْحَٰقَ وَيَعْقُوبَ ۚ مَا كَانَ لَنَآ أَن نُّشْرِكَ بِٱللَّهِ مِن شَىْءٍ ۚ ذَٰلِكَ مِن فَضْلِ ٱللَّهِ عَلَيْنَا وَعَلَى ٱلنَّاسِ وَلَٰكِنَّ أَكْثَرَ ٱلنَّاسِ لَا يَشْكُرُونَ ۝ يَٰصَٰحِبَىِ ٱلسِّجْنِ ءَأَرْبَابٌ مُّتَفَرِّقُونَ خَيْرٌ أَمِ ٱللَّهُ ٱلْوَٰحِدُ ٱلْقَهَّارُ ۝ مَا تَعْبُدُونَ مِن دُونِهِۦٓ إِلَّآ أَسْمَآءً سَمَّيْتُمُوهَآ أَنتُمْ وَءَابَآؤُكُم مَّآ أَنزَلَ ٱللَّهُ بِهَا مِن سُلْطَٰنٍ ۚ إِنِ ٱلْحُكْمُ إِلَّا لِلَّهِ ۚ أَمَرَ أَلَّا تَعْبُدُوٓا۟ إِلَّآ إِيَّاهُ ۚ ذَٰلِكَ ٱلدِّينُ ٱلْقَيِّمُ وَلَٰكِنَّ أَكْثَرَ ٱلنَّاسِ لَا يَعْلَمُونَ ۝

"And two young men entered the prison along with him. One of them said, 'I saw in a dream that I was pressing grapes,' and the other one said, 'I saw in a dream that I was carrying bread upon my head and birds were eating from it.' 'Inform us of the interpretation of this for indeed we see that you are one of the doers of good.' He said, 'No food will come to you to eat except that I will inform you about it fully before it comes to you. This is from the knowledge which my Lord has taught me as I have remained free of the religion of a people who do not believe in the oneness of Allaah and who are disbelievers in the Hereafter. Rather I follow the religion of my fathers, Ibraaheem, Ishaaq and Ya'qoob. It is not fitting that we should worship anything else along with Allaah. This is from Allaah's favour upon us and upon the people, yet most of the people do not give thanks for Allaah's favours. O my two companions in the prison, is it better that you worship many different lords, or that you worship only Allaah, the One, Who subdues and has full power over everything? You do not worship besides Allaah except idols which you call gods, which you and your forefathers give names to, for which Allaah has sent down no authority. Authority is for Allaah alone. He ordered that you worship none but Him, that is the Straight and true religion, yet most of the people do not know (and are people of *shirk*).'"[88]

This noble Prophet, *'alayhis-salaam*, lived in their palaces and was therefore well aware of the corruption of their administration and their rulers. He experienced at first hand their plots, their oppression, their unjust persecution and imprisonment by them. Furthermore he lived amongst an idolatrous nation who worshipped idols, cattle and stars. So where was correction to begin? What was the starting point?

---

[88] Soorah Yoosuf (12):36-40.

Did he begin calling to Allaah, whilst he was wrongfully imprisoned along with others who were oppressed like him, by inciting them and rousing them against the despotic and tyrant rulers? This would be without a doubt a political response, and was an opportunity open to him. Or did he begin his call from the starting point adopted by his noble forefathers, and at the head of them Ibraaheem, the chosen and beloved Friend of Allaah and the *Imaam* of the call to *tawheed*; which was the starting point for all the Messengers of Allaah? There is no doubt that the single way of correction and rectification in every time and place is the way of calling to correct *'aqeedah* and *tawheed* and that all worship should be made purely and sincerely for Allaah alone.

Therefore Yoosuf began from this starting point, following his noble fathers, proud of their *'aqeedah*, and deriding and exposing the foolishness of the idolaters and their practice of taking idols, cattle and stars as lords to be worshipped besides Allaah.

So after clearly explaining this, and openly calling to *tawheed* and to rejection of *shirk*, he emphasised his call and his argument by his saying,

إِنِ ٱلْحُكْمُ إِلَّا لِلَّهِ

"Authority and command is for Allaah alone."[89, 90]

---

[89] Soorah Yoosuf (12):40.

[90] This *Aayah* is one of the basic principles from the principles of *tawheed*, as Allaah has explained upon the tongue of Yoosuf, *'alayhis-salaam*. What is most unfortunate is that you see that many of the political reformers have explained it in a way that is far removed from its primary meaning, that all worship is to be made purely and sincerely for Allaah alone, and have instead explained it to have a political meaning, which is establishment of the state which they claim will establish Allaah's *Sharee'ah* upon the earth as His deputies/vicegerents. Then they go beyond bounds in this direction till they cause the people to forget the principal meaning of the *Aayah*, and they understand nothing from it except this new meaning, and there is no action and no ability except by the will of Allaah. They do the same with all or most of the *Aayaat* of *tawheed*.

Then he explained this authority and command to mean the *tawheed* of Allaah, and that He alone is to be worshipped:

$$ذَٰلِكَ ٱلدِّينُ ٱلْقَيِّمُ وَلَٰكِنَّ أَكْثَرَ ٱلنَّاسِ لَا يَعْلَمُونَ$$

"...That is the Straight and true religion, yet most of the people do not know (and are people of *shirk*)."[91]

Also Yoosuf, *'alayhis-salaam*, attained the highest position in this state[92] whilst calling to the *tawheed* of Allaah and establishing the clear proofs for his call and his Prophethood. Allaah, the Most High, says, in explanation of this,

$$وَقَالَ ٱلْمَلِكُ ٱئْتُونِى بِهِۦٓ أَسْتَخْلِصْهُ لِنَفْسِى ۖ فَلَمَّا كَلَّمَهُۥ قَالَ إِنَّكَ ٱلْيَوْمَ لَدَيْنَا مَكِينٌ أَمِينٌ ۝ قَالَ ٱجْعَلْنِى عَلَىٰ خَزَآئِنِ ٱلْأَرْضِ ۖ إِنِّى حَفِيظٌ عَلِيمٌ ۝$$

"The king of Egypt said, 'Bring him to me, I will make him my personal servant.' So when he spoke to Yoosuf, he said, 'Verily, this day you have with us a position of rank and full trust.' He said, 'Place me in charge of the storehouses and wealth of the land, indeed I will guard them faithfully and with full knowledge.'"[93]

---

[91] Soorah Yoosuf (12):40.
[92] Shaykhul-Islaam Ibn Taymiyyah, *rahimahullaah*, said in *al-Hisbah* (p.7), "Likewise Yoosuf the truthful and honest, was a minister for the Pharaoh of Egypt, and he and his people were *mushriks*. So Yoosuf performed whatever justice and good he was able to and called them as far as possible to correct *eemaan*."
[93] Soorah Yoosuf (12):54-55.

And he said, giving thanks to his Lord and Protector,

$$رَبِّ قَدْ ءَاتَيْتَنِي مِنَ ٱلْمُلْكِ وَعَلَّمْتَنِي مِن تَأْوِيلِ ٱلْأَحَادِيثِ فَاطِرَ ٱلسَّمَوَاتِ وَٱلْأَرْضِ أَنتَ وَلِيِّ فِي ٱلدُّنْيَا وَٱلْأَخِرَةِ تَوَفَّنِي مُسْلِمًا وَأَلْحِقْنِي بِٱلصَّالِحِينَ ۝$$

"O my Lord, You have bestowed upon me something of dominion and have taught me the interpretation of dreams. O Originator and Creator of the heavens and the earth, You are my Lord and Protector in this world and the Hereafter. Cause me to die as a Muslim and join me with the righteous."[94]

Furthermore Allaah says in explanation of his *da'wah*, upon the tongue of the Believer from the family of the Pharaoh:

$$وَلَقَدْ جَاءَكُمْ يُوسُفُ مِن قَبْلُ بِٱلْبَيِّنَاتِ فَمَا زِلْتُمْ فِي شَكٍّ مِّمَّا جَاءَكُم بِهِ حَتَّىٰ إِذَا هَلَكَ قُلْتُمْ لَن يَبْعَثَ ٱللَّهُ مِنْ بَعْدِهِ رَسُولًا كَذَٰلِكَ يُضِلُّ ٱللَّهُ مَنْ هُوَ مُسْرِفٌ مُّرْتَابٌ ۝$$

"And Yoosuf came to you previously (before Moosaa) with clear signs yet you have not ceased doubting about what he came to you with. Until when he died you said, 'Allaah will not send any Messenger after him.' This is the state of those whom Allaah leads astray, those who are disbelievers in Him and doubt the truthfulness of the Messengers."[95]

---

[94] Soorah Yoosuf (12):101.
[95] Soorah Ghaafir:(40):34.

So from the knowledge to be learned from the life-story of Yoosuf, *'alayhis-salaam*, which is presented to us in these noble *Aayaat* is that the call to *tawheed* is something very essential. Furthermore there is to be no leniency or relaxation in fighting against *shirk*, it is not permissible to keep silent about it, whatever the circumstances of the caller to Allaah; rather it is not permissible for any Muslim to ever accept it or be relaxed about it. So this shows the high station of *'aqeedah*, and its importance with Allaah, and with His Prophets and His Messenger. It also shows the very great difference and the distance between it and the details of Islaam.

It is not permissible for the Muslim, particularly the caller, to take up any position which violates his *'aqeedah* or is contrary to it, or that he is a fortune-teller, those who are *mushriks*, or that he is a custodian of their idols. If he does any of this then he is one of the misguided *mushriks*. With regard to the legislative aspect, if the Islamic state is established, it must apply the *Sharee'ah* of Allaah, otherwise:

﴿وَمَن لَّمْ يَحْكُم بِمَآ أَنزَلَ ٱللَّهُ فَأُوْلَٰٓئِكَ هُمُ ٱلْكَٰفِرُونَ ٤٤﴾

"And whoever does not judge by what Allaah has revealed then they are the ones guilty of infidelity (*kufr*)."[96]

The unbelief (*kufr*) here is explained in detail by the scholars of Islaam, from the Companions and others, that it may be major *kufr*, when the person disdains the *Sharee'ah* of Allaah and declares it lawful to judge by something else, and it may be lesser *kufr* (i.e., that which does not take a person out of Islaam) when he does not declare it lawful to judge by other than it, but gives in to his desires and because of that judges by other than what Allaah sent down.

---

[96] Soorah al-Maa'idah (5):44.

However when the Islamic state has not been established, then Allaah does not a burden a soul with more than it is capable of. So the Muslim may take up a position in a non-Muslim state with the condition that he establishes justice, and that he does not obey them in a matter which involves disobedience to Allaah, and does not judge by other than what Allaah sent down. This was what the Prophet of Allaah, Yoosuf, did. He took up a position as a deputy for a unbelieving king, and he did not judge according to his laws:

مَا كَانَ لِيَأْخُذَ أَخَاهُ فِي دِينِ ٱلْمَلِكِ

"He could not have taken and kept his brother according to the king's law."[97]

Furthermore, he established justice between the subjects and called them to the *tawheed* of Allaah. So this contains a decisive reply to those who give little importance to the *'aqeedah* of *tawheed*. Those who gloss over and accommodate when it comes to the *shirk* which has filled the world, and they regard the callers to *tawheed* and the enemies of *shirk* with contempt and scorn. They turn up their noses and are too proud to 'lower' themselves to the level of the callers to *tawheed*, and they are very wily and astute concerning political affairs, but nothing is more burdensome and disagreeable to their hearing and their hearts than listening to or saying a word regarding *tawheed* or *shirk*. These types of callers have caused themselves to fall into a deep abyss, whilst they think that they have reached the highest peaks. Can a people ever prosper whose stance with regard to the call of the Prophets is like this, unless they sincerely repent to Allaah from what they are upon?

---

[97] Soorah Yoosuf (12):76.

Moosaa

Moosaa, the one to whom Allaah spoke directly, the strong and trustworthy.

We see that his call was directed to *tawheed* and carried the lights of guidance and wisdom. Moosaa was brought up and was raised in the palaces of the greatest tyrant who claimed divinity. He knew the various types of corruption, unbelief, tyranny, injustice and despotism from what he witnessed in the palaces. He saw things which it is difficult to imagine or think possible. He also saw the enslavement of his people, the Children of *Israa'eel*, and their humiliation, and their women taken as slaves, and the killing of their children, to such an extent that it surpassed any oppression known to mankind. Allaah, the Most High, says,

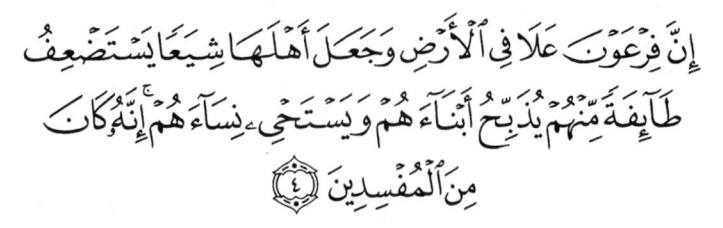

$$\text{إِنَّ فِرْعَوْنَ عَلَا فِي ٱلْأَرْضِ وَجَعَلَ أَهْلَهَا شِيَعًا يَسْتَضْعِفُ طَآئِفَةً مِّنْهُمْ يُذَبِّحُ أَبْنَآءَهُمْ وَيَسْتَحْيِ نِسَآءَهُمْ ۚ إِنَّهُۥ كَانَ مِنَ ٱلْمُفْسِدِينَ}$$

"Pharaoh exalted himself haughtily in the land, and divided its people into castes. He enslaved a group of them (i.e. the Children of *Israa'eel*), killing their sons and letting their women live. He was indeed one of the corrupt evil-doers."[98]

The people of Pharaoh were also people of *shirk* and idol-worship without a doubt.

---

[98] Soorah al-Qasas (28):4.

So how did Moosaa begin? Was his call directed to correction of the *'aqeedah* of this idolatrous nation? Or did it begin with a demand for the restoration of the rights of the Children of *Israa'eel*, and a struggle to gain rulership and authority from the hands of the tyrant, and at the head of them Pharaoh, who claimed divinity for himself?

The call of Moosaa was just like the call of his forefathers and brothers from the earlier Prophets. His Lord instructed him and inspired him with the principle of *tawheed*, and chose him to carry his revelation, and to establish worship of Him. Allaah, the Most High, says,

$$\text{إِذْ رَءَا نَارًا فَقَالَ لِأَهْلِهِ ٱمْكُثُوٓا۟ إِنِّىٓ ءَانَسْتُ نَارًا لَّعَلِّىٓ ءَاتِيكُم مِّنْهَا بِقَبَسٍ أَوْ أَجِدُ عَلَى ٱلنَّارِ هُدًى ۝ فَلَمَّآ أَتَىٰهَا نُودِىَ يَٰمُوسَىٰٓ ۝ إِنِّىٓ أَنَا۠ رَبُّكَ فَٱخْلَعْ نَعْلَيْكَ إِنَّكَ بِٱلْوَادِ ٱلْمُقَدَّسِ طُوًى ۝ وَأَنَا ٱخْتَرْتُكَ فَٱسْتَمِعْ لِمَا يُوحَىٰٓ ۝ إِنَّنِىٓ أَنَا ٱللَّهُ لَآ إِلَٰهَ إِلَّآ أَنَا۠ فَٱعْبُدْنِى وَأَقِمِ ٱلصَّلَوٰةَ لِذِكْرِىٓ ۝ إِنَّ ٱلسَّاعَةَ ءَاتِيَةٌ أَكَادُ أُخْفِيهَا لِتُجْزَىٰ كُلُّ نَفْسٍۭ بِمَا تَسْعَىٰ ۝}$$

"Has not the story of Moosaa come to you? When he saw a fire and said to his family, 'Remain where you are for I have seen a fire. Perhaps I can bring a firebrand from it or find someone who can show us the way.' So when Moosaa came to the fire his Lord called him, 'O Moosaa, I am your Lord. Remove your shoes, indeed you are in the purified valley of *Tuwaa*. I

have chosen you as My Messenger, so listen to and heed what I reveal to you. Indeed I am Allaah. None has the right to be worshipped but Me. So worship Me and do not worship anything else besides Me, and establish Prayer for My remembrance. Indeed the Final Hour is certainly coming, which I keep hidden from all except Myself, in order to reward each soul according to its good or bad deeds.'"[99]

So this was the beginning of his Messengership; he was inspired and ordered with the *'aqeedah* of *tawheed*. He was ordered to establish it in himself and to represent it in his life. Then he was entrusted with the duty of calling to this sublime principle and was sent by Allaah to the Pharaoh. Allaah furthermore explained to him the correct manner of giving *da'wah* and the wise way in which he was to face the Pharaoh. Allaah, the Most High, said:

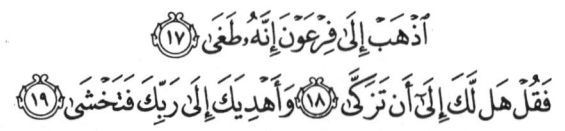

$$\text{اذْهَبْ إِلَىٰ فِرْعَوْنَ إِنَّهُۥ طَغَىٰ ۝ فَقُلْ هَل لَّكَ إِلَىٰٓ أَن تَزَكَّىٰ ۝ وَأَهْدِيَكَ إِلَىٰ رَبِّكَ فَتَخْشَىٰ ۝}$$

"Go to Pharaoh who has transgressed all bounds in his haughtiness, pride, unbelief, and say, 'Will you not purify yourself from the sin of unbelief and be obedient to your Lord? And that I guide you to the worship of your Lord, so that you may submit fearfully to Him and obey Him.'"[100]

He also supported him with his brother Haaroon in order for the proof to be established to the utmost, and He taught them to use gentleness and mildness in *da'wah* since that is the best way to attain the guidance of

---

[99] Soorah Taa Haa (20):9-15.
[100] Soorah an-Naazi'aat (79):17-19.

those whom Allaah wishes to guide:

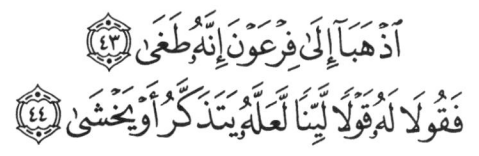

$$اذْهَبَا إِلَىٰ فِرْعَوْنَ إِنَّهُ طَغَىٰ ۝ فَقُولَا لَهُ قَوْلًا لَّيِّنًا لَّعَلَّهُ يَتَذَكَّرُ أَوْ يَخْشَىٰ ۝$$

"Go both of you to Pharaoh, indeed he has transgressed beyond all bounds, and speak mildly with him that he might accept admonition and fear and be obedient to his Lord."[101]

So they carried out the order of their Lord and called him to Allaah, hoping for him to be guided and purified, so that he should be one of those who fear Allaah and fear and beware of the evil consequences of *shirk* and oppression. But he did not respond to this wise and composed call. So Moosaa manifested the great signs and clear proofs of his Prophethood and the truthfulness of his Messengership. But the despotic tyrant Pharaoh merely increased in his transgression and rejection of the truth:

$$فَكَذَّبَ وَعَصَىٰ ۝ ثُمَّ أَدْبَرَ يَسْعَىٰ ۝ فَحَشَرَ فَنَادَىٰ ۝ فَقَالَ أَنَا رَبُّكُمُ الْأَعْلَىٰ ۝ فَأَخَذَهُ اللَّهُ نَكَالَ الْآخِرَةِ وَالْأُولَىٰ ۝$$

"But Pharaoh denied the signs which Moosaa came with and disobeyed his order for him to fear and obey his Lord. Then he turned away from what he ordered him (i.e. obedience to his Lord) and instead worked evil and corruption, and he gathered his people and his followers and said, 'I am your lord, the most high.' So Allaah seized him with punishment for his latter and his earlier saying."[102]

---

[101] Soorah Taa Haa (20):43-44.
[102] Soorah an-Naazi'aat (79):21-25.

The Escalation of the Tyranny of the Pharaoh and how Moosaa and his People Faced it with Patient Perseverance and Forbearance

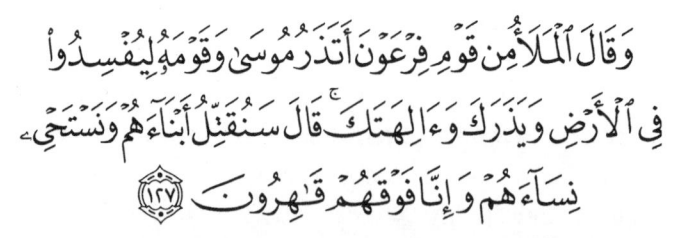

$$\text{وَقَالَ ٱلْمَلَأُ مِن قَوْمِ فِرْعَوْنَ أَتَذَرُ مُوسَىٰ وَقَوْمَهُۥ لِيُفْسِدُواْ فِى ٱلْأَرْضِ وَيَذَرَكَ وَءَالِهَتَكَ ۚ قَالَ سَنُقَتِّلُ أَبْنَآءَهُمْ وَنَسْتَحْىِۦ نِسَآءَهُمْ وَإِنَّا فَوْقَهُمْ قَٰهِرُونَ ۝}$$

"The chiefs of Pharaoh's people said, 'Will you leave Moosaa and his people to cause mischief in the land when they have abandoned worship of you and worship of your gods?' He said, 'We will kill their sons and let their women live, and will have full power over them.'"[103]

So what was the sin of Moosaa and his people in the view of these criminals? No crime except that they called to the *tawheed* of Allaah and to remain firm upon it, and to disbelieve in Pharaoh and his idols. Then what was the response of Moosaa with respect to these disgraceful and outrageous transgressions which exceeded all bounds in its barbarity and ferocity?!

His response was to remain firm upon correct belief, and to have patience and forbearance, and to seek the aid of Allaah in facing these calamities. Then he awaited the good outcome, and victory as a consequence and a good fruit of this remaining firm and this patient perseverance.

---

[103] Soorah al-A'raaf (7):127.

$$\text{قَالَ مُوسَىٰ لِقَوْمِهِ ٱسْتَعِينُوا بِٱللَّهِ وَٱصْبِرُوٓا۟ إِنَّ ٱلْأَرْضَ لِلَّهِ يُورِثُهَا مَن يَشَآءُ مِنْ عِبَادِهِۦ وَٱلْعَـٰقِبَةُ لِلْمُتَّقِينَ ۝}$$

"Moosaa said to his people, 'Seeks Allaah's help and be patient, the earth is Allaah's, He gives it as a heritage to whom He pleases from His servants. The final outcome is in favour of those who fear Allaah by avoiding disobedience of Him and doing what He orders.'"[104]

Then when no hope that the Pharaoh and his people would believe remained, and the suffering which the Children of *Israa'eel* were subjected to increased in severity, the sole request which Moosaa made to the Pharaoh was that he should allow the Children of *Israa'eel* the freedom to leave the land of Egypt and emigrate to wherever Allaah willed that they should go, in order to save them from the torment inflicted upon them.

$$\text{فَأْتِيَاهُ فَقُولَآ إِنَّا رَسُولَا رَبِّكَ فَأَرْسِلْ مَعَنَا بَنِىٓ إِسْرَٰٓءِيلَ وَلَا تُعَذِّبْهُمْ قَدْ جِئْنَـٰكَ بِـَٔايَةٍ مِّن رَّبِّكَ وَٱلسَّلَـٰمُ عَلَىٰ مَنِ ٱتَّبَعَ ٱلْهُدَىٰٓ}$$

"So go to the Pharaoh, saying, 'We are the Messengers sent by your Lord, to order you to free the Children of *Israa'eel*. So release them and cease tormenting them. Indeed we bring you a clear sign from your Lord, and peace and safety from Allaah's punishment are for those who follow the guidance.'"[105]

---

[104] Soorah al-A'raaf (7):128.
[105] Soorah Taa Haa (20):47.

It was a sublime call to the *tawheed* of Allaah containing light and wisdom. It was also accompanied by an eager desire for the guidance of those who were being called, and that they should be purified. It also contained a clear example of the utmost patience and forbearance in enduring great harm, and in facing tyranny and haughty oppression. It also shows the way to face the most difficult situations with wisdom and forbearance, whilst having the strongest hope in Allaah, that He will assist and grant victory to the Believers and destroy the unbelieving oppressors. Including clear lessons for those who make their call purely seeking the Face of Allaah and desire to rectify mankind and to turn to their Lord, and for them to be guided to His Straight Path.

Muhammad (ﷺ)

The noblest of all the Prophets and the last of them, Muhammad ibn 'Abdullaah (ﷺ). The one sent with the greatest, most complete and most comprehensive message. The one whom Allaah sent as a mercy for the worlds, and as a bringer of good tidings and a warner, and as a Caller to Allaah with His permission, and a shining light. He did not leave anything good except that he guided his *ummah* to it and pointed it out to them, nor anything evil except that he warned them against it. So which of the fundamentals of Islaam did this exalted Prophet begin with? What was the starting point for his *da'wah*? He (ﷺ) began with what all the Prophets began with, and started where they started in their *da'wah*: calling to the *'aqeedah* of *tawheed*, and calling for all worship to be made purely and sincerely for Allaah alone. He began with the testification, "None has the right to be worshipped except Allaah, Muhammad is the Messenger of Allaah," (*Laa ilaaha illallaah Muhammadur Rasoolullaah*). Can it be imagined that he or any of the other Prophets would begin with anything but this great principle, the foundation of all the divine Messages?! Allaah's Messenger (ﷺ) began with this fundamental principle, so the first thing which the people heard was, 'Witness that none has the right to be worshipped except Allaah.' So the proud and haughty said:

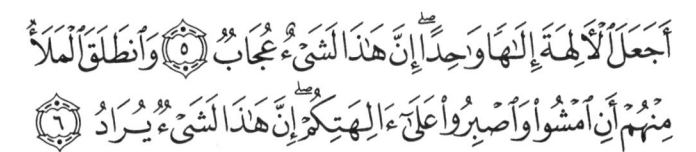

$$\text{أَجَعَلَ ٱلْآلِهَةَ إِلَٰهًا وَٰحِدًا ۖ إِنَّ هَٰذَا لَشَيْءٌ عُجَابٌ ﴿٥﴾ وَٱنطَلَقَ ٱلْمَلَأُ مِنْهُمْ أَنِ ٱمْشُوا۟ وَٱصْبِرُوا۟ عَلَىٰٓ ءَالِهَتِكُمْ ۖ إِنَّ هَٰذَا لَشَيْءٌ يُرَادُ ﴿٦﴾}$$

> "The unbelievers said, 'Has he made all that is to be worshipped a single God, who alone is to be called upon and hears all invocations. This is a very curious thing which we have not heard of.' So the leaders amongst them went off saying to one another, 'Continue in what you are upon and persist in wor-

shipping your idols. He only says this to gain ascendancy over us.'"[106]

He continued calling to this lofty principle and highest goal throughout the Meccan period of his Messengership, for thirteen years. He did not become weary or languid. He patiently bore all types of harm to propagate this principle, since no religious duties or pillars of Islaam were obligated upon him, except for the Prayer which was obligated in the tenth year of Prophethood, and apart from the excellent manners of keeping ties of relationship, truthfulness and chastity which he commanded his people with. However the core of his *da'wah* and the cause of dispute and opposition to him was that great fundamental principle. So Allaah charged this noble Prophet (ﷺ) with the particular duty of establishing this great principle. Allaah, the Most High, says:

$$\text{إِنَّآ أَنزَلْنَآ إِلَيْكَ ٱلْكِتَٰبَ بِٱلْحَقِّ فَٱعْبُدِ ٱللَّهَ مُخْلِصًا لَّهُ ٱلدِّينَ ۝ أَلَا لِلَّهِ ٱلدِّينُ ٱلْخَالِصُ ۚ وَٱلَّذِينَ ٱتَّخَذُوا۟ مِن دُونِهِۦٓ أَوْلِيَآءَ مَا نَعْبُدُهُمْ إِلَّا لِيُقَرِّبُونَآ إِلَى ٱللَّهِ زُلْفَىٰٓ إِنَّ ٱللَّهَ يَحْكُمُ بَيْنَهُمْ فِى مَا هُمْ فِيهِ يَخْتَلِفُونَ}$$

"**Indeed We have sent down the Book to you, O Muhammad (ﷺ), with the truth, so worship Allaah alone making all religion purely and sincerely for Him. Indeed the religion that is free of all taint of *shirk* is alone what is acceptable to Allaah. As for those who take and invoke helpers and protectors**

---

[106] Soorah Saad (38):5-6.

besides Allaah, then they say, 'We only worship them so that they should intercede for us and bring us nearer to Allaah.' Indeed Allaah will establish judgement between them regarding the matters of religion about which they dispute."[107]

Allaah, the Most High, says:

$$\text{قُلْ إِنِّي أُمِرْتُ أَنْ أَعْبُدَ ٱللَّهَ مُخْلِصًا لَّهُ ٱلدِّينَ ۝ وَأُمِرْتُ لِأَنْ أَكُونَ أَوَّلَ ٱلْمُسْلِمِينَ ۝ قُلْ إِنِّي أَخَافُ إِنْ عَصَيْتُ رَبِّي عَذَابَ يَوْمٍ عَظِيمٍ ۝ قُلِ ٱللَّهَ أَعْبُدُ مُخْلِصًا لَّهُ دِينِي ۝}$$

"Say, O Muhammad (ﷺ), 'Allaah has commanded that I should worship Him alone, purely and sincerely, not associating anything with Him, and I am commanded to be the first of this nation who submits to Him as a Muslim, making all worship purely for Him.' Say, O Muhammad, 'I fear should I disobey my Lord in this, the torment of a great Day.' Say, 'It is Allaah alone that I worship, making all of my worship purely and sincerely for Him, and not worshipping anything else besides Him.'"[108]

$$\text{قُلْ إِنَّ صَلَاتِي وَنُسُكِي وَمَحْيَايَ وَمَمَاتِي لِلَّهِ رَبِّ ٱلْعَالَمِينَ ۝ لَا شَرِيكَ لَهُۥ وَبِذَٰلِكَ أُمِرْتُ وَأَنَا۠ أَوَّلُ ٱلْمُسْلِمِينَ ۝}$$

---

[107] Soorah az-Zumar (39):2-3.
[108] Soorah az-Zumar (39):11-14.

"Say, O Muhammad (ﷺ), 'Indeed my Prayer, my sacrifice, my living and my dying are all purely and solely for Allaah, Lord of all the Worlds. There is no share of any of that for other than Him. That is what My Lord ordered me, and I am the first of this nation to submit to Allaah as a Muslim.'"[109]

He also commanded him to call all of the people to fulfil and implement this principle, and to proceed upon it. Allaah, the Most High, says:

$$\text{يَٰٓأَيُّهَا ٱلنَّاسُ ٱعْبُدُوا۟ رَبَّكُمُ ٱلَّذِى خَلَقَكُمْ وَٱلَّذِينَ مِن قَبْلِكُمْ لَعَلَّكُمْ تَتَّقُونَ ۝ ٱلَّذِى جَعَلَ لَكُمُ ٱلْأَرْضَ فِرَٰشًا وَٱلسَّمَآءَ بِنَآءً وَأَنزَلَ مِنَ ٱلسَّمَآءِ مَآءً فَأَخْرَجَ بِهِۦ مِنَ ٱلثَّمَرَٰتِ رِزْقًا لَّكُمْ ۖ فَلَا تَجْعَلُوا۟ لِلَّهِ أَندَادًا وَأَنتُمْ تَعْلَمُونَ ۝}$$

"O Mankind, single out your Lord with worship; He who created you and all those who came before you so that you may be of those who seek to avoid Allaah's punishment and anger; those whom Allaah is pleased with. He Who has made the earth a resting place for you and has made the sky a canopy, and sent down rain from the sky, and brought out with it crops and fruits from the earth as provision for you. So do not set up rivals with Allaah in your worship whilst you know that you have no Lord besides Him."[110]

---

[109] Soorah al-An'aam (6):162-163.
[110] Soorah al-Baqarah (2):21-22.

Allaah, the Most High, says:

$$\text{وَإِلَٰهُكُمْ إِلَٰهٌ وَاحِدٌ ۖ لَّا إِلَٰهَ إِلَّا هُوَ الرَّحْمَٰنُ الرَّحِيمُ ﴿١٦٣﴾}$$

"The God Who alone has the right to be worshipped is a Single God. So do not worship anything besides Him, nor associate anything in worship with Him, the Most Merciful, the Bestower of Mercy."[111]

Allaah, the Most High, says:

$$\text{قُلْ يَا أَيُّهَا النَّاسُ إِنِّي رَسُولُ اللَّهِ إِلَيْكُمْ جَمِيعًا الَّذِي لَهُ مُلْكُ السَّمَاوَاتِ وَالْأَرْضِ ۖ لَا إِلَٰهَ إِلَّا هُوَ يُحْيِي وَيُمِيتُ ۖ فَآمِنُوا بِاللَّهِ وَرَسُولِهِ النَّبِيِّ الْأُمِّيِّ الَّذِي يُؤْمِنُ بِاللَّهِ وَكَلِمَاتِهِ وَاتَّبِعُوهُ لَعَلَّكُمْ تَهْتَدُونَ ﴿١٥٨﴾}$$

"Say, O Muhammad (ﷺ), to all of the people, 'I am the Messenger of Allaah to you all. Allaah, to Whom belongs the dominion of the heavens and the earth and everything therein. None has the right to be worshipped but Him. He Who alone gives life and death. So affirm true faith in Allaah and in His sole right to worship, and believe in His Messenger, the Unlettered Prophet (Muhammad (ﷺ)) who believes in Allaah and His Words, and follow him, so that you may be rightly guided.'"[112]

---

[111] Soorah al-Baqarah (2):163.
[112] Soorah al-A'raaf (7):158.

The *Aayaat* in this regard are very many, and what we have quoted is an example showing the methodology of Allaah's Messenger (ﷺ) in calling to *tawheed*.

Then with regard to the *Sunnah*, there are many things clearly showing that Allaah's Messenger (ﷺ) began his *da'wah* with *tawheed* and completed it with it, and continued calling to it from the beginning to the end, throughout his (ﷺ) life.

(1) 'Amr ibn 'Abasah as-Sulamee, *radiyallaahu 'anhu*, who said, *"During the times of Ignorance I used hold that the people were upon error and futility, and they used to worship the idols, then I heard of a man in Makkah who received revelation. So I set out upon my riding beast and came to him. At that time he was in hiding due to oppression of his people. So I behaved in a way that enabled me to gain access to him in Makkah, which I did. So I said to him, 'What are you?' He replied, 'I am a Prophet.' So I said, 'And what is a Prophet?' He said, 'Allaah has sent me as a Messenger.' So I said, 'And what is it that He has sent you with?' He said, 'I have been sent to order the joining of ties of relationship, to break the idols, so that Allaah is worshipped alone and nothing at all is associated in worship along with Him.' So I said, 'And who is with you upon this?' He said, 'A free man and a slave.' He said, 'And at that time Aboo Bakr and Bilaal were with him from those who believed in him...'"*[113]

(2) When 'Amr ibn al-'Aas and 'Abdullaah ibn Rabee'ah al-Makhzoomee went to an-Najaashee, the ruler of Abyssinia, to speak to him in order to incite him against the Muslims who had emigrated to Abyssinia, they said, 'O king, some of our foolish youths have abandoned their religion and

---

[113] Reported by Muslim (Eng. trans. 2/395 no.1812) and Ahmad in *al-Musand* (4/112).

come to your land. They have split away from their own people and have not entered your religion. Rather they have come up with an innovated religion which is not known either to us or to you...' So the Najaashee asked the Muslims, 'What is this religion which you have split from your people and not entered my religion or the religion of any of these nations?!' So Ja'far ibn Abee Taalib was the one who replied, and he said to him, 'O king, we were a people from the people of ignorance who worshipped idols, and we ate unslaughtered meat and committed foul acts, and we cut off ties of relationship, treated our neighbours in an evil manner and the strong amongst us used to devour the weak. So we were upon that until Allaah sent a Messenger to us from amongst us. We knew his lineage, his truthfulness, his trustworthiness and his chastity. So he called us to Allaah, that we should single Him out and worship Him alone and renounce everything which we and our fathers used to worship besides Him, all stones and idols; he commanded us to speak the truth and to fulfil trusts; to join ties of relationship; to live in a good manner with our neighbours; to avoid forbidden acts and shedding blood; he forbade us from foul acts and from falsehood; and he forbade us from unlawfully devouring the wealth of orphans and falsely accusing chaste women. He ordered us to worship Allaah alone and not to worship anything along with Him...' He said, 'So he told him the affairs of Islaam,' 'So we attested to his truthfulness and believed him and followed him in that which he came with. So we worshipped Allaah alone, and did not worship anything else besides Him, and we made forbidden that which He forbade us, and declared lawful that which He allowed for us. So our people became enemies to us and tortured us and tormented us to turn back from our religion to the worship of idols, and so that we should allow the filthy actions which we used to allow. So when they oppressed us, treated us cruelly and made it unbearable for us, and came between us and our religion, then we left and came to your land, and we preferred you to others and wished to live in your company, and we hoped that we would not be oppressed while with you..."[114]

(3) Also amongst the questions which Hirqal (Heraclius) asked Aboo Sufyaan, at the time of the peace of Hudaybiyyah, about Allaah's Messenger (ﷺ) was that he asked Aboo Sufyaan, "What does he command you?" So Aboo Sufyaan replied, "He says, 'Worship Allaah alone and do not worship anything else along with Him, and abandon what your fathers say. And he orders Prayer, charity, chastity and the joining of ties of relationship.'"[115]

So these *ahaadeeth* clearly show us what the *da'wah* of Allaah's Messenger (ﷺ) was in both the Makkan and Madinan periods.

The Torture Endured by the Companions Because of their Adherence to *Tawheed*

The Companions of Allaah's Messenger (ﷺ) suffered the worst forms of torture because of their adherence to the correct *'aqeedah,* and their making all worship purely and sincerely for Allaah alone, and their rejection of *shirk* and *kufr*.

---

[114] Reported by Imaam Ahmad in his *Musnad* (1/202) and (5/290). Ahmad said, "Ya'qoob (meaning Ibraaheem ibn Sa'd az-Zuhree) narrated to us (reliable): My father narrated to us, from Muhammad ibn Ishaaq: Muhammad ibn Muslim ibn 'Ubaydillaah ibn Shihaab narrated to me: from Aboo Bakr ibn 'Abdir-Rahmaan ibn al-Haarith ibn Hishaam al-Makhzoomee: from Umm Salamah bint Abee Umayyah (meaning the Mother of the Believers, *radiyallaahu 'anha,*)." It is a chain of narration that is fully *saheeh*, except for Muhammad ibn Ishaaq, but he clearly states that he heard it directly and so his narration is *hasan* (good and acceptable).

[115] Reported by al-Bukhaaree (Eng. trans. 1/7/no. 6) and it is a long *hadeeth*.

From 'Abdullaah ibn Mas'ood, *radiyallaahu 'anhu*, who said, "The first people to openly proclaim their Islaam were seven: Allaah's Messenger (ﷺ), Aboo Bakr, 'Ammaar and his mother Sumayyah, Suhayb, Bilaal and al-Miqdaad. So as for Allaah's Messenger (ﷺ), Allaah gave him protection through his uncle Aboo Taalib. As for Aboo Bakr, Allaah gave him protection through his people. But as for the rest of them, the *mushriks* would take hold of them and dress them in iron armour and place them to scorch and roast in the sun. There was not one of them except that they responded to them except Bilaal, for his soul became as nothing to him for Allaah's sake, and his people had no respect for him. So they gave him to the children who used to drag him around the streets of Makkah and he would say repeatedly, '(He who has the right to worship is) One, One.'"[116]

In the *Seerah* of Ibn Hishaam[117] there occurs: 'Umayyah ibn Khalf used to take him (Bilaal) out in the midday heat of the sun, and throw him down upon his back, on the ground of the flat valley bed of Makkah, and he would order for a large rock to be placed on his chest. Then he would say, "By Allaah, you will stay like this until you die, unless you disbelieve in Muhammad (ﷺ) and you worship *al-Laat* and *al-'Uzzaa*." So he would say, whilst he was in that condition, "(He who alone has the right to worship is) One, One."

Sumayyah was tortured until death because of the *'aqeedah* of *tawheed* not because she was a political leader. From Mujaahid who said, "The first martyr in Islaam was Sumayyah the mother of 'Ammaar. Aboo Jahl thrust a spear into her abdomen."[118]

---

[116] Reported by al-Haakim in *al-Mustadrak* (3/284) and he declared it *saheeh* and adh-Dhahabee mentioned it in *Siyar A'laamin-Nubalaa* (1/348) and he said, "It has a *saheeh* chain of narration..."
[117] *Seerah* of Ibn Hishaam (1/318).
[118] *At-Tabaqaat* of Ibn Sa'd (8/264/265). He said, "Ismaa'eel ibn 'Umar, Abul-Mundhir related to us that Sufyaan ath-Thawree narrated to us from Mansoor from Mujaahid who said..." This is a *saheeh* chain of narration to Mujaahid.

Ibn Sa'd said, "She accepted Islaam early on in Makkah and she was one of those who was tortured to force them to abandon their religion. But she bore and endured it until Aboo Jahl came to her and thrust a spear into her abdomen and she died."[119]

The Great Importance Given to the *'Aqeedah* in the Madinan Period

After Allaah's Messenger (ﷺ) and his Companions migrated to al-Madeenah, and the Islamic state was established through the efforts of the *Muhaajireen* and the *Ansaar*, and upon the foundation of *tawheed*, then the greatest importance continued to be given to *tawheed*. The *Aayaat* of the Qur'aan continued to be sent down with it, and the directions and the orders of the Prophet (ﷺ) revolved around it.

(1) Allaah's Messenger (ﷺ) did not suffice even with all this. Rather he used to take pledge of allegiance from the greater Companions, not to mention the others, upon it from time to time. Whenever the opportunity arose, he would take their pledge of allegiance upon it. Allaah, the Most High, says,

$$\text{يَٰٓأَيُّهَا ٱلنَّبِيُّ إِذَا جَآءَكَ ٱلْمُؤْمِنَٰتُ يُبَايِعْنَكَ عَلَىٰٓ أَن لَّا يُشْرِكْنَ بِٱللَّهِ شَيْـًٔا وَلَا يَسْرِقْنَ وَلَا يَزْنِينَ وَلَا يَقْتُلْنَ أَوْلَٰدَهُنَّ وَلَا يَأْتِينَ بِبُهْتَٰنٍ يَفْتَرِينَهُۥ بَيْنَ أَيْدِيهِنَّ وَأَرْجُلِهِنَّ وَلَا يَعْصِينَكَ فِى مَعْرُوفٍ ۙ فَبَايِعْهُنَّ وَٱسْتَغْفِرْ لَهُنَّ ٱللَّهَ ۖ إِنَّ ٱللَّهَ غَفُورٌ رَّحِيمٌ}$$

> "When the Believing women come to give you their pledge that they will not associate anything in wor-

---
[119] *Tabaqaat Ibn Sa'd* (8/264).

ship with Allaah; nor steal; nor commit fornication; nor kill their children; nor attribute to their husbands children which are not theirs; nor disobey you, O Muhammad (ﷺ), in that which is good and commanded by Allaah; (and not wail over the dead), then accept their pledge and ask Allaah to forgive them. Indeed Allaah forgives those who repent to Him and is Most Merciful to them."[120]

Even though this *Aayah* is with regard to the women's pledge, Allaah's Messenger (ﷺ) also used to take pledge from the men upon its contents.

From 'Ubaadah ibn as-Saamit, *radiyallaahu 'anhu*, who said, *"Allaah's Messenger (ﷺ) was in an assembly (of his Companions) and said, 'Swear allegiance to me with the pledge that you will not associate anything in worship with Allaah, and that you will not steal, nor commit fornication, nor kill your children, (and upon the Aayah which was taken as a pledge from the women [60:12]). So whoever fulfils this pledge from you, then he will be rewarded by Allaah. And whoever falls into sin with any of that and is punished for it, then it is an expiation for it. And whoever falls into any of these sins and Allaah conceals his sin, then it is up to Allaah: if He wills He may forgive him, and if He wills He may punish him.'"*[121]

Also Ibn Katheer quotes a large number of *ahaadeeth* that Allaah's Messenger (ﷺ) used to take pledge from the women upon that which this *Aayah* contains.[122] From these *ahaadeeth* is that of 'Aa'ishah; the *hadeeth*

---

[120] Soorah al-Mumtahinah (60):12.
[121] Reported by al-Bukhaaree (Eng. trans. 1/21/no.17 and 5/151 no.233), and Muslim (Eng. trans. 3/924-925 nos. 4235-4238), and an-Nasaa'ee (7/128).
[122] See *Saheeh al-Bukhaaree* (Eng. trans. 6/385 no.414).

of Umayyah bint Ruqayqah;[123] the *hadeeth* of Umm 'Atiyyah;[124] the *hadeeth* of Salmaa bint Qays, one of the maternal aunts of the Messenger (ﷺ);[125] and the *hadeeth* of Raa'itah bint Sufyaan al-Khuzaa'iyyah.[126] Then he (i.e. Ibn Katheer) said, "And Allaah's Messenger (ﷺ) used to take this pledge from the women repeatedly." Then he quoted the *hadeeth* of Ibn 'Abbaas,[127] and other *ahaadeeth*.

He also used to take this pledge repeatedly from the men. This is indicated by the *hadeeth* of 'Ubaadah ibn as-Saamit which has preceded, and also by the *hadeeth* of 'Auf ibn Maalik al-Ashja'ee, *radiyallaahu 'anhu*, who said, *"We were with Allaah's Messenger (ﷺ) and numbered nine, eight or seven people, so he said, 'Will you not give your pledge to Allaah's Messenger?' So we said, 'We have already given you our pledge, O Messenger of Allaah!' Then he said, 'Will you not give your pledge to Allaah's Messenger?' So we stretched out our hands and said, 'We will indeed give you our pledge, O Messenger of Allaah, but what will our pledge be?' He said, 'That you will worship Allaah and not worship anything else besides Him; the five obligatory Prayers; that you obey (and he said a word quietly); and that you do not ask the people for anything.' So I have as a result seen some of those people, their whip would fall down from their hand (while riding) and he would not ask anyone to pick it up for him."*[128]

---

[123] Reported by Ahmad (6/357) and an-Nasaa'ee (7/149).
[124] Reported by al-Bukhaaree (Eng. trans. 6/386 no. 415).
[125] Reported by Ahmad (6/379-380, 422-433) and its chain of narration contains Saleet ibn Ayyoob about whom al-Haafidh ibn Hajr said, *"Maqbool,"* (i.e. acceptable if supported), and adh-Dhahabee said in *al-Kaashif* (1/388), "Declared reliable by some," so it is *hasan* due to its supports.
[126] *Musnad Ahmad* (6/365).
[127] Reported by al-Bukhaaree (Eng. trans. 6/388 no.418).
[128] Reported by Muslim (Eng. trans. 2/498 no.2270), Aboo Daawood (Eng. trans. 2/431 no.1638) and others.

(2) He (ﷺ) used to send callers, teachers, judges and governors, to kings and tyrants, and to various areas, calling to *tawheed*. From Anas, *radiyallaahu 'anhu*, the servant of Allaah's Messenger (ﷺ), "The Prophet of Allaah (ﷺ) sent letters to Kisraa (Chosroes), and Caesar, and the Najaashee (Negus) and to every tyrant ruler calling them to Allaah. And this Negus was not the one whom the Prophet (ﷺ) prayed Funeral Prayer for."[129] This point is shown very clearly by the text of his letter to the Caesar, and that his purpose was to call to *tawheed*. Its text is:

"In the Name of Allaah, the Most Merciful, the Bestower of Mercy.

From Muhammad, the Slave of Allaah and His Messenger, to Hiraql, the Emperor of the Byzantines.

Peace and safety are for those who follow the Guidance. To proceed: I invite you with the call of Islaam. Accept Islaam and you will be safe, and Allaah will grant you a double reward. But if you turn your back upon it, then you will carry the burdens of the sins of your subjects."[130] And he (ﷺ) said, *"Whoever calls to guidance then there is for him a reward similar to the reward of those who follow him, nothing being reduced from their reward. And whoever calls to misguidance, then there is a burden of sin*

---

[129] Reported by Muslim (Eng. trans. 3/971 no.4382), at-Tirmidhee (no.2716), and Ahmad (3/336) from the *hadeeth* of Jaabir with the wording, *"And Allaah's Messenger (ﷺ) sent letters five years before he died to Kisraa and Caesar, and to every tyrant ruler."*

[130] i.e. his followers from the weak and others, since he became a reason for their continuing upon *shirk*. This is from Allaah's Justice, and His way with regard to the rulers, that they carry their own burden of sin and also the burden of sin of those who follow them in deviating from *tawheed* and the truth, and fighting against it. Allaah, the Most High, says:
"They will bear the burden of their own sins in full on the Day of Resurrection and the sin of those whom they lead astray." [Soorah an-Nahl (16):25].

upon him similar to the sin of those who follow him, nothing being reduced from their sins."

$$\text{قُلْ يَٰٓأَهْلَ ٱلْكِتَٰبِ تَعَالَوْاْ إِلَىٰ كَلِمَةٍ سَوَآءٍۭ بَيْنَنَا وَبَيْنَكُمْ أَلَّا نَعْبُدَ إِلَّا ٱللَّهَ وَلَا نُشْرِكَ بِهِۦ شَيْـًٔا وَلَا يَتَّخِذَ بَعْضُنَا بَعْضًا أَرْبَابًا مِّن دُونِ ٱللَّهِ ۚ فَإِن تَوَلَّوْاْ فَقُولُواْ ٱشْهَدُواْ بِأَنَّا مُسْلِمُونَ ۝}$$

"O People of the Book, come to a word of justice between us, that we will single Allaah out with all worship and will not worship anything besides Him and disassociate ourselves from everything that is worshipped besides Him. Nor will we take one another as lords besides Allaah by obeying one another in that which involves disobedience to Allaah. So if they turn away, then say, 'Bear witness that we are Muslims, submitting to Allaah and making our worship purely and sincerely for Him and not worshipping anything else besides Him.'"[131]

When the letter reached the Caesar he sent for Aboo Sufyaan ibn Harb and some riders of Quraysh. They were at that time trading in the area of Palestine/Syria, and were within the time of the truce period agreed between Allaah's Messenger (ﷺ) and the unbelievers of Quraysh. So they came to Caesar at Jerusalem and he asked Aboo Sufyaan a number of questions. From them was that he asked, "What does he (i.e. Muhammad (ﷺ)) command you?" Aboo Sufyaan said, "I replied, 'He says, "Worship

---

[131] Soorah Aal-'Imraan (3):64. Both of them are part of a single *hadeeth* reported by al-Bukhaaree (Eng. trans. 1/7 no.6) and it is a long *hadeeth*, abridged, and Ahmad (1/262).

Allaah alone and do not worship anything else besides Him and abandon the saying of your fathers." He orders prayer, truthfulness, chastity and joining ties of relationship.'"[132]

(3) Furthermore he used to organise armies to fight *Jihaad* in the path of Allaah in order to establish and raise high the word of *tawheed*, *"He who fights in order that Allaah's Word is the highest then he is the one who is fighting in the Path of Allaah."*

From Buraydah ibn al-Husayyib, *radiyallaahu 'anhu*, who said, "When Allaah's Messenger (ﷺ) appointed the chief of a raiding party or an army, he used to counsel him to have taqwaa of Allaah concerning himself and with regard to good treatment of the Muslims with him, and he said, *'When you meet your enemy from the mushriks then call them to accept one of three things, whichever of them they agree to, then accept it and leave them alone: (i) Invite them to accept Islaam. If they accept that then accept it from them, and leave them alone. Invite them in that case to leave their homes and to migrate to the land of the Muhaajirs... (ii) But if they refuse (to accept Islaam), then ask them to pay the jizya tax. If they agree to that then accept that from them and leave them alone. (iii) But if they refuse then seek the aid of Allaah and fight them. And if you besiege a fortified place and they ask you to allow them to surrender upon the judgement of Allaah, then do not allow them to surrender upon that since you do not know what Allaah's judgement concerning them is. Rather allow them to surrender in accordance with what you judge in the matter. Then decide as you wish concerning them.'"*[133]

---

[132] *Ibid.*

[133] Reported by Muslim (Eng. trans. 3/943 no.4294), and Aboo Daawood (Eng. trans. 2/722 no.2606) and others.

Like the *hadeeth* of Buraydah is the *hadeeth* of an-Nu'maan ibn Muqarrin al-Muzanee, *radiyallaahu 'anhu*, which is indicated by Muslim, Aboo Daawood and Ibn Maajah, who all said, "'Alqamah said: I narrated it to Muqaatil ibn Hayyaan. He said: Muslim ibn Haysam narrated to me, from an-Nu'maan ibn Muqarrin from the Prophet (ﷺ) with its like."

(4) Furthermore he (ﷺ) sent Mu'aadh to Yemen as a Governor, a judge and a teacher. Allaah's Messenger (ﷺ) said to him, *"You are a going to a people from the People of the Book, so let the first thing you call them to be the testification that none has the right to be worshipped except Allaah, (and in a narration: that they should single Allaah out with all worship), and I am the Messenger of Allaah. So if they obey you in that, then inform them that Allaah has made five Prayers obligatory upon them in each day and night. So if they obey you in that, then inform them that Allaah has obligated upon them a charity which is to be taken from their rich and given to their poor. If they obey you in that, then beware of taking the best parts of their wealth, and beware of the supplication of the oppressed, because there is no screen between it and Allaah."*[134]

There is no doubt that he used to give this same advice to all the callers, governors and judges whom he sent out.

(5) *Jihaad* was prescribed for the establishment of *tawheed* and to purify the earth from the scourge of *shirk*. Allaah, the Most High, says:

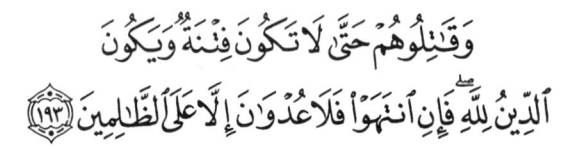

$$\text{وَقَٰتِلُوهُمْ حَتَّىٰ لَا تَكُونَ فِتْنَةٌ وَيَكُونَ ٱلدِّينُ لِلَّهِ ۖ فَإِنِ ٱنتَهَوْا۟ فَلَا عُدْوَٰنَ إِلَّا عَلَى ٱلظَّٰلِمِينَ ﴿١٩٣﴾}$$

"Fight the *mushriks* until there remains no worship of anything besides Allaah, and all worship is for

---

[134] Reported al-Bukhaaree (Eng. trans. 5/445 no.634 and 9/348 no.469) and Muslim (Eng. trans. 1/14-15 nos. 27-28).

Allaah alone and His religion is uppermost. So if they desist from *shirk* and enter into Islaam then let there be no transgression except those that worship others along with Allaah"[135]

Ibn Jareer (at-Tabaree), *rahimahullaah*, said in his *Tafseer* (2/194-195): "Allaah, the Most High, says to His Prophet (ﷺ), وَقَـٰتِلُوهُمْ حَتَّىٰ لَا تَكُونَ فِتْنَةٌ وَيَكُونَ ٱلدِّينُ لِلَّهِ Meaning so that there is no *shirk* with Allaah, and no one besides Him is worshipped; and worship of the idols, false gods and those set up as rivals is extinguished. And worship and obedience is for Allaah alone to the exclusion of idols and images... Qataadah said, 'So that there is no *shirk*.' He quotes his chain of narration with this explanation from Qataadah, Mujaahid, as-Suddee and Ibn 'Abbaas. He said, 'What is meant by *Deen* (religion) which Allaah mentions in this place is: Worship and obedience to Allaah in what He orders and forbids.' He said, 'With this meaning there occurs the saying of al-A'shee: He caused the (tribes of) ar-Ribaab to submit and become obedient when they hated obedience - Achieving it through continual fighting and attacks.'

Then he quoted his chain of narration of ar-Rabee' who said concerning, وَيَكُونَ ٱلدِّينُ لِلَّهِ Meaning: "Until none but Allaah is worshipped," which is the meaning of *laa ilaaha illallaah* (none has the right to be worshipped except Allaah). That is what Allaah's Messenger (ﷺ) fought for and called to."

From Aboo Hurayrah, *radiyallaahu 'anhu*, who said that Allaah's Messenger (ﷺ) said, *"I have been ordered to fight the people until they say laa ilaaha illallaah (none has the right to be worshipped except Allaah). So whoever says: laa ilaaha illallaah, then his wealth and his person is*

---

[135] Soorah al-Baqarah (2):193.

safe from me, except due to any right of it, and his reckoning is with Allaah."[136]

Also the Chief of the Believers 'Umar, *radiyallaahu 'anhu*, said to Aboo Bakr, the *Khaleefah* of Allaah's Messenger (ﷺ), when he resolved to fight the apostates and also those with them who refused to hand over the *zakaat*, 'Umar, *radiyallaahu 'anhu*, said, "How can you fight those people when Allaah's Messenger (ﷺ) said, 'I have been ordered to fight the people until they testify that none has the right to be worshipped except Allaah, so whoever says this then his wealth and his person are safe from me except due to any right of it, and his reckoning is with Allaah.'" So Aboo Bakr, *radiyallaahu 'anhu*, said, "By Allaah, I will fight those who seek to separate between the Prayer and the *zakaat*. Indeed the *zakaat* is a right due upon wealth. By Allaah, were they to hold a single young goat from me which they used to pay to Allaah's Messenger (ﷺ), I would fight them for it."[137]

From Jaabir ibn 'Abdillaah, *radiyallaahu 'anhumaa*, who said that Allaah's Messenger (ﷺ) said, *"I have been ordered to fight the people until they say, 'None has the right to be worshipped except Allaah.' So when they say that none has the right to be worshipped except Allaah then their blood and their property are safe from me except due to a right pertaining to it, and their reckoning is with Allaah."* Then he recited,

$$فَذَكِّرْ إِنَّمَا أَنتَ مُذَكِّرٌ ۝ لَّسْتَ عَلَيْهِم بِمُصَيْطِرٍ ۝$$

"Indeed We have only sent you, O Muhammad (ﷺ), as an admonisher to them. You are not to force them to believe against their will."[138, 139]

---

[136] Reported by Muslim (Eng. trans. 1/16 no.30) and at-Tirmidhee (no. 3341) and Ibn Maajah (no. 3928).
[137] Reported by al-Bukhaaree (Eng. trans. 9/46 no.59) and Muslim (Eng. trans. 1/15 no.29).
[138] Soorah al-Ghaashiyah (88):21-22.
[139] Reported by Muslim (Eng. trans. 1/17 no.32), at-Tirmidhee (no. 3341) and Ibn Maajah (no. 3928).

From Ibn 'Umar, *radiyallaahu 'anhumaa*, who said that Allaah's Messenger (ﷺ) said, *"I have been ordered to fight the people until they bear witness that none has the right to be worshipped except Allaah, and that Muhammad is the Messenger of Allaah, and they establish the Prayer, and pay the zakaat. So if they do that then their blood and their wealth are safe from me except due to its right, and their reckoning is with Allaah."*[140]

So it may be noticed that the *ahaadeeth* of 'Umar, Aboo Bakr, Aboo Hurayrah and Jaabir are restricted to mentioning the matter of *tawheed* and do not mention the other matters. So perhaps the reason for this is the very great concern which the Messenger (ﷺ) gave to this matter so that he would mention it to them time after time on its own, as an indication of its greatness and importance. Also because of the fact that he (ﷺ) realised that they understood that all the other affairs of Islaam follow on from it, and are required by it and are from its rights, particularly the pillars of Islaam and *eemaan*.

I say, because of the fact that Allaah's Messenger (ﷺ) often used to mention only that which related to *'aqeedah*, 'Umar used this saying as an evidence. Then the reply of Aboo Bakr to support his stance, was to make a direct analogy between the *zakaat* and the Prayer, "By Allaah, I will fight anyone who makes a difference between the Prayer and the *zakaat*..." So if he knew the narration as it was reported by Ibn 'Umar he would have used that as a clear and decisive proof.

Also if 'Umar knew of the narration as reported by his son he would not have raised any objection to the saying of Aboo Bakr. Then if those present at the time, including Aboo Hurayrah, knew the narration of Ibn 'Umar, then they would have mentioned it to the two *Shaykhs*.[141] So perhaps

---

[140] Reported by al-Bukhaaree (Eng. trans. 1/25 no.24) and Muslim (Eng. trans. 1/17 no. 33).
[141] i.e. Aboo Bakr and 'Umar.

the reason behind this was indeed as we have said, the great importance which the Messenger (ﷺ) gave to *'aqeedah*, and his propagation of it, and the frequency with which he spoke about it.

Then also because the most prominent and most important aspect of the teachings which the Prophets conveyed from their Lord was *Tawheedul-Uloohiyyah* (singling out Allaah with all worship), and this was the greatest reason for strife between the Prophets and their enemies.

Furthermore the most significant of the aspects of falsehood and misguidance, against which the Prophets (*'alayhimus-salaatu was-salaam*) fought, and which the *mushriks* who denied the truth of their message furiously fought to defend, in every nation was: the worship of images and idols, and the building of tombs upon the graves of the pious and the Prophets, and veneration of them, and making offerings to them, and attachment of people's hearts to them, both of the rulers and the ruled, an attachment of hope and fear, desiring and anticipating that they would intercede for them with Allaah, enabling the accomplishment of their wishes. This was indeed major *shirk* which will not be forgiven, so we must mention, along with that which we have already quoted whilst speaking about the methodology of the Prophets, particularly when we spoke concerning Ibraaheem, the *Imaam* of the Pious and the destroyer of the worthless idols, something about the full scale war which Allaah's Messenger (ﷺ) waged against major *shirk* which was seen in his smashing the idols physically and by blocking up all the ways which Satan uses to lead his followers to worshipping them and taking them as rivals to Allaah, by using the terms 'gods' or *'awliyaa'* (pious ones beloved to Allaah) or hiding beneath any of the misleading titles they use.

So from this war which is clearly seen in the Qur'aan and was waged by the Messenger of the One Who sent the Qur'aan, is the saying of Allaah, the Most High,

أَفَرَءَيْتُمُ ٱللَّـٰتَ وَٱلْعُزَّىٰ ﴿١٩﴾ وَمَنَوٰةَ ٱلثَّالِثَةَ ٱلْأُخْرَىٰٓ ﴿٢٠﴾ أَلَكُمُ ٱلذَّكَرُ وَلَهُ ٱلْأُنثَىٰ ﴿٢١﴾ تِلْكَ إِذًا قِسْمَةٌ ضِيزَىٰٓ ﴿٢٢﴾ إِنْ هِىَ إِلَّآ أَسْمَآءٌ سَمَّيْتُمُوهَآ أَنتُمْ وَءَابَآؤُكُم مَّآ أَنزَلَ ٱللَّهُ بِهَا مِن سُلْطَـٰنٍ إِن يَتَّبِعُونَ إِلَّا ٱلظَّنَّ وَمَا تَهْوَى ٱلْأَنفُسُ وَلَقَدْ جَآءَهُم مِّن رَّبِّهِمُ ٱلْهُدَىٰٓ ﴿٢٣﴾

"Have you seen, O *mushriks*, (the idols:) *al-Laat*, *al-'Uzzaa*, and the other one *Manaat*, the third of them.[142] You prefer and love the male offspring for yourselves and then falsely attribute daughters,

---

[142] **Translator's Note:** *Al-Laat* had its origin in a man of the tribe of *Thaqeef* who used to mix gruel for pilgrims in the times of ignorance near to a certain rock in Taa'if. Then after his death the people built a tomb around the rock, upon his grave. They then worshipped this and gave it the name *al-Laat* which they invented by twisting the name of Allaah. Allaah's Messenger (ﷺ) sent al-Mugheerah ibn Shu'bah and Aboo Sufyaan to destroy it. They did so and in its place the mosque of Taa'if was built.

As for *al-'Uzzaa*, then it was in the form of a tree surrounded by a curtained building in a palm grove between Taaiif and Makkah. The Quraysh used to venerate it. An-Nasaa'ee reports in his *Tafseer* (2/357 no.567) that when Allaah's Messenger (ﷺ) conquered Makkah he sent Khaalid ibn al-Waleed to it. He found that it was built around three trees, so he cut them down and destroyed the building. He then went to the Prophet (ﷺ) and informed him, but he said, "Return for you have done nothing." So he returned and saw the keepers of the idol fleeing into the hills saying, "O '*Uzzaa*!" So Khaalid came and found a naked female with dishevelled hair, throwing dust upon her head. So he struck her with his sword and killed her, then he returned to the Prophet (ﷺ) and informed him. So he said, "That was *al-'Uzzaa*."

As for *Manaat* then it was situated at *Mushallal*, near to Qudayd, between Makkah and al-Madeenah. It was venerated by various tribes in the times of ignorance. Allaah's Messenger (ﷺ) sent 'Alee to demolish it in the year of the Conquest of Makkah. Ibn Ishaaq said in his *Seerah*, "The Arabs took other structures besides the *Ka'bah*, buildings which =

which is something you hate for yourselves, to Allaah. This is indeed an unjust division. Rather these idols are mere names which you *mushriks* and your forefathers have invented. Allaah has sent down no proof for that. Rather they follow only conjecture and their own desires, even though clear guidance has come to them from their Lord proving the futility of worshipping these idols and that worship is the right of Allaah alone."[143]

So this is a clear statement of contempt for the idols which they worshipped, and war against them. Also, Allaah, the Most High, says,

$$\text{فَاجْتَنِبُوا الرِّجْسَ مِنَ الْأَوْثَانِ وَاجْتَنِبُوا قَوْلَ الزُّورِ ۝ حُنَفَاءَ لِلَّهِ غَيْرَ مُشْرِكِينَ بِهِ وَمَن يُشْرِكْ بِاللَّهِ فَكَأَنَّمَا خَرَّ مِنَ السَّمَاءِ فَتَخْطَفُهُ الطَّيْرُ أَوْ تَهْوِي بِهِ الرِّيحُ فِي مَكَانٍ سَحِيقٍ}$$

"So shun the filth of worshipping idols and shun false speech. Worship Allaah alone in *tawheed* making worship purely for Him, and not worshipping anything besides Him. And whoever worships anything else along with Allaah, then he is like one who fell down from the sky and was ripped to pieces by the

---

they worshipped and venerated just as they honoured the *Ka'bah*. These shrines had keepers and guards, and offerings would be made to them just as with the *Ka'bah*. The people would also make *tawaaf* around them and make sacrifices there..." (*Tafseer Ibn Katheer* and *Tayseerul-'Azeezil-Hameed*, (p.177)).

[143] Soorah an-Najm (53):19-23.

birds, or like one cast by the wind in a far distant place."[144]

Allaah, the Most High, says,

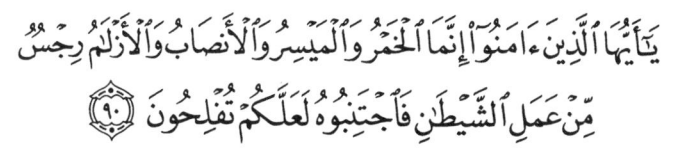

$$\text{يَٰٓأَيُّهَا ٱلَّذِينَ ءَامَنُوٓاْ إِنَّمَا ٱلْخَمْرُ وَٱلْمَيْسِرُ وَٱلْأَنصَابُ وَٱلْأَزْلَٰمُ رِجْسٌ مِّنْ عَمَلِ ٱلشَّيْطَٰنِ فَٱجْتَنِبُوهُ لَعَلَّكُمْ تُفْلِحُونَ ۝}$$

"O you who believe, intoxicants, gambling, stone altars erected for sacrifice and divining-arrows are an abomination from the handiwork of Satan. So shun all of that so that you may be successful."[145]

From 'Amr ibn 'Abasah, *radiyallaahu 'anhu*, and his *hadeeth* has preceded, and in it there occurs, *"I said, 'Did Allaah send you as a Messenger?' He said, 'Yes,' I asked, 'With what message did he send you?' He replied, 'That Allaah should be singled out and worshipped in tawheed, and that nothing should be worshipped besides Him, and to smash the idols and to join ties of relationship.'"*[146]

Also in the *hadeeth* of Ja'far which has preceded there occurs, "...until Allaah sent a Messenger to us from amongst us. We knew his lineage and his truthfulness and his chastity. He called us to single out Allaah in *tawheed* and to worship Him alone, and to renounce the stones and idols and whatever we and our fathers used to worship besides Him..."[147]

In the *hadeeth* of Aboo Sufyaan and his conversation with Heraclius, the King of the Byzantines, there occurs, "He says, (i.e., the Messenger (ﷺ)),

---

[144] Soorah al-Hajj (22):30-31.
[145] Soorah al-Maa'idah (5):90.
[146] Reported by Muslim (Eng. trans. 2/395 no.1812) as has preceded.
[147] Reported by Ahmad (1/202 and 5/290) and is *hasan* as has preceded.

'Worship Allaah alone and do not worship anything along with Him, and renounce what the forefathers say...'"[148]

In the *hadeeth* of Aboo Umaamah, *radiyallaahu 'anhu*, there occurs, "*Indeed Allaah sent me as a mercy for the worlds, and as a guide for the worlds, and my Lord, the Mighty and Majestic, ordered me to destroy all musical instruments and flutes, and idols and the cross, and such things from the days of Ignorance...*"[149]

Then the leaders of Quraysh went out of their minds in anger, unable to put up with the attack of Allaah's Messenger (ﷺ) against their idols, whether it was concerning the Qur'aan sent down to him, or his *da'wah* in secret, or his *da'wah* in the open. This was something about which there could be no indulgence, and it was something which had to be due to his true and sincere call.

From Ibn 'Abbaas, *radiyallaahu 'anhumaa*, who said, "*When Aboo Taalib became ill a group of Quraysh entered upon him, amongst them Aboo Jahl, and they said, 'The son of your brother abuses our gods, and does such and such, and says such and such. So if only you were to send a message forbidding him.' So he sent a message and the Prophet (ﷺ) came and entered the house... Aboo Taalib said to him, 'O son of my brother! Why is it that your people complain about you? They claim that you abuse their idols and say such and such?!' They spoke a great deal against him, and Allaah's Messenger (ﷺ) spoke and said, 'O Uncle! I only desire that they should say a single phrase which if they say it, then the Arabs will become obedient to them and the non-Arabs will pay the Jizyah tax to them.' So they were very surprised at what he said and they*

---

[148] Reported by al-Bukhaaree (Eng. trans. 1/7 no.6) as has preceded.
[149] Al-Haithumee says in *Majma'az Zawaa'id* (5/72), "Reported by Ahmad and at-Tabaraanee and its chain contains 'Alee ibn Yazeed (i.e. al-Alhaanee) who is weak." [Translator's Note]

said, 'A single phrase? Yes, by your father, even ten.' So they asked, 'And what is it?' Aboo Taalib said, 'And which saying is it, O son of my brother?' So he (ﷺ) said, 'None has the right to be worshipped except Allaah.' So they stood up, shaking their clothes saying, 'Does he declare that worship should be for a single God?! This is something bizarre.'"[150]

Also from Jaabir, *radiyallaahu 'anhu,* who said, "The Quraysh gathered together one day and said, 'See who is the most knowledgeable of you with regard to sorcery, divining and poetry, then let him go to this man who splits our united body, causes schism between us and abuses our religion. So let him speak to him and see how best to reply to him.' So they said, 'We do not know anyone but 'Utbah ibn Rabee'ah.' So they said, 'Then it is to be you O Abul-Waleed.' So 'Utbah went to him and said, 'O Muhammad (ﷺ)! Are you better or 'Abdullaah?'[151] Allaah's Messenger (ﷺ) remained silent. 'Are you better or 'Abdul-Muttalib?'[152] Again Allaah's Messenger (ﷺ) remained silent. So he said, 'If you claim that they are better than you, then they certainly worshipped the idols which you abuse. If however you claim that you are better than them, then speak so that we may hear what you have to say. Indeed we have never seen a youngster who has boded evil for his people more so than yourself. You have split our unity and caused schism in our affair, and you have abused our religion and shamed us in front of the Arabs. It has spread amongst them that there is a sorcerer within Quraysh, and a diviner within Quraysh.

---

[150] *Musnad Ahmad* (1/362) and at-Tirmidhee (no.3232) and its chain of narration contains Yahyaa ibn 'Umaarah and it is said: Ibn 'Abbaad who is mentioned by Ibn Hibbaan in *ath-Thiqaat*. Ibn Hajr says in *Tahdheebut-Tahdheeb* (11/259), "Acceptable (if supported)," and refer to, *at-Taqreeb* (2/354). Adh-Dhahabee says in *al-Kaashif* (3/224), "Declared reliable by some." It is also reported by Ibn Jareer (23/165) with his chain of narration to al-A'mash: 'Abbaad narrated to us: from Sa'eed ibn Jubayr: from Ibn 'Abbaas, and I do not find any biography for 'Abbaad. Its chain of narration also contains weakness, but may be suitable to be supported to the level of *hasan*.
[151] i.e. the father of Allaah's Messenger (ﷺ). [Translator's Note]
[152] i.e. the grandfather of Allaah's Messenger (ﷺ). [Translator's Note]

By Allaah we do not expect that we will have to wait for the time it takes a newborn to cry out before we will fight amongst ourselves with swords and wipe ourselves out. O man, if it is poverty that is your problem, then we will gather wealth for you until you will be the richest man of Quraysh. If it is that you have a need to marry, then choose whichever of the women of Quraysh you like and we will marry you ten of them.' So Allaah's Messenger (ﷺ) said, 'Have you finished?' He said, 'Yes.' So Allaah's Messenger (ﷺ) said:

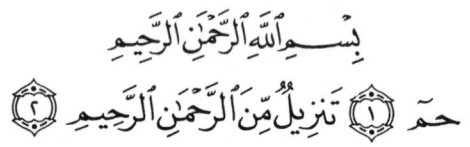

بِسْمِ ٱللَّهِ ٱلرَّحْمَٰنِ ٱلرَّحِيمِ

حمٓ ۝ تَنزِيلٌ مِّنَ ٱلرَّحْمَٰنِ ٱلرَّحِيمِ ۝

"In the name of Allaah, the Most Merciful, the Bestower of Mercy. *Haa Meem*. This Qur'aan is the Revelation sent down by the Most Merciful, the Bestower of Mercy...

until he reached

فَإِنْ أَعْرَضُوا۟ فَقُلْ أَنذَرْتُكُمْ صَٰعِقَةً مِّثْلَ صَٰعِقَةِ عَادٍ وَثَمُودَ ۝

So if these *mushriks* turn away from the proof which We have made clear to them, O Muhammad (ﷺ), then say, 'I warn you of a terrible punishment like that which befell 'Aad and Thamood.'"[153]

'Utbah said, 'Enough! Enough! Do you have nothing other than this?' He said, 'No.' So he returned to Quraysh and they said, 'What has occurred?' He said, 'I didn't leave anything which I thought that you would wish to say except that I said it to him.' They said, 'Did he respond to you?' He said, 'No, by the one who caused the *Ka'bah* to be built, I did not under-

---

[153] Soorah Fussilat (41):1-13.

stand anything which he said except that he warned you of a terrible punishment like that of 'Aad and Thamood.' They said, 'Woe to you, the man speaks to you in Arabic and you don't understand what he says?!' He said, 'No, by Allaah, I did not understand anything that he said except for his mention of the terrible punishment.'"[154]

So this war was fought with words and the soul, with biting attacks and belittlement and derision, by overcoming the falsehood and ignorance of the *mushriks*. At the same time, establishing the proof against them so that whoever went to destruction did so aware of the clear proof, and those who lived did so upon the clear proof. So from the results of this war, and from the results of this clear declaration was that Allaah guided many of the Arabs from the Quraysh and from the other tribes, and from *Aws* and the *Khazraj*. Allaah granted them clear discernment and they realised the reality of *tawheed* and its status. They also knew the vileness of committing *shirk* with idols or anything else, and also, at the same time, its seriousness and evil consequences for the *mushriks* in this world and the Hereafter.

---

[154] *Al-Muntakhab min Musnad 'Abd Ibn Humayd* (no.1141) and *Musnad Abee Ya'laa al-Mawsulee* (no.1812) both of them from Aboo Bakr ibn Abee Shaybah: 'Alee ibn Muhammad narrated to us: from al-Ajlah: from adh-Dhayyaal ibn Hurmulah al-Asadee: from Jaabir, *radiyallaahu 'anhu,* from the Prophet (ﷺ). Ibn Katheer said in his *Tafseer* (7/151), after quoting the *hadeeth* with his chain of narration from 'Abd ibn Humayd and Aboo Ya'laa: "Al-Baghawee reports it in his *Tafseer* with his chain of narration from Muhammad ibn Fudayl: from al-Ajlah, who is Ibn 'Abdullaah al-Kindee, and he is declared somewhat weak from adh-Dhayyaal..." However al-Haafidh (Ibn Hajr) says about him in *at-Tuqreeb* (1/46), "Generally acceptable *Shee'ee* from the seventh level." Adh-Dhahabee said in *al-Kaashif* (1/99), "He was declared reliable by Ibn Ma'een and others and declared weak by an-Nasaa'ee and was a *Shee'ee*." As for his Shaykh, adh-Dhayyaal, then al-Haafidh (Ibn Hajr) says of him in *Ta'jeelul-Manfa'ah* (p.84), "He reports from Jaabir and Ibn 'Umar and al-Qaasim ibn Mukhaymirah. Fitr ibn Khaleefah, Husayyin, al-Ajlah and Hajjaaj ibn Arlhat narrate from him. And Ibn Hibbaan declared him reliable." The rest of the narrators of the chain are reliable.

So these were the great and good fruits which came as a result of the *Jihaad* of Allaah's Messenger (ﷺ) and his Companions and their steadfastness in the field of true *da'wah* to Allaah, and their intensive striving against the idols and false objects of worship. Then when Allaah's Messenger (ﷺ) took *tawheed* to a new practical level which was to physically annihilate, smash and eradicate the idols and purify the earth from them, being fully aware of their seriousness, since they are the primary source of danger for every generation of mankind since the dawn of history until the end of history, just as the leader of those upon the true and straight religion said:

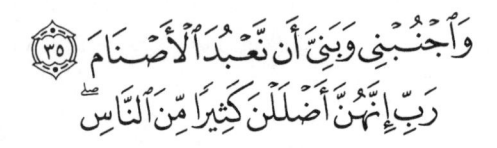

$$\text{وَٱجْنُبْنِى وَبَنِىَّ أَن نَّعْبُدَ ٱلْأَصْنَامَ ۝ رَبِّ إِنَّهُنَّ أَضْلَلْنَ كَثِيرًا مِّنَ ٱلنَّاسِ}$$

"And keep me and my sons away from worshipping idols, O my Lord, they have indeed caused the misguidance of many people."[155]

Therefore the greatest Messenger (ﷺ) resolved to carry out the task of purifying the earth from idols, and to level the graves since tombs are the partner of the idols in causing the misguidance of mankind.

From 'Abdullaah ibn Mas'ood, *radiyallaahu 'anhu*, who said, "The Prophet (ﷺ) entered Makkah and there were three hundred and sixty idols erected around the *Ka'bah*. So he began striking them with a stick which he had in his hand and was saying, *'The truth has arrived and falsehood has perished. The truth has arrived and falsehood cannot begin or return.'"*[156]

---

[155] Soorah Ibraaheem (14):35-36.
[156] Reported by al-Bukhaaree (Eng. trans. 3/369 no.658 and 5/406 no.583 and 6/206 no.244) and Muslim (Eng, trans. 3/978 no.4397) and at-Tirmidhee (no.3138) and Ahmad (1/377).

Allaah's Messenger (ﷺ) prepared an attachment to go from al-Madeenah to the tribe of Khath'am to attack Dhul-Khalasah, which they did. From Jareer ibn 'Abdullaah, *radiyallaahu 'anhu*, who said, "There was a house[157] called Dhul-Khalasah, or the *Yemeni Ka'bah* or the *Shaamee Ka'bah*, and the Prophet (ﷺ) said to me, *'Will you not relieve me of Dhul-Khulasah?'* So I set out with a hundred and fifty riders of the Ahmas tribe. So we broke it down and killed whomever we found there. Then I came to the Prophet (ﷺ) and informed him, so he made supplication for blessing for us and for the tribe of Ahmas."[158]

The wording used by al-Bukhaaree, Muslim and Ahmad is, *"Will you not relieve me of Dhul-Khalasah?"* See the wording used by the Prophet (ﷺ)?! It was as if the existence of idols deprived him of sleep and disturbed him, so that he could not settle or be at ease.

So I am amazed at the situation of many callers today who see the manifestation of *shirk* in front of their eyes, yet it does not cause them any concern whatsoever and they do not give any attention to it. Indeed what is even worse is that they complain about those who criticise it and who feel pained by this evil state of affairs which remains from the days of ignorance.

Also, from Abut-Tufayl 'Aamir ibn Waathilah who said, *"When Allaah's Messenger (ﷺ) conquered Makkah he sent Khaalid ibn al-Waleed to some date palm trees where al-'Uzzaa was to be found. It was constructed around three trees, so he cut them down and destroyed the building. Then he came to the Prophet (ﷺ) and told him, but he said, 'Go back, for you have done nothing.' So Khaalid returned, and when the keepers*

---

[157] i.e. a house like a shrine, which contained idols.
[158] Reported by al-Bukhaaree (Eng. trans. 5/450-452 no.641-643), Muslim (Eng. trans. 4/1320 nos. 6052-6054), Aboo Daawood (Eng. trans. 2/777 no. 2766) and Ahmad (4/360-362).

of the shrine saw him they fled to the hills, saying, 'O 'Uzzaa! O 'Uzzaa!' So Khaalid came and found a naked woman with bedraggled hair, casting dust upon her head. So Khaalid transfixed her with the sword and killed her. Then he returned to Allaah's Messenger (ﷺ) and informed him, so he said, 'That was al-'Uzzaa.'"[159]

Also *Manaat* was the idol worshipped by *Aws* and *Khazraj* and those who followed their religion in Yathrib. So Allaah's Messenger (ﷺ) sent Aboo Sufyaan to demolish it, or it is said, 'Alee ibn Abee Taalib.[160] Furthermore Thaqeef requested that Allaah's Messenger (ﷺ) leave the major idol, *al-Laat*, and not destroy it for three years. Allaah's Messenger (ﷺ) refused. So then they asked him to leave it for a year, but he continued to refuse. Finally they asked him to leave it for a month only after their arrival, but he refused to leave it for any period of time. What they wanted by this was to remain safe from the initial reaction of their foolish people, their womenfolk and their offspring... but Allaah's Messenger (ﷺ) refused except that he should send Aboo Sufyaan ibn Harb and al-Mugheerah ibn Shu'bah to destroy it.[161]

From 'Uthmaan ibn Abil-'Aas, "That Allaah's Messenger (ﷺ) ordered that the mosque of Taa'if be built in the place where their idol formerly stood."[162] Ibn Jareer said,[163] "They extracted its name from the name of

---

[159] Reported by an-Nasaa'ee in his *Tafseer* within *al-Kubraa*, as occurs in *Tuhfatul-Ashraaf* (4/235): 'Alee ibn al-Mundhir related to us: Ibn Fudayl related to us: al-Waleed ibn Juma'i narrated to us... And this is a *hasan* chain of narration.
[160] The *Seerah* of Ibn Hishaam (1/85-86).
[161] Ibn Hishaam's *Seerah* (2/540-541), Ibn Jareer (3/140), *al-Bidaayah wan-Nihaayah* (5/32), *Uyoonul-Athar* of Ibn Sayyidun-Naas (2/228) and *Zaadul-Ma'aad* (3/499-500).
[162] Ibn Maajah (no.743) and Aboo Daawood (Eng. trans. 1/117 no.450) and its narrators are reliable except for Muhammad ibn 'Abdullaah ibn 'Iyaad, who is acceptable if supported.
[163] In his *Tafseer* (27/58-59) and it occurs in Ibn Hishaam's *Seerah* (pp.78-79), and he speaks at length about the idols of the Arabs and the things which they used to worship, and the form which their worship took.

Allaah, so they said, '*al-Laat*' seeking to make it feminine, and High is Allaah and far removed from their saying." He then reports with his chains of narration from Qataadah, Ibn 'Abbaas, Mujaahid and Ibn Zayd that *al-Laatta* was the title of the man who used to produce a broth to feed the pilgrims. Then when he died they became devoted to his grave, and worshipped it. Imaam al-Bukhaaree said, Muslim ibn Ibraaheem narrated to us that Abul-Ashab narrated to us that Abul-Jawzaa narrated to us from Ibn 'Abbaas, *radiyallaahu 'anhumaa*, with regard to Allaah's saying (in Soorah an-Najm)[164] "*al-Laat* was a man who used to mix broth for the pilgrims."[165]

From Thumaamah ibn Shufayy who said, "We were with Fudaalah ibn 'Ubayd in the land of the Romans at Rhodes and a companion of ours died. So Fudaalah gave orders concerning the grave, and it was levelled, then he said, 'I heard Allaah's Messenger (ﷺ) ordering that they be levelled.'"[166]

From Jaabir ibn 'Abdullaah, *radiyallaahu 'anhumaa*, who said, "Allaah's Messenger (ﷺ) forbade that graves should be plastered, or that they should be sat upon, or that anything should be built upon them."[167]

From Aboo Marthad al-Ghanawee who said, "I heard Allaah's Messenger (ﷺ) say, '*Do not pray towards graves, and do not sit upon them.*'"[168]

---

[164] "**Have you considered al-Laat and al-'Uzza**" [Soorah an-Najm (53):19]
[165] Al-Bukhaaree (Eng. trans. (6/361 no.382).
[166] Reported by Muslim (Eng. trans. 2/459 no.2114), Aboo Daawood (Eng. trans. 2/915 no.3213) and an-Nasaa'ee (4/88).
[167] Reported by Muslim (Eng. trans. 2/459 no.2116), Aboo Daawood (Eng. trans. 2/916 no.3219) and an-Nasaa'ee (4/87 and 88).
[168] Reported by Muslim (Eng. trans. 2/460 no.2122) and Aboo Daawood (Eng. trans. 2/917 no.3223).

From Aboo Hurayrah, *radiyallaahu 'anhu,* who said, "Allaah's Messenger (ﷺ) said, *'O Allaah, do not make my grave an idol which is worshipped. Allaah's Wrath is severe against people who take the graves of their Prophets as places of Prayer.'*"[169]

Then this heedfulness and attention given by the Prophet (ﷺ) to the dangers of idols and tombs continued right to the final moment of the life of the sincere and trustworthy Messenger (ﷺ). From Jundub ibn 'Abdullaah al-Bajalee, *radiyallaahu 'anhu,* who said, "I heard Allaah's Messenger (ﷺ) five days before he died, saying, *'I am free before Allaah of having taken a single special and beloved friend from amongst you, since Allaah has taken me as a special beloved friend just as He took Ibraaheem as a special beloved friend. And if I were to take a special beloved friend from my ummah, then I would have taken Aboo Bakr as a special beloved friend. Indeed the people who came before you used to take the graves of their Prophets and the Pious from them as places of Prayer. But do not take the graves as places of worship, since I forbid you from that.'*"[170]

Also at this point of death, and after having chosen the company of the highest Angels, his greatest preoccupation was with the danger of the trial which graves and tombs caused to this *ummah*, most of whom are in ignorance of the attention and importance which the Prophet (ﷺ) gave to this, and are ignorant of the danger of this devastating trial.

---

[169] Reported by Maalik in *al-Muwattaa* (Eng. trans. no.416) in *mursal* form, and Ahmad (2/246): Sufyaan narrated to us: from Hamzah ibn al-Mugheerah: from Suhayl ibn Abee Suhayl ibn Abee Saalih: from his father: from Aboo Hurayrah, *radiyallaahu 'anhu,* from the Prophet (ﷺ). It is also reported by Ibn Sa'd in *at-Tabaqaat* (2/240-241) by way of Maalik and (2/241-242) by way of Sufyaan from Hamzah. It is also reported by Aboo Nu'aym in *al-Hilyah* (7/317) by way of Sufyaan from Hamzah.

[170] Reported by Muslim (Eng .trans. 1/269 no.1083) and others.

From Usaamah ibn Zayd, *radiyallaahu 'anhumaa*, that Allaah's Messenger (ﷺ) said during his illness which he died from, *"Enter my Companions upon me."* So they entered upon him and he was covering his face with a Ma'aarifee[171] cloak, he uncovered his face and said, *"Allaah's curse is upon the Jews and the Christians, they took the graves of their Prophets as places of Prayer."*[172]

So now we ask the question: Since it is the case that the call of the Messengers, *'alayhimus-salaatu was-salaam,* comprised all that is good, and warned against all that is evil, then why is it that we see in what Allaah relates in His Book, and we find in the *Sunnah* and the *Seerah* of our Prophet Muhammad (ﷺ) that their call to *tawheed,* and the war which they waged against *shirk* and its manifestations, and its causes and means, took up a very large part of their call, and occupied a great deal of their lives, to the point that it was as if it was their sole preoccupying concern?

But as for their stance with regard to the tyrannical and despotic rulers, then that was a secondary matter since *shirk* is the greatest of all oppression, and because their goal was to make the people slaves and worshippers of their Lord, the Perfect and Most High, it was not merely to remove one ruler and replace him with another. Allaah, the Most High, says:

$$إِنَّ ٱللَّهَ لَا يَغْفِرُ أَن يُشْرَكَ بِهِ وَيَغْفِرُ مَا دُونَ ذَٰلِكَ لِمَن يَشَآءُ$$

---

[171] *Ma'aafir* is a tribe in Yemen.
[172] Reported by Ahmad (5/214) and at-Tirmidhee in *al-Kabeer* (1/127 no.393) and at-Tayaalisee in his *Musnad* (p.88 no.634). Its chain of naration contains Qays ibn ar-Rabee' al-Asadee about whom al-Haafidh says, "Generally acceptable, but his memory deteriorated when he grew old and his son entered into his narrations things which were not from it." Its chain also contains Kulthoom al-Khuzaa'ee about whom al-Haafidh says, "Acceptable if supported." However it is suitable as a witness.

"Indeed Allaah does not forgive association of anything in worship with Him, but He forgives what is lesser than *shirk* to whomever He pleases."[173]

إِنَّهُۥ مَن يُشْرِكْ بِٱللَّهِ فَقَدْ حَرَّمَ ٱللَّهُ عَلَيْهِ ٱلْجَنَّةَ وَمَأْوَىٰهُ ٱلنَّارُ

"Indeed whoever associates anything in worship with Allaah then Allaah has forbidden Paradise for him, and his abode will be the Fire."[174]

وَمَن يُشْرِكْ بِٱللَّهِ فَكَأَنَّمَا خَرَّ مِنَ ٱلسَّمَآءِ فَتَخْطَفُهُ ٱلطَّيْرُ أَوْ تَهْوِى بِهِ ٱلرِّيحُ فِى مَكَانٍ سَحِيقٍ

"And whoever worships anything else along with Allaah, then he is like one who fell down from the sky and was ripped to pieces by the birds, or like one cast by the wind to a far distant place."[175]

Thus intellect, wisdom and the natural way therefore necessitates that the starting point is to wage war against the danger of *shirk*, and that the call of the Prophets and their followers should continue fighting it for as long as anything of it remains, or any form or manifestation of it continues. So if a nation is afflicted by matters damaging to its *'aqeedah*, and *shirk* which destroys its *'aqeedah*, and also is beset by economic and political problems, then where is wise treatment of the problems to begin?! As for the Prophets, then they did not begin except with applying their full efforts to treating problems facing *'aqeedah*. Beginning by seeking to treat the most dangerous problem is a matter about which all humans with intellect agree upon. For example, if a person with intellect

---

[173] Soorah an-Nisaa (4):48.
[174] Soorah al-Maa'idah (5):72.
[175] Soorah al-Hajj (22):31.

saw a snake and an ant moving towards a person, then his intellect would lead him to hasten to repel or kill the snake due to the greater danger which it poses to a person. It is not possible that he would divert his attention to the ant, nor even to a thousand such ants. Also if a number of people possessing intellect saw that a fierce lion and a number of rats attacked them all at once, then they would all strive together to prevent the attack of the lion and they would forget all the rats, even if a group of frogs came with them. And if a group of travellers came to a point where they had no choice but to take one of two roads: the first passed by volcanoes which were emitting flames and fire, and flinging out rocks and boulders. Then the second road passed through areas of thorny bushes, and sunbaked ground and was subject to the heat of the sun. Then anyone with intellect would not choose except to take the second road.

So now let us think about the most severe problems and ills. I mean the problems in political affairs, social affairs and economic affairs, and the worst of these is corruption in matters relating to rulership and judgement. Then let us weigh this against corruption in matters of *'aqeedah*. Are these two things equal in weight with Allaah and with the Prophets, or is it the case that one is more severe, dangerous and worse in its consequences?!! In the scale of Allaah and the scale of the Prophets the most dangerous of these two, and the one which has the greater demand for attention throughout the ages, and with all the Messengers, is *shirk* and its manifestations, whose evil and corruption cannot be matched by any other evil no matter how great. So upon this we repeat and say, "All of the Prophets began with correction of matters of *'aqeedah*, and by waging war upon *shirk* and its manifestations," and this is what is demanded by wisdom and intellect and that is due to the following reasons:

Firstly, that corruption relating to matters of the *'aqeedah* of the people: *shirk*, false superstitions and beliefs, and the various types of misguidance, is thousands of times more dangerous than the corruption resulting from the corruption in rulership and other affairs. Indeed if we do not say and firmly believe this then we have without knowing it discredited and belittled the Messengers, and we seek Allaah's refuge from misguidance. Indeed this corruption encompasses the ruler and the ruled. So the rulers themselves in every time and place, except for the Believers from them, humble themselves to the idols, false-gods and tombs. They construct them, protect them, worship them and present offerings to them. They firmly believe that they have some supernatural power over and above their own authority. So they hold that these things cause harm and benefit for them due to the unseen power and authority which they think they possess, or at the very least they think they can intercede with Allaah in order for their problems to be reduced. The clearest example of the submission of the rulers to the idols is the example of the despot who claimed divinity, the Pharaoh, who said, boasting:

$$فَقَالَ أَنَا رَبُّكُمُ ٱلْأَعْلَىٰ ۝$$

"I am your Lord, the Most High."[176]

And he said:

$$مَا عَلِمْتُ لَكُم مِّنْ إِلَٰهٍ غَيْرِي$$

"I know of no other god for you besides me."[177]

Since the leaders of his people said to him:

$$أَتَذَرُ مُوسَىٰ وَقَوْمَهُ لِيُفْسِدُوا۟ فِى ٱلْأَرْضِ وَيَذَرَكَ وَءَالِهَتَكَ$$

"Will you leave Moosaa and his people to cause mischief in the land when they have abandoned worship of you and worship of your gods?"[178]

---

[176] Soorah an-Naazi'aat (79):24.
[177] Soorah al-Qasas (28):38.
[178] Soorah al-A'raaf (7):127.

Also Namrood, the king of the Chaldeans who claimed lordship for himself. When Ibraaheem, *'alayhis-salaam,* broke the idols, Namrood sought to burn Ibraaheem to take revenge for these idols, because they were the gods which he worshipped. Likewise the kings of India and Persia worship idols and worship fire. The kings of Rome in the past and the present-day rulers of Europe and America worship the cross and worship images. And how many of the past and present-day rulers of the Muslims are afflicted by the trial caused by the dead, so that they build tombs over them, and their hearts are attached to them in love, hope and fear. They fall into that which Allaah's Messenger (ﷺ) feared for his *ummah* and which he warned against. So the seriousness and the soundness of the methodology will therefore be clear to you, and also the importance of the firm stance taken by the Messenger (ﷺ) with regard to idols and tombs. Furthermore the wisdom of Ibraaheem will become clear to you, and the depth of his thinking and its extent when he made the enduring call which resounds in all corners and in every generation.

$$\text{وَاجْنُبْنِي وَبَنِيَّ أَن نَّعْبُدَ ٱلْأَصْنَامَ ۝ رَبِّ إِنَّهُنَّ أَضْلَلْنَ كَثِيرًا مِّنَ ٱلنَّاسِ ۖ فَمَن تَبِعَنِي فَإِنَّهُۥ مِنِّي ۖ وَمَنْ عَصَانِي فَإِنَّكَ غَفُورٌ رَّحِيمٌ ۝}$$

"And keep me and my sons far removed from worshipping the idols. O my Lord, they have caused the misguidance of many of the people. So whoever follows me in what I am upon (*eemaan* in Allaah, making worship purely for Allaah and disassociation from the worship of idols) then he is from my people (upon my way and religion), and whoever disobeys me, then indeed You are the Most Forgiving, Most Merciful."[179]

---

[179] Soorah Ibraaheem (14):35-36.

So you see Ibraaheem, who was fully upon the truth and the right way, seeking Allaah's refuge from the evils and danger of the idols, and not seeking His refuge from the evils and danger of the rulers, despite the level of their corruption and their danger.

Secondly, the people were upon a single religion (Islaam), upon guidance, but then they diverged from it, so Allaah sent the Prophets as bringers of good tidings of reward for the obedient Believers, and warners of Allaah's punishment for the disobedient unbelievers.

Allaah, the Most High, says:

$$\text{وَمَا نُرْسِلُ ٱلْمُرْسَلِينَ إِلَّا مُبَشِّرِينَ وَمُنذِرِينَ فَمَنْ ءَامَنَ وَأَصْلَحَ فَلَا خَوْفٌ عَلَيْهِمْ وَلَا هُمْ يَحْزَنُونَ}$$

"We do not send Our Messengers except with good news for the obedient that Paradise and success on the Day of Resurrection is the reward for obedience to Me, and with a warning for those who disobey and reject My commands that We will punish them, so that they may die aware of that. So whoever believes the Messengers and acts righteously in this world by following what they are upon then there will be no fear upon them when they meet their Lord, nor will they grieve about what they left behind in the world."[180]

Allaah, the Most High, says:

---

[180] Soorah al-An'aam (6):48.

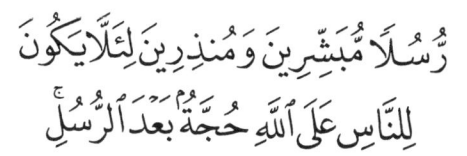

$$رُسُلًا مُبَشِّرِينَ وَمُنذِرِينَ لِئَلَّا يَكُونَ لِلنَّاسِ عَلَى ٱللَّهِ حُجَّةٌ بَعْدَ ٱلرُّسُلِ$$

"Messengers who were sent with the good news of Allaah's reward for those who obey Allaah, do as He commands and believe in His Messengers, and warners of Allaah's punishment for those who disobey Allaah, contravene His commands and disbelieve in His Messengers, so that those who disbelieve in Allaah and worship others besides Him may have no excuse to avoid punishment after the sending of the Messengers."[181]

Allaah's Messenger (ﷺ) said, *"There is no one to whom granting excuse is more beloved than Allaah, therefore He sent the bringers of good-tidings and the warners."*[182]

Allaah, the Most High, says:

$$فَهَلْ عَلَى ٱلرُّسُلِ إِلَّا ٱلْبَلَٰغُ ٱلْمُبِينُ$$

"So are the Messengers charged with anything but to clearly convey the Message?"[183]

Allaah, the Most High, says:

$$وَمَا عَلَى ٱلرُّسُلِ إِلَّا ٱلْبَلَٰغُ ٱلْمُبِينُ$$

"The Messenger's duty is but to clearly convey the Message."[184]

---

[181] Soorah an-Nisaa (4):165.
[182] Reported by al-Bukhaaree (Eng. trans. (9/378 no.512), Muslim (Eng. trans. 2/782 no.3572), Ahmad (4/238) and ad-Daarimee (no.2233).
[183] Soorah an-Nahl (16):35.
[184] Soorah an-Noor (24):54.

Allaah, the Most High, says:

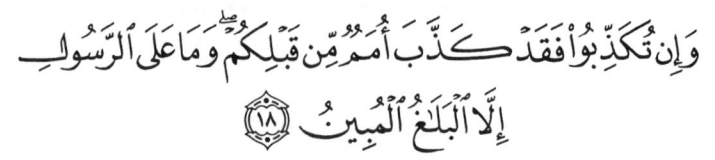

$$\text{وَإِن تُكَذِّبُواْ فَقَدْ كَذَّبَ أُمَمٌ مِّن قَبْلِكُمْ وَمَا عَلَى ٱلرَّسُولِ إِلَّا ٱلْبَلَٰغُ ٱلْمُبِينُ}$$

"So if you deny Our Messenger, O people, and reject his command for you to worship your Lord and to free yourselves from the worship of idols, then nations before you denied their Messengers who called them to the truth, so Allaah sent His punishment upon them and will do the same with you. The Messenger's duty is but to clearly convey the Message."[185]

So this duty of warning and bringing good tidings and conveying the Message is a very exalted, sublime and lofty duty. It is enough in this regard that it was the duty of the Prophets and fully concorded with their lofty station, since it the hardest and the greatest task taken up by mankind. It was then taken up by their inheritors from the true and sincere callers who follow their methodology, therefore Allaah's Messenger (ﷺ) said, *"The people who are most severely tried are the Prophets, then those most like them, then those most like them."* We have also already mentioned the extent of the difficulties faced by the caller to *tawheed* and that others are unable to persevere in this sphere.

Thirdly, Allaah, the One free of all imperfections, and the Most High, did not start by commanding and making it a duty upon them, as is seen from the stories of their lives, that they should establish states and cause the downfall of others, and this is perfect wisdom since the call to establish a state attracts the seekers of this world, and those who seek after self-elevation and positions of power, and those who have personal goals and

---

[185] Soorah al-'Ankaaboot (29):18.

grudges, and aspirations and ambitions.[186] So these types of people quickly respond to the call to establish a state which they think will enable them to attain their goals, their desires and their ambitions.

Due to the like of these considerations, and Allaah knows best, and due to other reasons known by Allaah, the Creator, the All-Knowing, the All-Wise, the calls of the Prophets and their methodologies were far removed from using these flashy and attractive slogans or those which clearly appeal to short-term ambitions and desires. Rather they followed a methodology which is wise, unblemished and noble. It involves being tried and tested. So they are followed upon this way and believed in by every true and sincere person free of selfish ambitions and personal goals. Such a person does not desire through his *eemaan*, his *tawheed* and his obedience to Allaah's Messenger (ﷺ) except Paradise and the Pleasure of his Lord. He does not fear except from His Anger and His severe punishment. Therefore they are only followed generally by the poor, the needy and the weak. Allaah, the Most High, says, quoting what the people of Nooh said:

$$\textarabic{قَالُوٓا۟ أَنُؤْمِنُ لَكَ وَٱتَّبَعَكَ ٱلْأَرْذَلُونَ ۝}$$

"They said, 'Are we to believe in you, O Nooh, and affirm what you call us to, when it is only the lowly people who follow you?'"[187]

He said concerning the people of Saalih:

---

[186] As has happened with many political calls, and from the latest of them the call of the *Ikhwaanul-Muslimeen* who have been joined by the like of those called "the free officers" and many people with self interest.

[187] Soorah ash-Shu'araa (36):111.

$$\text{قَالَ ٱلْمَلَأُ ٱلَّذِينَ ٱسْتَكْبَرُوا۟ مِن قَوْمِهِۦ لِلَّذِينَ ٱسْتُضْعِفُوا۟ لِمَنْ ءَامَنَ مِنْهُمْ أَتَعْلَمُونَ أَنَّ صَٰلِحًا مُّرْسَلٌ مِّن رَّبِّهِۦ ۚ قَالُوٓا۟ إِنَّا بِمَآ أُرْسِلَ بِهِۦ مُؤْمِنُونَ ۝ قَالَ ٱلَّذِينَ ٱسْتَكْبَرُوٓا۟ إِنَّا بِٱلَّذِىٓ ءَامَنتُم بِهِۦ كَٰفِرُونَ ۝}$$

"The heads of the people who haughtily rejected Faith said to those who they held to be lowly, to those who believed in and followed Saalih and what he came with, 'Do you really know that Saalih is one sent by Allaah?' They said, 'We indeed attest and believe in the truth and guidance which Allaah has sent him with.' The haughty ones said, 'We deny and disbelieve that which you believe in.'"[188]

Also amongst the questions which Heraclius asked Aboo Sufyaan was, "Is it the noble of the people who follow him or the weak amongst them?" Aboo Sufyaan replied, "Rather it is the weak amongst them." So Heraclius said, "I asked you 'Is it the noble of the people who follow him or the weak amongst them,' and you mentioned that it is the weak amongst them, and it is they who are the followers of the Messengers." So the call to establish a state is far far easier, and people respond more quickly to it since most people are seekers after this world and followers of desires.

---

[188] Soorah al-A'raaf (7):75-76.

Also because of the reasons, the consequences and the difficulties in the way of the calls of the Messengers we find that they are not followed except by a small number of people. So Nooh remained, for nine hundred and fifty years,[189] calling to Allaah, yet despite this, "None but a few believed along with him."[190]

From Ibn 'Abbaas, *radiyallaahu 'anhumaa,* who said, *"Allaah's Messenger (ﷺ) said, 'The nations were presented before me, and I saw a Prophet and with him was a small group of people, and I saw a Prophet along with one man or two men, and a Prophet accompanied by nobody. Then I saw a huge crowd of people and I thought that they were my ummah. So it was said to me, "This is Moosaa and his people. But rather look to the horizon." So I looked and saw a huge crowd, so it was said to me, "This is your ummah, and from them are seventy thousand who will enter Paradise without any reckoning.""*[191]

As for Ibraaheem, the chosen and beloved Friend of Allaah, who refuted and silenced the *mushriks* with irrefutable and clear proofs. Allaah says regarding him and those who believed along with him:

$$\text{فَـَٔامَنَ لَهُۥ لُوطٌۘ وَقَالَ إِنِّى مُهَاجِرٌ إِلَىٰ رَبِّىٓۖ إِنَّهُۥ هُوَ ٱلْعَزِيزُ ٱلْحَكِيمُ}$$

"So Loot believed in him and attested to the truth of what he came with, and Ibraaheem said, 'Indeed I will emigrate (to the land of *Shaam*) for the sake of my Lord. Indeed He is the All-Mighty, the All-Wise.'"[192]

---

[189] Soorah al-'Ankaaboot (29):14.
[190] Soorah Hood (11):40.
[191] Reported by al-Bukhaaree (Eng. trans. 7/407 no.606 and 8/359 no.549) and Muslim (Eng. trans 1/141 no.625) and Ahmad (1/271).
[192] Soorah al-'Ankaaboot (29):26.

With regard to Loot and those who were saved from the punishment along with him, and perhaps they were his daughters alone:

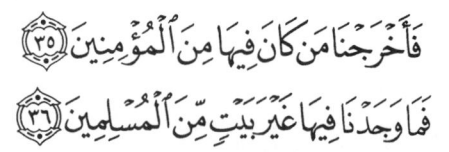

$$\text{فَأَخْرَجْنَا مَن كَانَ فِيهَا مِنَ ٱلْمُؤْمِنِينَ ۝ فَمَا وَجَدْنَا فِيهَا غَيْرَ بَيْتٍ مِّنَ ٱلْمُسْلِمِينَ ۝}$$

"So We brought out those who were Believers from the town, and We did not find there except a single household of Muslims."[193]

But none of this diminishes the rank of the Prophets by the slightest degree, rather they are upon the highest rank and are the noblest and most distinguished of the people and the most honourable. They stand above all the people in manhood, bravery, excellence of language and eloquence, and in their clarity of explanation, their sincerity and sacrifice.

They also established their duty of calling to *tawheed*, propagating the Message, giving the good tidings and the warnings, and they fulfilled this in the most complete manner. So the fact that they had few followers or some of them had no followers, is purely the fault of the nations which refused to accept the call since, in their view, they did not satisfy their lowly goals. Then it may be that they respond to his call, or a large number of them do so, and so they gain a state, as a goodly fruit due to their *eemaan*, their affirmation of what the Prophet came with, and their righteous actions.

They thus establish the obligation upon them of fighting *Jihaad* to raise up the Word of Allaah, and of following and applying the *Sharee'ah* and the prescribed punishments and other matters prescribed for them by Allaah. This is what happened with our Prophet Muhammad (ﷺ) and his

---

[193] Soorah adh-Dhaariyaat (51):35-36.

noble Companions. Allaah crowned their *eemaan*, their righteous actions, and their exemplary perseverance when facing the harm and oppression of the *mushriks*, by aiding them and making their *Deen* uppermost, and by establishing them upon the earth as Allaah, the Most High, says:

$$\text{وَعَدَ ٱللَّهُ ٱلَّذِينَ ءَامَنُواْ مِنكُمْ وَعَمِلُواْ ٱلصَّٰلِحَٰتِ لَيَسْتَخْلِفَنَّهُمْ فِى ٱلْأَرْضِ كَمَا ٱسْتَخْلَفَ ٱلَّذِينَ مِن قَبْلِهِمْ وَلَيُمَكِّنَنَّ لَهُمْ دِينَهُمُ ٱلَّذِى ٱرْتَضَىٰ لَهُمْ وَلَيُبَدِّلَنَّهُم مِّنۢ بَعْدِ خَوْفِهِمْ أَمْنًا يَعْبُدُونَنِى لَا يُشْرِكُونَ بِى شَيْئًا وَمَن كَفَرَ بَعْدَ ذَٰلِكَ فَأُو۟لَٰٓئِكَ هُمُ ٱلْفَٰسِقُونَ ۝}$$

> **"Allaah has promised those who truly believe (have true *eemaan*) amongst you, and act in obedience to Allaah and His Messenger, that He will grant them rulership upon the earth just as He granted it to those before them, and that He will establish their religion for them grant them authority to practice the religion which He chose for them and ordered. And He will certainly change their situation to one of security, after their fear, providing that they worship and obey Me, not associating anything else in worship with Me."**[194]

Then sovereignty was offered to Allaah's Messenger (ﷺ) in Makkah but he refused and he continued calling to *tawheed* and waging war against *shirk* and the idols. So when Quraysh became troubled by the call of Allaah's Messenger (ﷺ) they sent 'Utbah ibn Rabee'ah and he came to

---

[194] Soorah an-Noor (24):55.

Allaah's Messenger (ﷺ) and said, "O son of my brother, you know the excellence you hold amongst us with regard to your position in the tribe and your lineage, but you have brought a matter which is very serious for your people. Because of it you have split their united body, caused their youth to behave foolishly and you have abused their idols with it, and their religion. You have also declared their forefathers to be infidels because of it. So listen to me and I will offer you some things which you may consider, and hopefully some of them will be acceptable to you." So Allaah's Messenger (ﷺ) said, "Speak, O Abul-Waleed, I will listen." He said, "O son of my brother, if what you desire by this matter that you have come with is wealth, then we will gather wealth for you from our wealth until you are one of the richest of us. **And if you wish by it for high position, then we will give you such authority that we will not do anything without your approval, and if you wish by it for sovereignty, then we will make you sovereign over us.** But if it is the case that what comes to you is a demon which you see and cannot get rid of, then we will seek after a medical cure for you and will expend our money until we can get you cured of it. Since a demon may take hold of a person until he is cured and relieved of it," or as he said. Allaah's Messenger (ﷺ) was listening to him, then he said, "Have you finished, O Abul-Waleed?" He said, "Yes." He said, "Then listen to me." He said, "I will do so." He said:

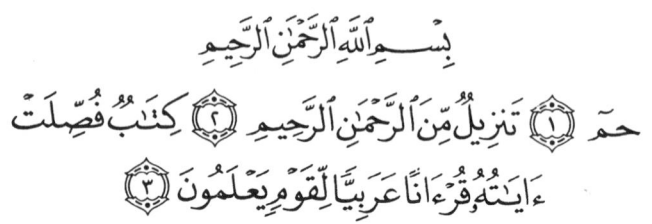

بِسْمِ اللَّهِ الرَّحْمَنِ الرَّحِيمِ

حمٓ ۝ تَنزِيلٌ مِّنَ الرَّحْمَٰنِ الرَّحِيمِ ۝ كِتَٰبٌ فُصِّلَتْ ءَايَٰتُهُۥ قُرْءَانًا عَرَبِيًّا لِّقَوْمٍ يَعْلَمُونَ ۝

"In the name of Allaah, the Most Merciful, the Bestower of Mercy. *Haa Meem.* This Qur'aan is the Revelation sent down by the Most Merciful, the Bestower of Mercy. A Book whose *Aayaat* are made

clear, a recital in pure Arabic for those who know (the pure Arabic language), bringing them good tidings of Paradise if they believe in it and act upon it, and as a warning to those who disbelieve in it and do not act in obedience to Allaah, that they will receive punishment and dwell forever in Hell in the Hereafter. But most of them turn away haughtily and refuse to listen to it."[195]

Then Allaah's Messenger (ﷺ) continued reciting it to him. When 'Utbah heard it he remained silent and sat with his hands behind his back, resting upon them and listening. So when Allaah's Messenger (ﷺ) came to the *Aayah* of prostration in it he prostrated and then said, "You have heard what you have heard O Abul-Waleed, so now it is up to you..." So 'Utbah went back to Quraysh and when he sat with them they said, "What has happened with you, O Abul-Waleed?" He said, "What happened is that I heard the like of which, by Allaah, I have never heard. By Allaah, it is not sorcery, nor poetry, nor divining. O Quraysh, obey me and let the decision be mine. Leave the man and let him continue in what he is upon. Keep away from him since, by Allaah, his saying which I heard will come to have great importance. So if the (other) Arabs kill him, then you will be rid of him due to the action of others, and if he conquers the Arabs, then his sovereignty is your sovereignty, his power is your power and you will be the ones fortunate with regard to him." They said, "By Allaah, he has performed magic upon you with his tongue, O Abul-Waleed." He said, "This is my opinion with regard to him, you may do whatever you see fit."[196]

---

[195] Soorah Fussilat (41):1-4.
[196] Reported by Ibn Ishaaq in his *Seerah*, he said, "Yazeed ibn Abee Ziyad narrated to me: from Muhammad ibn Ka'b al-Qurazee who said: It was related to me that 'Utbah ibn Rabee'ah..." And he reported the narration: *as-Seerah* of Ibn Hishaam (1/293-294). It also has a supporting witness in the *hadeeth* of Jaabir which is reported by 'Abd ibn Humayd and Aboo Ya'laa which has preceded.

Ibn Ishaaq reports with his chain of narration to Ibn 'Abbaas that a group of Quraysh gathered and made an offer close to the offer made by 'Utbah and his saying to Allaah's Messenger (ﷺ). So he (ﷺ) answered them by saying, *"I am not afflicted by what you say. I have not come with that which I have come with seeking your wealth, nor seeking status above you, nor sovereignty over you, but rather Allaah has sent me as a Messenger to you, and has sent down a Book to me, and has ordered me to be a bringer of good tidings and a warner to you. So I have conveyed to you the revealed Messages from my Lord, and I have sincerely advised you. So if you accept what I have brought to you then you will have your share in this world and the Hereafter. But if you refuse to accept it from me then I will patiently await Allaah's Order, until Allaah judges between me and you..."*[197]

Likewise Allaah's Messenger (ﷺ) rejected the request of one of the tribes that they should be in charge of the affairs after his death, if the report is authentic. Ibn Ishaaq said that az-Zuhree narrated to me that Allaah's Messenger (ﷺ) came to Banoo 'Aamir ibn Sa'sa'ah and called them to Allaah, the Mighty and Majestic, and presented himself to them. So a man from them called Bayharah ibn Firaas said, "By Allaah, if I were to take hold of this young man from Quraysh I would devour the Arabs with him," then he said, "If we give you our pledge of allegiance upon your affair, then Allaah gives you victory over those who oppose you, then will we be in authority after you?" He said, "The affair is for Allaah, He places authority wherever He wills." So he said to him, "Are we to risk our necks before the Arabs for you, then when Allaah grants you victory, authority will be for other than us?! We have no need of your affair." So they rejected him.[198]

---

[197] *As-Seerah* of Ibn Hishaam (1/295-296): Ibn Ishaaq said: A person of knowledge narated to me: from Sa'eed ibn Jubayr and 'Ikrimah the *mawlaa* of Ibn 'Abbaas: from 'Abdullaah ibn 'Abbaas, *radiyallaahu 'anhumaa,* who said, "A group of Quraysh gathered: 'Utbah ibn Rabee'ah, Shaybah ibn Rabee'ah and Aboo Sufyaan..." And this strengthens the previous narration, each of them supporting the other.

[198] Ibn Hishaam's *Seerah* (1/424-425) and *as-Seeratun-Nabawiyyah* of adh-Dhahabee (pp.189-190).

A Summary of the *Da'wah* of the Prophets

The Prophets, *'alayhimus-salaatu was-salaam*, did not come to bring about the downfall of one state and to replace it with another. They did not seek after sovereignty, nor did they organise parties for that. Rather they came for the guidance of mankind and to save them from misguidance and *shirk*, and to take mankind out of darkness and into light and to remind them of the days when Allaah has sent favours upon them. If rule and sovereignty had been offered to them, they would have rejected it and continued upon their *da'wah*. Indeed Quraysh offered sovereignty to Allaah's Messenger (ﷺ) and he refused it. It was also offered to him that he should be a Prophet-king or a Slave-Messenger, so he chose that he should be a Slave-Messenger. From Aboo Hurayrah, *radiyallaahu 'anhu*, who said, *"Jibreel sat with Allaah's Messenger (ﷺ) and looked to the heavens and saw an Angel descending, so Jibreel said, 'This Angel has never descended since he was created until now.' So when he descended he said, 'O Muhammad! Your Lord has sent me to you, saying, "Shall He make you a Prophet-king or a Slave-Messenger?"" Jibreel said, 'Show humbleness to your Lord, O Muhammad.' He said, 'Rather a Slave-Messenger.'"*[199]

So he did not used to take pledge of allegiance from the Ansaar or others except for Paradise, despite the fact that the pledge of the Ansaar was given in the most severe and difficult circumstances, yet it contained no promise of positions of authority, nor sovereignty, nor leadership, nor wealth, nor any other temporal gain.

---

[199] Reported by Ahmad (2/231) and Ibn Hibbaan, as occurs in *al-Mawaarid* (no.2137), both of them by way of Muhammad ibn Fudayl: from 'Umaarah ibn al-Qa'qaa: from Aboo Zur'ah: from Aboo Hurayrah, *radiyallaahu 'anhu*. Al-Albaanee said in his *as-Saheehah* (3/4), "This is a chain of narration *saheeh* to the standard of Muslim, and it has a witnessing narration from the *hadeeth* of Ibn 'Abbaas reported by al-Baghawee in *Sharhus-Sunnah* (13/248-249) and its chain of narration is weak."

'Ubaadah ibn as-Saamit, *radiyallaahu 'anhu*, said, "I am one of those chiefs who gave the 'Aqabah pledge to Allaah's Messenger (ﷺ)," and he said, "We gave the pledge that we would not worship anything else besides Allaah, nor steal, nor fornicate, nor kill a person whose killing Allaah had made unlawful, except rightfully, nor rob each other, nor disobey, and (then) Paradise would be ours."[200]

From Aboo Mas'ood al-Ansaaree, *radiyallaahu 'anhu*, who said, *"Allaah's Messenger (ﷺ) went along with his uncle al-'Abbaas to seventy of the Ansaar, beneath the tree. So he said, 'Let the one of you who is to speak do so, but he should not make his speech long since the mushriks have a spy watching you, and if they come to know about you they will expose you.' So their speaker, who was Aboo Umaamah said, 'Ask, O Muhammad, for your Lord whatever you wish, then ask for yourselves and your Companions whatever you wish. Then inform us what reward there is for us with Allaah, the Mighty and Majestic, and what is due to us from you if we do that.' So he said, 'For my Lord, the Mighty and Majestic, I ask that you do not worship anything besides Him, and for myself and my Companions I ask that you grant us shelter and assist us, and defend us as you defend yourselves.' They said, 'So what is there for us if we do that?' He said, 'Paradise is for you.' They said, 'Then we will do that for you.'"*[201]

From Jaabir ibn 'Abdullaah, *radiyallaahu 'anhumaa*, who said, "Allaah's Messenger (ﷺ) spent ten years in Makkah following up the people in

---

[200] Reported by al-Bukhaaree (Eng. trans. 9/6 no.12) and Muslim (Eng. trans. 3/925 no.4238).

[201] Reported by Ahmad in his *Musnad* (4/119-120), saying: Yahyaa ibn Abee Zakariyyaa ibn Abee Zaaidah narrated to us: My father narrated to me: from 'Aamir - meaning ash-Sha'bee, then he reported it with this chain of narration from Mujaalid: from 'Aamir ash-Sha'bee: from Aboo Mas'ood al-Ansaaree. Then he reports it with this chain of narration from Ismaa'eel ibn Abee Khaalid: from ash-Sha'bee who said, "Neither old men nor young men had heard a speech like it."

the places where they settled in 'Ukaaz and Majannah and in the times of pilgrimage at Minaa, and he would say, *'Who will shelter me, who will assist me, so that I may convey the Messages of my Lord, and Paradise will be his?'* To the point that a man would arrive from Yemen or from Mudarr and come to his people, and they would say: 'Beware of the young man of Quraysh, do not let him put you to trial.' He would walk amongst them and they would point at him - until Allaah sent us to him from Yathrib and we gave shelter to him and affirmed the truthfulness of his Message. A man from us would go out and believe in him and be taught the Qur'aan by him, then he would go back to his family and they would accept Islaam as a result of his Islaam. To the point that there did not remain a single household amongst the Ansaar except that it contained a number of Muslims who openly manifested their Islaam. Then they all performed *'Umrah*, so we said, 'For how long will we leave Allaah's Messenger (ﷺ) cast out amongst the mountains of Makkah in a state of fear?!' So a group of seventy of our men travelled to him and came to him at the time of the pilgrimage. We agreed to meet him in the ravine at 'Aqabah. So we came in ones and twos until we had all gathered and we said, 'O Messenger of Allaah. May we give you pledge of allegiance?' He said, 'Give me the pledge that you will hear and obey, in that which is pleasing to you and in that which is burdensome, in difficulty and in ease, and that you order the good and forbid the evil, and that you speak for Allaah's sake and do not fear the reproach of anyone when speaking for Allaah's sake, and that you assist me, and defend me when I come to you just as you would defend yourselves and your wives and your children, and Paradise is yours.' He said, 'So we stood and gave him the pledge and As'ad ibn Zuraarah took his hand, and he was the youngest of them, so he said, 'Do not be hasty, O People of Yathrib, for we have not travelled this long distance except because we know that he is Allaah's Messenger (ﷺ), and that fulfilment today will mean splitting away from the rest of the Arabs, and that the best of you will be killed, and that the sword will be used against you. So either you are a people who will withstand that, and your reward will be with Allaah, or you are a people who fear that you may prove to be cowardly, then you should make this clear, and it will be an excuse for you with Allaah.' They said, 'Withhold, O Sa'd, for by Allaah, we will not abandon this pledge ever, nor will we be robbed of it.' So he took it from us upon these conditions, and promised us Paradise in return for that."[202]

So here also he would cultivate his Companions upon the Book and the *Sunnah*, and upon *eemaan*, sincerity and purity of intention for Allaah in every action, far from political methods and from tempting them with positions of authority. He did not give any of them, either before or after they entered Islaam, any wish or hope for a position of authority in the State. So with regard to 'Umar ibn al-Khattaab, *radiyallaahu 'anhu*, one of the greatest of the Companions and the strongest personality amongst them, Allaah's Messenger (ﷺ) did not promise him any position of authority, nor did he himself have any desire for that at all, until the day of Khaybar, twenty years after the beginning of the Messengership, when Allaah's Messenger (ﷺ) surprised them by saying, "I will give the flag tomorrow to a man who loves Allaah and His Messenger. Allaah will grant victory at his hand." So 'Umar, *radiyallaahu 'anhu*, and the rest of the Companions spent the night wondering whom he would give it to, and

---

[202] Reported by Imaam Ahmad (3/322) who said, "'Abdur-Razzaaq narrated to us: Ma'mar related to us: from Ibn Khuthaym: from Abuz-Zubayr: from Jaabir, and (3/339): Ishaaq ibn 'Eesaa narrated to us: Yahyaa ibn Sulaym narrated to us: from 'Abdullaah ibn 'Uthmaan ibn Kuthaym: from Abuz-Zubayr: that he narrated to him from Jaabir..." and he mentioned the *hadeeth*. It is reported by Ibn Hibbaan in his *Saheeh*, as occurs in *Mawaariduz-Zamaan* (p.408), and al-Haakim (2/624) and he declared it *saheeh* and adh-Dhahabee agreed, and Abuz-Zubayr's narration is witnessed to by Imaam ash-Sha'bee, *rahimahullaah*: al-Bazzaar, *rahimahullaah*, said, "Muhammad ibn Ma'mar narrated to us: Qubaysah narrated to us: Sufyaan narrated to us: from Jaabir and Aboo Daawood, who is Abee Hind: from ash-Sha'bee: from Jaabir who said, 'Allaah's Messenger (ﷺ) said to the chiefs amongst the Ansaar, "You will shelter me?" They said, "Yes, then what is there for us?" He said, "Paradise.""

'Umar, *radiyallaahu 'anhu*, said, "I never had any love for leadership except on that day."[203]

So what was it that those noble Companions hoped for?! Was it leadership itself, or was it that great rank of loving Allaah and His Messenger? So why did 'Umar ibn al-Khattaab not love leadership if it was indeed something which Allaah's Messenger (ﷺ) endeared to them, and trained them for and caused them to desire it?!

From Aboo Hurayrah, *radiyallaahu 'anhu*, who said that Allaah's Messenger (ﷺ) said, *"You will indeed desire for leadership, but it will be a cause of regret on the Day of Resurrection. So what a good wet nurse it is, but what an evil weaning one it is."*[204] So he forbade seeking for it and desiring it.[205]

'Abdur-Rahmaan ibn Samurah, *radiyallaahu 'anhu*, said that Allaah's Messenger (ﷺ) said to me, *"O 'Abdur-Rahmaan! Do not ask for leadership, since if you are given it having requested it, then you will be left alone to*

---

[203] Reported by Muslim (Eng. trans. 4/1285 no.5917) from Aboo Hurayrah and (no. 5918) from Sahl ibn Sa'd and its wording includes, "So they spent the night wondering which of them would be given it." and "A man who loves Allaah and His Mesenger, and who is loved by Allaah and His Messenger." and (no.5915) from Sa'd ibn Abee Waqqaas, and its wordiing is, "I will give the flag to a man who loves Allaah and His Messenger." He said, "So we hoped for that." And the reason for this was their eagerness for this high station before Allaah, not a desire for leadership itself. It is also reported by al-Bukhaaree (Eng. trans. 4/156 no. 253 and 5/43 no. 51).

[204] Reported by al-Bukhaaree (Eng. trans. 9/196 no.262) and Ahmad (2/4048). Ibn Hajar said in *Fathul-Baaree* (13/126), "'What a good wet nurse it is' due to the status, wealth and implementation of ones word that go with it, and attainment of physical and imagined delights that are enjoyed whilst it is attained, and, 'what an evil weaning one it is,' due to the cutting off of all these upon death or due to other causes, and due to the serious consequences of it in the Hereafter."

[205] Publisher's note: Also refer to "The Evil of Craving for Wealth and Status" by Haafidh Ibn Rajab (Al-Hidaayah Publishing and Distribution, U.K.).

discharge it, but if you are given it without requesting it you will be helped (by Allaah) in it."[206]

Indeed on top of all this he firmly implanted the Islamic principle that positions of authority are prohibited for those who earnestly desire and crave after them. From Aboo Moosaa al-Ash'aree, *radiyallaahu 'anhu,* who said, "I entered upon the Prophet (ﷺ) along with two men from the sons of my uncle, so one of the two men said, 'O Messenger of Allaah! Appoint us to take charge of one of the lands which Allaah, the Mighty and Majestic, has given you authority over.' The other man also said the same. So he (ﷺ) said, *'We do not appoint to that position anyone who asks for it, nor anyone who is keen to have it.'"* In a wording of Muslim there occurs, *"What do you say, O Aboo Moosaa, or 'Abdullaah ibn Qays?"* He said, "So I said, 'By Him Who sent you with the truth, they did not disclose to me what they had in their minds, nor was I aware that they were going to seek this appointment.'" He said, "And it is as if I can still see his (i.e., the Prophets (ﷺ)) tooth-stick between his lips." So he said, *"We shall not, or, do not appoint to authority in this affair of ours anyone who desires it. Rather you go, O Aboo Moosaa."* So he sent him to Yemen, and then sent Mu'aadh in addition to him. And in the version of an-Nasaa'ee there occurs, *"We do not seek the assistance in this affairs of ours of those who request it."*[207]

Al-Haafidh ibn Hajar said, "al-Mu'allib said, 'Desire for leadership is the cause for people fighting each other for it to the point that they shed blood and make wealth and private parts lawful, and therefore great corruption results in the land. Then the reason for regret is that he may be killed, deposed or die and then regret having entered into it in the first

---

[206] Reported by al-Bukhaaree (Eng. trans. 9/194 no.260) and Muslim (Eng. trans. 3/1013 no.4487).
[207] Reported by al-Bukhaaree (Eng. trans. 9/196 no.263), Muslim (Eng, trans. 3/104 no.4490) and an-Nasaa'ee (8/198).

place. Since he will be held to account for the evils he has committed and that which he craved for will be lost to him as soon as he leaves it.' He said, 'And an exception to this is the case of one who has to take it on due to the fact that the ruler dies and no one else is to be found to take over but him, and if he does not take over then this will cause corruption and chaos.'"[208] But leadership and the office of judge are matters which are essential, and vital to the life of the Muslims, and necessary for the protection of blood and wealth.

However it is obligatory that in choosing the governors and the judges that we follow the methodology of Allaah's Messenger (ﷺ), so these positions are not to be given to those who ask for them, or desire them, or put themselves forward, in elections for example, since this pertains to desiring these positions.

Rather the ones to be chosen are those who are suitable in knowledge, piety and those who do not desire such a position. Then we must also benefit from this Prophetic methodology in our education and training. So we should not bring up the youth to have love for leadership, authority and position. If we bring them up upon love of these things, then we have acted contrary to the way and guidance of Allaah's Messenger (ﷺ) and have led the youth to that which will only destroy them. Then what success can we expect in this world or the Hereafter if we act contrary to the methodology of Allaah's Messenger (ﷺ)?

وَيَقُولُونَ ءَامَنَّا بِٱللَّهِ وَبِٱلرَّسُولِ وَأَطَعْنَا ثُمَّ يَتَوَلَّىٰ فَرِيقٌ مِّنْهُم مِّنۢ بَعْدِ ذَٰلِكَ وَمَا أُو۟لَٰٓئِكَ بِٱلْمُؤْمِنِينَ ۝ وَإِذَا دُعُوٓا۟ إِلَى ٱللَّهِ وَرَسُولِهِۦ لِيَحْكُمَ بَيْنَهُمْ إِذَا فَرِيقٌ مِّنْهُم مُّعْرِضُونَ ۝

---

[208] *Fathul-Baaree* (13/126).

"And the Hypocrites say, 'We believe in Allaah and His Messenger, and are obedient to Allaah and His Messenger.' Then they turn away from Allaah's Messenger (ﷺ) to others for judgement, and they are not Believers. And if they are called to the Book of Allaah and to His Messenger for judgement about that which they dispute in, then a group of them turn away from acceptance of the truth."[209]

In what has preceded, we have come to know the methodology of the Prophets in calling to *tawheed* and in fighting against *shirk* and its manifestations and causes, and that it is a methodology built upon intellect, wisdom and the true and inborn nature. We have also come to know the proofs for this - both the general proofs and the proofs in detail - from the Book and the *Sunnah*, and from the intellectual angle. So now we ask: Is it permissible for those who call to Allaah, in any time, to turn away from the methodology of the Prophets in calling to Allaah? The answer: In light of what has preceded and what will come, it is not permissible in the *Sharee'ah*, nor intellectually, that anyone should turn away from this methodology and prefer a different way.

Firstly, This is the straight and upright way which Allaah laid down for all the Prophets, from the first to the last of them. And Allaah, the One who laid down this methodology, is the Creator of mankind, and the One Who knows everything about human nature, and knows what is most beneficial for their souls and their hearts:

أَلَا يَعْلَمُ مَنْ خَلَقَ وَهُوَ ٱللَّطِيفُ ٱلْخَبِيرُ ﴿١٤﴾

"How can He Who created not know when He is the One Who knows the innermost secret of His servants and is fully aware of them and their actions?!"[210]

---

[209] Soorah an-Noor (24):47-48.
[210] Soorah al-Mulk (67):14.

Secondly, The Prophets adhered to it and followed it, which shows clearly that it is not an area for *ijtihaad* (independent interpretation and judgement), so we do not find:
(1) any Prophet beginning his call with *Sufism*;
(2) another one beginning with philosophy and theological rhetoric (*kalaam*);
(3) and others beginning with politics.

Rather we find that they all followed a single methodology, and all gave the same primary importance to the *tawheed* of Allaah.

Thirdly, Allaah made it obligatory upon our noble Prophet, whom Allaah made it obligatory upon us to follow, that he should follow them and their methodology. So He said, after mentioning eighteen of them:

$$أُو۟لَٰٓئِكَ ٱلَّذِينَ هَدَى ٱللَّهُ فَبِهُدَىٰهُمُ ٱقْتَدِهْ$$

"They are those whom Allaah has guided, so follow the way and guidance which they were upon."[211]

And he followed their way by beginning with *tawheed* and giving the greatest importance to it.

Fourthly, since their call in its most complete form was to be seen in the call of Ibraaheem, *'alayhis-salaatu was-salaam,* Allaah further emphasised the matter and ordered our Prophet Muhammad (ﷺ) to follow his methodology. He says:

$$ثُمَّ أَوْحَيْنَا إِلَيْكَ أَنِ ٱتَّبِعْ مِلَّةَ إِبْرَٰهِيمَ حَنِيفًا ۖ وَمَا كَانَ مِنَ ٱلْمُشْرِكِينَ ۝$$

---

[211] Soorah al-An'aam (6):90.

> "Then We revealed to you, O Muhammad (ﷺ), that you should follow the religion of Ibraaheem who was a Muslim upon the true religion and was not one of those who worshipped idols and associated partners with Allaah."[212]

So the order to follow him covers adherence to his religion which is *tawheed* and fighting against *shirk*. It also covers following his methodology in beginning by calling to *tawheed*. Then Allaah, the Most High, further emphasised this order also by ordering the *ummah* of Muhammad (ﷺ) to follow the way and the religion of this Prophet who was upon the true religion. So He, the Most High, says:

$$ قُلْ صَدَقَ ٱللَّهُ فَٱتَّبِعُواْ مِلَّةَ إِبْرَٰهِيمَ حَنِيفًا وَمَا كَانَ مِنَ ٱلْمُشْرِكِينَ ﴿٩٥﴾ $$

> "Say, O Muhammad (ﷺ), Allaah has indeed spoken the Truth, so follow the religion of Ibraaheem who was upright, upon the religion of Islaam, and he did not make any share of his worship for any created being."[213]

Therefore the *ummah* of Islaam is commanded to follow his religion and way. So just as it is not permissible to act contrary to his religion, then likewise it is not permissible to turn away from his methodology in calling to *tawheed* and fighting *shirk* and its manifestations and causes.

Fifthly, Allaah, the Most High, says:

$$ فَإِن تَنَٰزَعْتُمْ فِى شَىْءٍ فَرُدُّوهُ إِلَى ٱللَّهِ وَٱلرَّسُولِ إِن كُنتُمْ تُؤْمِنُونَ بِٱللَّهِ وَٱلْيَوْمِ ٱلْءَاخِرِ ذَٰلِكَ خَيْرٌ وَأَحْسَنُ تَأْوِيلًا ﴿٥٩﴾ $$

---

212 Soorah an-Nahl (16):123.
213 Soorah Aal-'Imraan (3):95.

> "So if you disagree in any of the affairs of your religion, then refer it back to the Book of Allaah and the *Sunnah* of His Messenger, if you truly believe in Allaah and the Last Day. That is better for you in this world and the Hereafter, and better in its final consequences."[214]

Thus if we refer back to the Qur'aan we are informed that all of the Messengers had as their *'aqeedah* the *'aqeedah* of *tawheed* and that their call began with *tawheed*, and that *tawheed* is the most important and greatest thing which they came with. We also find that Allaah ordered our Prophet (ﷺ) to follow them and to follow their methodology. Then if we also refer back to the Messenger (ﷺ), we find that his call from start to finish gave the greatest importance to *tawheed* and to fighting *shirk* and its manifestations and causes, and we have already seen this in what has preceded.

Sixthly, Allaah created the creation and organised and ordered it with laws governing its nature, and laws and prescriptions relating to and ordering its behaviour. So He caused it to proceed upon natural laws which are such that if they were broken then this creation would end in destruction. He made the heavens and the earth, the planets and the stars, the sun and the moon and provided laws by which they proceed, and if they were to be broken then this creation would cease to be. From these natural laws laid down by Allaah is that animals, humans and others cannot live except with a spirit and a body. So if the spirit leaves the body then the body dies and rots, and this body must be buried so that other animals are not harmed by its stench. Also from the creational laws laid down by Allaah in the world of plants is that trees cannot stand and survive except upon a trunk, so if the trunk is cut off then the branches die.

---

[214] Soorah an-Nisaa (4):59.

With regard to the world of prescribed laws, no system of prescribed laws can stand except based on belief/creed (*'aqeedah*). So if a system of prescribed laws has no *'aqeedah*, then it will be ruined and will not remain as a correct and sound system of prescribed laws. So, for example, the prescribed laws followed by Ibraaheem, *'alayhis-salaatu was-salaam*, remained for centuries amongst the Arab nation, then when 'Amr ibn Luhayy al-Khuzaa'ee entered *shirk* into it, then it became an idolatrous system of laws and its reality changed and it became corrupted and ruined. This was because it was the *'aqeedah* of *tawheed* which provided its firm foundation upon which it stood. From Aboo Hurayrah, *radiyallaahu 'anhu*, who said that Allaah's Messenger (ﷺ) said, *"I saw 'Amr ibn 'Aamir al-Khuzaa'ee dragging his intestines in the Fire. He was the first one who introduced the practice of setting animals free for the sake of their deities."*[215] So Aktham said, "Perhaps the fact that I resemble him[216] will cause harm to me, O Messenger of Allaah?" He (ﷺ) said, *"No, you are a Believer and he was an unbeliever. He was the first one who altered the religion of Ismaa'eel. He created the idols, and established the practice of keeping the milk of certain animals for the deities, and of freeing animals for the sake of the idols, and of freeing for their idols the she camels which gave birth to female camels as their first and second deliveries, and of freeing for their idols male camels completing their allotted number of sirings."*[217]

After 'Amr ibn Luhayy corrupted the *'aqeedah* supporting the *Sharee'ah* which Ibraaheem came with and which was followed by Ismaa'eel, then it

---

[215] Reported by al-Bukhaaree (Eng. trans. 6/116/no.148), Muslim (Eng. trans. 2/426/no.1966 and 4/1485/no.6839) and Ahmad (2/257).

[216] i.e. physical resemblance. [Translator's Note]

[217] Ibn Hishaam said in his *Seerah* (1/76): Ibn Ishaaq said: And Muhammad ibn Ibraaheem at-Taymee narrated to me that Aboo Saalih as-Sammaan narrated to him that he heard Aboo Hurayrah say: I heard Allaah's Messenger (ﷺ) say... and mentioned the *hadeeth*. So Ibn Ishaaq clearly states that he heard it directly, and the rest of the narrators are reliable so it is a *hasan* (good) chain of narration at the very least.

became an idolatrous religion, and the Arabs became idol worshippers, even though they continued to associate themselves and attach themselves to Ibraaheem and his religion and his code of laws, and even though they still clung to a few remnants of what he came with such as honouring the *Ka'bah*, and performing *tawaaf* around it, and making *hajj* and *'umrah*, and standing in 'Arafah and Muzdalifah, and making sacrifices, and other acts of devotion to Allaah. Likewise the message of Moosaa and 'Eesaa was a message of *tawheed* and a revealed system of laws. But when they lost their basis of *tawheed* due to the saying of the Jews: ''Uzayr is the son of Allaah,' and the saying of the Christians: 'The Messiah is the son of Allaah,' then they became religions of unbelievers, which it is not permissible to attribute to Allaah, nor to those noble Prophets.

Allaah, the Most High, says:

قَٰتِلُوا۟ ٱلَّذِينَ لَا يُؤْمِنُونَ بِٱللَّهِ وَلَا بِٱلْيَوْمِ ٱلْءَاخِرِ وَلَا يُحَرِّمُونَ مَا حَرَّمَ ٱللَّهُ وَرَسُولُهُۥ وَلَا يَدِينُونَ دِينَ ٱلْحَقِّ مِنَ ٱلَّذِينَ أُوتُوا۟ ٱلْكِتَٰبَ حَتَّىٰ يُعْطُوا۟ ٱلْجِزْيَةَ عَن يَدٍ وَهُمْ صَٰغِرُونَ ۝ وَقَالَتِ ٱلْيَهُودُ عُزَيْرٌ ٱبْنُ ٱللَّهِ وَقَالَتِ ٱلنَّصَٰرَى ٱلْمَسِيحُ ٱبْنُ ٱللَّهِ ذَٰلِكَ قَوْلُهُم بِأَفْوَٰهِهِمْ يُضَٰهِـُٔونَ قَوْلَ ٱلَّذِينَ كَفَرُوا۟ مِن قَبْلُ قَٰتَلَهُمُ ٱللَّهُ أَنَّىٰ يُؤْفَكُونَ ۝

"Fight those who do not believe in Allaah, and do not believe in the Hereafter, nor consider unlawful that which Allaah and His Messenger declare unlaw-

ful, nor obey Allaah truly by following Islaam, from the People of the Book (Jews and Christians), until they pay the *jizyah* tax in a state of being subdued and debased. For the Jews said that 'Uzayr is the son of Allaah and the Christians said that the Messiah is the son of Allaah. That is merely the false saying of their tongues, like the saying of the idolaters before them. Allaah's curse is upon them. How can they deviate from the truth which is manifest?"[218]

From Aboo Sa'eed al-Khudree, *radiyallaahu 'anhu*, from the Prophet (ﷺ) who said, *"On the Day of Resurrection a caller will call out that every nation should follow that which it used to worship. So none will remain from those who used to worship others besides Allaah, idols and false deities, except that they will fall into the Hell-Fire until none remain except those who used to worship Allaah, the righteous and the impious, and the remainder of the People of the Book. So the Jews will be called and it will be said to them: 'Whom had you used to worship?' They will say: 'We used to worship 'Uzayr, the son of Allaah.' So it will be said to them: 'You have lied, Allaah did not take any wife, nor any son, so what do you want?!' So they will say: 'We are thirsty, O our Lord, so give us something to drink.' So they will be directed: 'Will you not then drink?' And they will be gathered and taken to the Hell-Fire, which will be like a mirage, some parts of it devouring others, and they will fall into it. Then the Christians will be called, and it will be said to them: 'Whom had you used to worship?' They will say: 'We used to worship the Messiah, the son of Allaah.' So it will be said to them: 'You have lied, Allaah did not take any wife, nor any son.' It will be said to them: 'What do you want?' So they will be treated like the others, until none remain except those who used to worship Allaah (alone), the righteous and the*

---

[218] Soorah at-Tawbah (9):29-30.

impious. The Lord of the Worlds will come to them in a form closest to what they will expect. Then it will be said to them: 'Why are you waiting? Every nation has followed what it used to worship.' They will say: 'We separated ourselves from the people in the world despite being in need of them, and we did not associate ourselves with them, and we are waiting for our Lord whom we used to worship.' So He will say: 'I am your Lord.' So they will say twice: 'We do not worship anything besides our Lord.'"[219]

The point in question which is seen in both of the *Aayaat* and the *hadeeth* is that the messages of Moosaa and 'Eesaa, two messages comprising *tawheed* and *eemaan* were corrupted by the Jews and the Christians, by their worship of 'Uzayr and 'Eesaa and their sayings about them. So because of this they became idolaters and unbelievers, and these two messages, due to their abominable action and their foul distortions, turned into false and idolatrous religions, which it is not permissible to attribute to Allaah, nor to those two noble Messengers, even though very many of the laws from the prescribed law of Moosaa and 'Eesaa still remained.

It will be clear to the reader that the *'aqeedah* of *tawheed* is the relation to all of the prescribed law systems of the Prophets, including the final Prophet (ﷺ) like the relation of the foundation to the building. The building cannot stand without the foundation, and it is like the trunk of the tree, it cannot stand without it. Or like the spirit with relation to the body: the body cannot live without the spirit. So the person with intellect must compare and judge all other calls with these intellectual and *Sharee'ah* proofs in order to see which of them are upon the way of the Prophets and which are far removed from that. I wish to add three examples which will increase our understanding of the prescribed ways laid down and commanded by Allaah, and that the organisation and order found in them

---

[219] Reported by al-Bukhaaree (Eng. trans. 6/85/no.105) and Muslim (Eng. trans. 1/117/no.352).

is something required, and must be followed, and that it is not permissible to turn aside from it.

1. The Prayer. Allaah's Messenger (ﷺ) taught the Prayer by practical examples, and he said: *"Pray as you have seen me praying"*[220] So he (ﷺ) began by standing, then the *takbeer*, then the recitation, then the *rukoo'*, then the *sujood*, and he did this in every *rak'ah*. He performed the second *rak'ah* in the same way, followed by the *tashahhud*, then at the end of the Prayer the final *tashahhud*, followed by *salaam*.

So if a *Jamaa'ah* now said that it is better in this age, or that it is obligatory that we should begin the Prayer with the *salaam* and finish it with the *takbeer*, or that we should say the *tashahhud* in the place of *Faatihah* and vice versa; if this *Jamaa'ah* did this, or any of these things, then would this Prayer be correct, and would it be Islamic?!

2. The Hajj. Allaah's Messenger (ﷺ) performed *Hajj* and taught the people the rites of *Hajj*, and said, *"Take your rites of pilgrimage from me."* He made the standing in *Arafah* in a specific place, at a specific time, the ninth day, and he made the night-stay in *Muzdalifah* on a particular night, and he made the Day of Sacrifice, and the days and nights of *Tashreeq* in a particular time and place. He also made the *Tawaaful-Ifaadah* at a particular time, and he laid down a particular place for the *Sa'ee* between *Safaa* and *Marwaa*, its starting point and finishing point were laid down. So if a *Jamaa'ah* wished to change any of these rites and alter their time or place, for example saying, "We want the *Tawaaful-Ifaadah* to be performed on the ninth day, and to be done between *Safaa* and *Marwaa*, and we want to move the standing in *'Arafah* to the eighth or the tenth day, and that it should be done in *Muzdalifah* or *Minaa*, and

---

[220] Reported by al-Bukhaaree (Eng. trans. 1/345/no.604, and 8/24/no.37, and 9/266/no.352), Muslim (1/327/no.1423), an-Nasaa'ee (2/8), ad-Daarimee (no.1256) and Ahmad (3/436), all of them from Maalik ibn al- Huwayrith, *radiyallaahu 'anhu*.

we want the sacrifice to be done in *'Arafah*, or we want to bring some rites forward and delay others according to what will be helpful and according to the situation of the pilgrims." Then would this be an Islamic *Hajj*, or would it rather be an evil distortion and a disfigurement of this rite?!!

3. The Main Point. Allaah's Messenger (ﷺ) began his *da'wah* with *tawheed*, and likewise all the Messengers. He also used to command his governors and *daa'ees* to begin by calling to *tawheed*. There are many examples showing this, from them is his saying to Mu'aadh when he sent him to Yemen: *"You are going to a People from the People of the Book, so let the first thing which you call them to be the testification that none has the right to be worshipped except Allaah. So if they accept that from you, then inform them that Allaah has obligated upon them five Prayers in every day and night. So if they accept that then inform them that Allaah has obligated upon (them) a charity which is to be taken from their rich and given to their poor."*[221]

So do you not see that it was an organised call and an ordered *Sharee'ah*?! It begins with the most fundamental principle and then moves on to what is next in importance, then what follows in importance. So why do we fail to understand this precise organisation? Why do we fail to comply with it? **And why do we understand that it is obligatory upon us to comply with the way laid and prescribed by Allaah and the precise organisation in matters of worship and its parts, but we do not understand the way laid down and prescribed by Allaah and the precise organisations in the field of *da'wah*, which was followed closely by all of the Prophets in succession?** How is it that we make it permissible to act contrary to this great and fundamental methodology and to turn aside from it?! This is a very serious matter and the callers

---

[221] Its reference has preceded.

must re-examine their minds and change their standpoints. Has the Islamic *ummah*, and in particular its callers, benefited from this great methodology, the methodology of the Prophets, in giving importance to *tawheed* and in making it the starting point for their *da'wah*?!! The answer is that the state of the *ummah* is a very painful and bitter one. If a person were to die due to pain and grief at this dark and painful situation, then that would be fully appropriate. How is that?!! Indeed many of the people of the *ummah* of Islaam, which includes its *daa'ees* and its thinkers, are ignorant of this methodology, and some of them merely pretend to be ignorant of it. The devils have come between them and have led them away from it. Instead they have taken up methodologies contrary to the methodology of the Prophets, methodologies which are disastrous for their religion and their worldly life. How appropriate is the saying of the truthful and trusted Messenger (ﷺ) to them, *"You will certainly follow the ways of those who came before you, handspan by handspan, and cubit by cubit, even to the point that if they were to enter a lizard's hole you would enter it."* We said, *"O Messenger of Allaah, (do you mean) the Jews and the Christians?"* He said, *"Who else."*[222] And his (ﷺ) saying, *"The Jews split into seventy one sects, and the Christians split into seventy two sects, and this ummah will split into seventy three sects, all of them in the Fire except one, and that is the Jamaa'ah."*[223] And in a word-

---

[222] Reported by al-Bukhaaree (Eng. trans. 4/440 no.642 and 9/314 no.422), Muslim (Eng. trans. 4/1403 no. 6448) and Ahmad (3/84,89 and 94) from the *hadeeth* of Aboo Sa'eed from the Prophet (ﷺ). And Ibn Maajah (no.3994) and Ahmad (2/327) from the *hadeeth* of Aboo Hurayrah. Muhammad Fu'aad said in *az-Zawaa'id*, "Its *isnaad* is *saheeh* and its narrators are reliable." Ibn Abee 'Aasim reports it in *as-Sunnah* (1/36,37) from the *hadeeth* of Aboo Hurayrah, 'Abdullaah ibn 'Amr and Aboo Sa'eed, some of that being *saheeh* and some *hasan*.

[223] Reported by Aboo Dawood (Eng. trans. 3/1290 no.4580), Ahmad (4/102), ad-Daarimee (2/158) and al-Haakim (1/128) from the *hadeeth* of Mu'aawiyah, *radiyallaahu 'anhu*. Ibn Maajah (no.3993) from the *hadeeth* of 'Awf ibn Maalik. Ibn Abee 'Aasim reports it in *as-Sunnah* (1/32), and al-Albaanee said, "Its *isnaad* is good." Aboo Daawood also reports it (Eng. trans. 3/1290 no.4579), at-Tirmidhee (no.2640), Ahmad (2/332) and Ibn Maajah (no.3991) from the *hadeeth* of Aboo Hurayrah. Ibn Abee 'Aasim also reports =

ing, *"Which is that, O Messenger of Allaah?"* He said, *"That which I and my Companions are upon."*[224]

So the people have become like the scum found upon the surface of floodwater just as Allaah's Messenger (ﷺ) said, *"It is about to happen that the nations invite one another to come upon you just as those invited to a meal come together to eat from the dish." So someone said, "Is that because of our small number on that day?" He said, "Rather on that day you will be many, but you will be like the scum found upon floodwater, and Allaah will pluck away fear of you from the hearts of you enemies, and Allaah will cast wahn into your hearts." Someone said, "And what is wahn?" He said, "Love of this world and hatred of death."*[225]

Certainly they have become like the scum upon floodwater, and the nations have invited each other to attack them just as those invited to a meal come together to eat from the dish. They have attacked them within their own lands, humbled them, subjugated them, taken possession of them and their lands, plundered their riches, and corrupted their manners - all of this is a result of being far from the methodology prescribed by Allaah, the methodology of the Prophets. Then when fully submerged in this painful state and when it was too late, many people opened their eyes and awoke from their slumbers. So they began shouting out to the

---

it (1/36) and al-Albaanee said, "It is *saheeh*." Ahmad reports it (3/120,145) from the *hadeeth* of Anas through two chains, and it has many witnessing narrations, some of which are to be found in *as-Saheehah*. Ibn Abee 'Aasim reports it in *as-Sunnah* (1/32) and al-Albaanee said, "The *hadeeth* is certainly *saheeh* since it has six chains of narration and witnesses reported from a group of the Companions."

[224] Reported by at-Tirmidhee (no.2641) from the *hadeeth* of 'Abdullaah ibn 'Amr ibn al-'Aas.

[225] Reported by Aboo Daawood (Eng. trans. 3/1196 no.4284), Ahmad (5/278) and Aboo Nu'aym in *al-Hilyah* (1/182). It also has a witness in the *hadeeth* of Aboo Hurayrah, reported by Ahmad (2/359), so it is *saheeh*, and it is declared *saheeh* by al-Albaanee. Refer to *as-Saheehah* (no.958).

people, "Return to Allaah, for these are the ways to salvation." They began writing and delivering speeches, giving directions to the people, making plans and outlining the means to attain might, honour and salvation. Each of them strove and acted according to what appeared to them to be the truth. So I say in truth: They put forward a great deal in the field of manners, society, politics and economics, and they are many and represent a number of different orientations. If their efforts were united and they began with what the Messengers began with, and they earnestly strove to follow their methodology, then their *ummah* would escape from what it has fallen into and they would be able to reach what they desire. The most significant of these orientations are three:

The first is represented by a group who follow the methodology of the Messengers in its *'aqeedah* and its *da'wah*, and who cling onto the Book of their Lord and the *Sunnah* of their Prophet, and who follow in the footsteps of the Pious Predecessors (*as-Salafus-Saalih*) in their *'aqeedah*, their worship and their *da'wah*. This is the orientation which it is obligatory upon the Muslims to adopt, in obedience to the saying of Allaah, the Most High,

وَٱعْتَصِمُواْ بِحَبْلِ ٱللَّهِ جَمِيعًا وَلَا تَفَرَّقُواْ

"And hold fast, all of you together to the Rope of Allah and be not divided."[226]

They must do this so that their efforts can achieve success and so that they attain the Pleasure of their Lord, and so that they achieve strength in order to attain the honour, nobility and success which they desire. A point to be held against them is that they have not expended the necessary monetary and physical efforts needed to broadcast the true *da'wah*, and have not presented the truth vigorously in the form of *da'wah* and publications such as benefit the rank and loftiness of their *da'wah*.

---

[226] Soorah Aal-'Imraan (3):103.

The second is represented by a group who direct their attention to some of the actions of Islaam, and are dominated by *Soofee* tendencies which have seriously undermined the *'aqeedah* of *tawheed* in the souls of many of its followers, and have produced that which is to be held against them in their creed (*'aqeedah*) and their worship. Shaykh Taqiyyuddeen al-Hilaalee and Shaykh Muhammad Aslam, a graduate of the Islamic University, and others have written critiques directed to this group, and it is binding upon them to benefit from this and to return to the truth and the correct way.

The third, is represented by a group which directs its attention to the political, economic and social aspects of Islaam. It has put forward a good deal, and what they have forwarded is known by what is to be found in the libraries, upon the pulpits and in the Universities. They are to be thanked for the efforts they have expended. From the criticisms that need to be made of this orientation is that they have written a great deal in the political field in the name of Islamic Politics, and the call to the supremacy and authority of Allaah, and the establishment of the Islamic state. They urge the Islamic *ummah,* especially its youth, to devote all their efforts and to mobilize their potential in order to realise this goal. They use very forceful and captivating methods, so as to captivate the hearts and seize the minds. They have written a great deal of good and beneficial things in the field of Islamic economics and about the virtues of Islaam, such things as are needed by the *ummah,* particularly at this time, and this is something for which they deserve praise.[227] But at the same time they are to be criticised for the fact that while giving importance to these aspects, they have clearly neglected the right of *'aqeedah*. If they had directed the same vigour and importance to the correction of *'aqeedah* upon the

---

[227] I wrote these words at a time when my view was still obscured and deceived, and much of this has been uncovered and cleared, and it has become clear to me that most of what they have put forward is in reality harmful and injurious.

methodology of the Prophets, and had utilised their efforts and their pens to uproot practices of *shirk* and its manifestations, and innovations, and false superstitions and fables, then they would have been able to achieve a great deal of good for Islaam and the Muslims, and they would have set about the matter in the correct manner. Then they would have truly been upon the methodology of the Prophets, *'alayhimus-salaatu was-salaam.* So since their *da'wah* and their intellectual writings are as I have described, and I am one of the many readers of these writings, I wished to put forward some observations to the leaders of this orientation, bearing in mind the heavy responsibility which they bear before Allaah, Who said in the clear and decisive *Aayaat* of His Book,

وَإِذْ أَخَذَ ٱللَّهُ مِيثَٰقَ ٱلَّذِينَ أُوتُواْ ٱلْكِتَٰبَ لَتُبَيِّنُنَّهُۥ لِلنَّاسِ وَلَا تَكْتُمُونَهُۥ

"Remember when Allaah took the covenant from the People of the Book that they would explain it to the people and not hide it."[228]

This a duty to be done following the way of the scholars of this *ummah* and its sincere callers, beginning with the Companions and continuing right up to the sincere scholars of this present time. So I hope those who are inclined to this orientation will have good thoughts about their brother and share his feelings concerning the heavy responsibility which we bear before Allaah, and open their hearts to criticism which I hope will lay the foundation for and will lead to good and benefit the Islamic *ummah*. I also hope that they will understand that the Companions of Allaah's Messenger (ﷺ) used to discuss some of his decisions with him and he would open his heart to discussion and would give up his own view if he saw that something else was more correct, from the view and opinions put

---

[228] Soorah Aal-'Imraan (3):187.

forward by his Companions, and sometimes the Qur'aan was sent down in support of their views.

From the greater leaders of this orientation is the thinker Abul-A'laa al-Maududi.[229] There are very serious and severe criticisms to be made concerning him, and it is not permissible for a Muslim who fears Allaah and respects Islaam, which raises its followers above veneration of people and their ideas, to remain silent about this. So from these criticisms are:

Firstly: He did not make the starting point of his *da'wah* the starting point of the Prophets, *'alayhimus-salaatu was-salaam,* which was the call to *tawheed*, and to make all worship purely for Allaah, and to fight against *shirk* and its manifestations. This was despite the fact that his country which he grew up in is one of Allaah's lands having the severest need for the call of the Prophets, and the situation there greatly demands it. It is a land rooted in many centuries of idolatry, where idols, cows, rocks, monkeys and private parts are worshipped. In it are found the lowest, foulest and most despicable forms of idolatry. Then the Muslims in this land, except for a few of them, are some of those furthest removed from understanding Islaam and from *tawheed*. Their beliefs are greatly influenced by the beliefs of their neighbours, the idol-worshippers. How often a person will see an idol worshipped by the idolaters garlanded with flowers - and opposite it you will see a mosque of the Muslims containing a decorated tomb, likewise garlanded with flowers. Incense is burned around it and it is dressed with silk. The Muslims come to them with the utmost devotion, with extreme fear, humility and respect, along with their belief that the pious in the graves know the Hidden and the Unseen and have some control over the creation.[230] So have you ever

---

[229] Refer to the treatise, *Ash-Shaqeeqaan: al-Maududi wal-Khomeini* (The Two Brothers: Maududi and Khomeini), and you will see some of his deviated beliefs (p.17) and how he closely resembles the *Raafidee Shee'ah*, and how he has served their ideology, which is something acknowledged by the leader of the *Shee'ah* (p.31 and p.33).

[230] A person such as this is not termed a Muslim, unless he does it out of ignorance, and has not had the proof established against him. (al-Fawzaan)

seen a land upon Allaah's earth throughout history, in the present or the past, having a greater need for *da'wah* to *tawheed* than this land?!

Secondly: He gave most importance to the political aspects and this took up a very large proportion of his *da'wah*, and gave it a greater emphasis than that given to it by Islaam and which was understood by the scholars of the *Salaf* of this *ummah*, the scholars of *hadeeth* and *fiqh*, and he laid down for himself and his followers a goal not laid down by Allaah and His Messengers, and which He did not make a duty upon them or their followers, since it is beyond human capability. Maududi said, speaking about this goal:

(a) "Perhaps it has become clear to you from our books and treatises that **the final goal** which we aim for in our present struggle is **to cause a revolution overthrowing the leadership**, and what I mean by that is that which we wish to attain and be successful in achieving in this world, is to purify the earth from the filth of wicked leaders and their supremacy, and to establish the system of pious and rightly-guided leadership (imaamate). So this continuous struggle and striving is seen by us to be the greatest and most effective way of attaining the Pleasure of the Lord, the Most High, and of seeking His Face, the Most High, in this world and the Hereafter."[231]

Hopefully the bright, intelligent and knowledgeable reader who memorises the Qur'aan and recites it during the night and at each end of the day, and considers the call of the Prophets, from the first to the last of them, will not know that this is supposed to be the goal of the Messengers for which they struggled. Nor will he understand that this striving and effort is the greatest and most effective way of attaining Allaah's Pleasure and seeking His Face. Rather the greatest and most effective way of

---

[231] *Al-Usasul-Akhlaaqiyah lil-Harakatil-Islaamiyyah*, p.16.

attaining the Pleasure of the Lord is by following the methodology of the Prophets in their *da'wah*, and following in their footsteps by purifying the earth of corruption and *shirk*, and the greatest means is *eemaan* with its well-known pillars and Islaam with its pillars which are also well known.

Then[232] Maududi knows fully well the state of the people of India with regard to their ignorance of Islaam and the innovations and misguidance which they are upon. He knows full well that there is within them remnants of the beliefs, manners and customs of their previous religions. He has himself has spoken about this in his book "Waaqi'ul Muslimeen-wa-Sabeelun Nuhood-Bihim" (The State of the Muslims and the Means for their Revival), in a section in which he talks of the shortcomings and negligence of the rulers with regard to Islamic education, and that the institutions that are established for education only benefit the higher and middle levels of people. He said, "The ignorant and the deluded have continued in a state of total ignorance about the teachings of Islaam, deprived to a great extent of its effect of reform and rectification. The reason for this is that non Muslims used to enter into Allaah's religion as whole nations and tribes, but many of the false and futile practices and customs of the days of ignorance which they used to be upon before Islaam are still widespread amongst them today. Indeed not even their thoughts and beliefs have completely changed; so even now many of the beliefs of the *mushriks* remain and the false ideas which they inherited from the religions of their unbelieving forefathers. The most that can be said to have changed after they entered into Islaam is that they brought new gods into the history of Islaam. These were the same gods which they worshipped before, except that they chose new names using Islamic terminology for their ancient idolatrous actions.

---

[232] This portion of the text, beginning here until point (b), was missed from the printed Arabic version and was inserted upon the instructions of Shaykh Rabee' (the author) from his handwritten manuscript copy. [Publisher's Note]

"They then continued to behave as before, the only thing that changed was the outward appearance. If you wish to see proof of what I say, then closely examine the religious state of the people of one area of your land, and then look into history and research the religion which the people of this area used to practice before Islaam. You will realise that there are many things which are very similar, in both beliefs and actions, to the previous religion except that they have taken on a different form and appearance. So those areas in which the Buddhist religion, for example, was found before Islaam, and where the people used to worship relics of Buddha: here there would be one of his teeth, there would be some of his bones and so on - which would be worshipped by the people, and from which they would seek to derive blessings. Then today you will find that the people in those areas do the same thing with the hair from the head of the Prophet (ﷺ), or with his footprints, or they seek blessings from any relics left behind by the righteous Muslims and worshippers from amongst them. Likewise if you were to examine many of the practices and customs which have found their way into the Islaam practised by some tribes, and were then to see the practices and customs of the non Muslim people of the same tribes - you would find that there is very little difference between them. Is this not a clear proof that those who were in charge of the Muslims and their social affairs in past generations fell far short of their duty in that they did not aid and assist those who strove individually to propagate Islaam..."[233]

So Maududi was fully aware of the state of his land. He knew its history, and he knew the extent to which the beliefs of the Muslims were connected to and influenced by the beliefs of their forefathers and indeed present day idolaters. Then he criticised the Muslim rulers of the past for falling short in their duty of propagating Islaam, and failing to assist those individuals who strove to propagate Islaam, and for failing in their duty of

---

[233] *Waaqi'ul Muslimeen-wa-Sabeelun Nuhood-Bihim*, pp130-132.

establishing Islamic education. So this profound understanding should have lead him to see the strength of the methodology of the Prophets in calling to tawheed, and that all worship should be made purely for Allaah, and in concentrating upon giving importance to the Muslims' *'aqeedah* in order to save them from the claws of the shirk of Hinduism, Buddhism and their like. Indeed it was upon him that he should desist from opposing the callers to *tawheed* at the very least - if he was not going to assist them with the strength he was given in *da'wah* and writing - and that he should assemble his followers in this field instead of applying huge resources in the field of politics and economics. Furthermore, if the people were to die having certainty upon all of his books written about politics and economics, then would that save them from the idolatry which they are upon, and then would that save them from the Fire.

Then with whom will he establish the system of righteous and rightly guided rulership[234] when he has opened up the doors for anyone to enter into his *Jamaa'ah* and organisation. The door is open for the Bareilawi - the extreme grave worshipper, and for the Raafidee Shee'ah, and for the Deobandi, and for the Salafee - so that the sick are mixed with the healthy. Then the result of this, as is seen, is that sickness overcomes them all and

---

[234] What we say is something well known, and for those who do not know I will quote the following evidence. The Pakistani newspaper "The Jang" published an interview by Mahmood Ash-Shaam with the vice President of Jamaati-Islaami in Karachi, Professor Ghafoor Ahmad, on the 25th April 1984, and this is a translation of it: "What do you think of the people's opposition to Jamaati-Islaami on the grounds of *madhhabs*?" Professor Ghafoor Ahmad: "Yes, it is true that the *Jamaa'ahs* of *madhhabs* oppose us in many matters, indeed it seems that they do not think we are Muslims. However religious *Jamaa'ahs* should not make the religion a means to cause disagreements and separation. But the situation today is that the disagreements blaze away in the mosques also, on the basis of *'aqeedah*, and this leads to disputes and arguments. As for the matter of beliefs (*'aqaa'id*) of the Jamaati-Islaami, then it contains individuals from the Ahlul-Hadeeth, the Deobandis, the Shee'ah and the Bareilawis. Furthermore, I myself am a Bereilawi, and the fact that a person is a Bareilawi does not prevent him from joining Jamaati-Islaami."

its germs are spread to the healthy, so at the very least their tongues and pens are afflicted and become paralysed and unable to give *da'wah* to and write concerning *tawheed* and the *Sunnah*, and unable to fight against innovation and *shirk*. This is one of the results of this form of gathering together and the programmes and outlines laid down for it. So will the like of these people be able to purify the earth from corruption, and to establish the system of righteous and rightly guided rulership, which in his view the Companions of Muhammad (ﷺ) were not able to establish after the four rightly guided Caliphs, nor were the sons of the Muhaajiroon and the Ansaar: since Maududi holds - and in that he is following the severest enemies of the Companions and those who love and ally themselves with them - that rulership after 'Uthmaan and 'Alee was based upon principles of the days of ignorance instead of the principles of Islaam. So if the rulership of those whom Allaah's Messenger (ﷺ) and his rightly guided Caliphs and his noble Companions were pleased with was a rulership based upon principles of the days of ignorance, then what can we expect from an organisation (*jamaa'ah*) which gathers the most alien orientations and the furthest of them away from the way of the Prophets.

(b) And he said, "One of the reasons for regret is that we see the people today, all of them, the Muslims and the non-Muslims, are heedless of this thing that we have made our goal and have set our sights upon. As for the Muslims, then it is because they regard it as a purely political goal, and they hardly realise its status and importance in the religion. Then as for the non-Muslims due to their being brought up with blind hatred towards Islaam, and their ignorance and lack of knowledge about its teachings, then they certainly do not know that the leadership of the wicked and evildoers is the source of all disasters and calamities that afflict mankind, and that the well-being and happiness of mankind rests solely upon the reins of authority over the worldly affairs lying in the hands of the righteous and just."[235]

That which he takes as his goal and the goal of his followers and what they set their sights upon is something important, but it is something other than the goal of the Prophets. But rather what is greater and more deserving of attention is to strive for the guidance of the people, and to call them all, the weak and the strong, to *tawheed*. This was the goal of the Prophets and those who seek to rectify the affairs.

As for his saying, "'The leadership of the wicked and evildoers is the source of all disasters and calamities that afflict mankind…"
Then I say: This may be one reason and alongside it are other causes: the unbelief of the nations in Allaah, and their commission of *shirk*, and their rejection of the guidance brought by the Prophets.

Allaah, the Most High, says:

$$\text{وَإِذَا أَرَدْنَا أَن نُّهْلِكَ قَرْيَةً أَمَرْنَا مُتْرَفِيهَا فَفَسَقُوا فِيهَا فَحَقَّ عَلَيْهَا الْقَوْلُ فَدَمَّرْنَاهَا تَدْمِيرًا ﴿١٦﴾}$$

"And when We wished to destroy a town (of transgressors) We ordered those in authority to be obedient, but they were disobedient and transgressed, so Allaah's threat of punishment became certain for them, so we destroyed them totally."[236]

---

[235] *Al-Usasul-Akhlaaqiyah lil-Harakatil-Islaamiyyah*, pp.16-17.
[236] Soorah al-Israa (17):16.

He, the Most High, says:

$$\text{وَمَا أَصَابَكُم مِّن مُّصِيبَةٍ فَبِمَا كَسَبَتْ أَيْدِيكُمْ وَيَعْفُو عَن كَثِيرٍ ۝}$$

"And any misfortune which strikes you in this world in your selves, family and wealth, then it is as a punishment from Allaah for the sins which you have committed, and your Lord forgives many of your sins and does not punish you for them."[237]

He, the Most High, says:

$$\text{وَكَأَيِّن مِّن قَرْيَةٍ عَتَتْ عَنْ أَمْرِ رَبِّهَا وَرُسُلِهِ فَحَاسَبْنَاهَا حِسَابًا شَدِيدًا وَعَذَّبْنَاهَا عَذَابًا نُّكْرًا ۝}$$

"And how many towns transgressed against the orders of their Lord and His Messengers, so We gave them a severe reckoning and punished them with a tremendous and terrible punishment (Hell-fire)."[238]

So because of transgression of the people, the rulers and the ruled, the rich and the poor, Allaah sends disasters, misfortunes and calamities upon them. He sends upon them wars of destruction, deadly diseases, devastating famines, thunderbolts, torrents, removal of blessings from the earth and so on. Then the worship of idols present in India and elsewhere is more hateful to Allaah and to His Prophets and the righteous rectifiers than the oppression of the rulers, even though it also serious and hateful to Allaah.

---

[237] Soorah ash-Shooraa (42):30.
[238] Soorah at-Talaaq (65):8.

Therefore you see what Ibraaheem said:

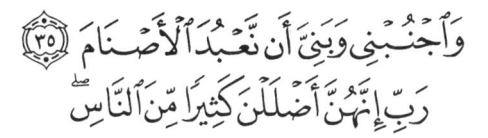

$$\textrm{وَاجْنُبْنِي وَبَنِيَّ أَن نَّعْبُدَ الْأَصْنَامَ ۝ رَبِّ إِنَّهُنَّ أَضْلَلْنَ كَثِيرًا مِّنَ النَّاسِ}$$

"And keep me and my sons away from worshipping idols. O my Lord they have indeed caused the misguidance of many people."[239]

It was in his time that the most oppressive, arrogant and corrupt ruler lived. But Ibraaheem, *'alayhis-salaam*, took as his goal the call to *tawheed* and the obliteration of *shirk*. So when the word of *tawheed* becomes manifest and the voice of *shirk* is wiped out then the condition of the people, both the rulers and the ruled, is rectified.

(c) He also said, "So if someone today wishes to purify the earth and change the corruption to well-being, unrest to security, corrupt manners to righteous manners, sins to good deeds, then it will never be enough for him to call them to good, and to admonish them to have *taqwaa* and fear of Allaah, and to encourage them upon good manners. Rather it is a duty upon him to gather what he is able with regard to the resources of righteous people, and form them into an organised group and a strong community, such as will enable him to snatch the reins of authority from those who are in charge of the civilisations in this world, and bring about the revolution aspired for, to attain leadership of the world and rulership (imaamate)." So how is it that these people in a sorry condition turn away from the methodology of the Prophets, and leave alone the most severe sickness afflicting the nations, which is *shirk*? They take no notice of this, and instead they want to gather righteous people into organised groups and a strong community, in order to attain what they have laid down as

---

[239] Soorah Ibraaheem (14):35-36.

their goal and have set their sights upon! So tell me, by your Lord, where will these resources of righteous people come from when we have conceitedly turned away from the *'aqeedah* of the Prophets and their methodology in raising the people (*tarbiyah*) and in *da'wah*?! Will they fall down from the sky for us?!

(d) Maududi says, 'Indeed the matter of leadership and rulership is the most important matter in human life and the most fundamental principle. The importance of this matter and its seriousness is not something new to this age, rather it is something which is tied to human life and which human life is dependent upon since the most ancient of times, and what an excellent witness to this is the common saying, 'The people are upon the religion of their kings.' So because of this it is reported in the *hadeeth*, 'The scholars of the *ummah* and its leaders are the ones responsible for its well-being or its corruption.'[240]"[241]

This is the view of this great thinker! Whereas I bear witness before Allaah that if I had merely heard it reported by a truthful person I would have thought that he was perhaps mistaken in attributing it to this thinker. But what can I or anyone else say when it occurs in his book, *al-Usasul-Akhlaaqiyyah lil-Harakatil-Islaamiyyah*, which he gave as a lecture to a gathering of the committee members of the Islamic University and its helpers and those influenced by it. He gave the talk in a crowded conference more than forty years ago, and the people, particularly his followers, circulated it whilst giving it a warm welcome and respecting it, from that day till this.

---

[240] I am very surprised at his using as proof for the most serious matter, the "most important matter," a common saying, and another saying whose author is unknown, which he thought was a *hadeeth*.
[241] *Al-Usasul-Akhlaaqiyyah*, pp.21-22.

But in reality the most important matter is that which all of the Prophets, *'alayhimus-salaatu was-salaam,* came with, and that is the matter of *tawheed* and *eemaan*. This is summed up by Allaah, in His Saying:

$$\text{وَمَآ أَرْسَلْنَا مِن قَبْلِكَ مِن رَّسُولٍ إِلَّا نُوحِىٓ إِلَيْهِ أَنَّهُۥ لَآ إِلَٰهَ إِلَّآ أَنَا۠ فَٱعْبُدُونِ ۝}$$

"We did not send any Messenger before you, O Muhammad (ﷺ), except that We revealed to him that none has the right to be worshipped except Allaah, so make all of your worship purely for Him."[242]

$$\text{وَلَقَدْ بَعَثْنَا فِى كُلِّ أُمَّةٍ رَّسُولًا أَنِ ٱعْبُدُوا۟ ٱللَّهَ وَٱجْتَنِبُوا۟ ٱلطَّٰغُوتَ}$$

"We sent a Messenger to every nation, ordering them that they should worship Allaah alone, obey Him and make their worship purely for Him, and that they should avoid everything worshipped besides Allaah."[243]

$$\text{وَلَقَدْ أُوحِىَ إِلَيْكَ وَإِلَى ٱلَّذِينَ مِن قَبْلِكَ لَئِنْ أَشْرَكْتَ لَيَحْبَطَنَّ عَمَلُكَ وَلَتَكُونَنَّ مِنَ ٱلْخَٰسِرِينَ ۝ بَلِ ٱللَّهَ فَٱعْبُدْ وَكُن مِّنَ ٱلشَّٰكِرِينَ ۝}$$

---

[242] Soorah al-Ambiyaa (21):25.
[243] Soorah an-Nahl (16):36.

> "And We have revealed to you, O Muhammad (ﷺ), and to the Messengers before you that if you commit *shirk* with Allaah then your actions will be nullified and you will be one of those destroyed. Rather worship Allaah alone, and be one of those thankful for Allaah's favours, of being guided to worship Him alone, and being free of worshipping idols and false gods."[244]

This is the most important matter which caused the struggle between the Prophets and the misguided nations, and due to it those who drowned were drowned, those who were destroyed were destroyed, those who were swallowed up in earthquakes were swallowed up, and those who were punished were punished, and we have already quoted the many proofs for this in what has preceded, so refer to that.

(e) Then he says, "The true goal of the religion is to establish the system of righteous and rightly guided leadership (imaamate)"[245]

I say, rather the true goal of the religion, and the purpose for the creation of *Jinn* and mankind, and the purpose for the sending of the Messengers, and the sending down of the Books, is the worship of Allaah, and that all the religion (*Deen*) be made purely for Him. Allaah, the Most High, says:

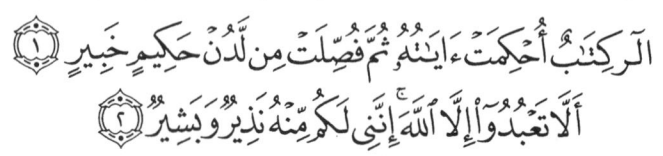

$$\text{الٓرۚ كِتَٰبٌ أُحۡكِمَتۡ ءَايَٰتُهُۥ ثُمَّ فُصِّلَتۡ مِن لَّدُنۡ حَكِيمٍ خَبِيرٍ ۝ أَلَّا تَعۡبُدُوٓاْ إِلَّا ٱللَّهَۚ إِنَّنِي لَكُم مِّنۡهُ نَذِيرٌ وَبَشِيرٌ ۝}$$

> "*Alif Laam Raa.* This is the Book whose *Aayaat* are perfected and free from falsehood, and fully explained, from the One All-Wise, and All-Knowing.

---

[244] Soorah az-Zumar (39):65-66.
[245] *Al-Usasul-Akhlaaqiyyah*, p.22.

> **Making clear that you should worship none but Allaah alone, attributing no partner to Him. Say, O Muhammad (ﷺ), to the people, 'I am a warner to you from Allaah, warning of His punishment for those who disobey Him and those who worship the idols, and a bringer of good tidings of His reward for those who obey Him and make worship purely for Him.'"**[246]

So since this is Maududi's view of leadership, rulership and imaamate, i.e. that it is the true goal of the religion and is the most important matter in the life of mankind, and the most fundamental principle, then it is fitting here that I quote Shaykhul-Islaam Ibn Taymiyyah's refutation of Ibnul-Mutahhir al-Hullee, one of the *Imaamee Raafidees*, who went to extremes and beyond bounds with regard to the matter of imaamate. Shaykhul-Islaam said, "The *Raafidee* author said, 'To proceed, this is a noble treatise and fine saying, comprising the most important of the rulings of the religion, and the most excellent of all the affairs of the Muslims, which is the issue of imaamate, which causes through its attainment the achievement of the level of highest esteem, and it is one of the pillars of *eemaan*, which produces the right to everlasting life in Paradise, and freedom from the Anger of the Most Merciful...'[247] (So Shaykhul-Islaam, *rahimahullaah*, said) So it is to be said that speech with regard to this is necessary from a number of angles:

Firstly: That it is to be said: One who says that the question of imaamate is the most important of the rulings of the religion is a liar according to the consensus (*ijmaa'*) of the Muslims, both the *Sunnis* and the *Shee'ah*. Indeed it is *kufr* (unbelief) since the matter of *eemaan* in Allaah and His Messenger is more important than the question of the imaamate, and this is something known necessarily from the religion of Islaam. So the

---

[246] Soorah Hood (11):1-2.
[247] *Minhaajus-Sunnah* (1/20).

unbeliever does not become a Believer until he testifies that none has the right to be worshipped except Allaah, and that Muhammad (ﷺ) is the Messenger of Allaah. This was what Allaah's Messenger (ﷺ) fought the unbelievers for, firstly, as is well-reported in the *Saheehs* and elsewhere, that he said, *"I have been ordered to fight the people until they testify that none has the right to be worshipped except Allaah, and that I am the Messenger of Allaah, and they establish the Prayer, and pay the Zakaat. So if they do that then their blood and their wealth is safe from me, except due to a right pertaining to it.'"*[248]

"And Allaah, the Most High, says:

$$\text{فَإِذَا ٱنسَلَخَ ٱلْأَشْهُرُ ٱلْحُرُمُ فَٱقْتُلُواْ ٱلْمُشْرِكِينَ حَيْثُ وَجَدتُّمُوهُمْ وَخُذُوهُمْ وَٱحْصُرُوهُمْ وَٱقْعُدُواْ لَهُمْ كُلَّ مَرْصَدٍ فَإِن تَابُواْ وَأَقَامُواْ ٱلصَّلَوٰةَ وَءَاتَوُاْ ٱلزَّكَوٰةَ فَخَلُّواْ سَبِيلَهُمْ}$$

"**So when the Sacred Months are completed then kill the *mushriks* wherever you find them on the earth, and take them captive, and prevent them from travelling freely in the land, and seek to ambush them wherever possible. But if they repent and leave their worship of others besides Allaah and their denial of Allaah's Messenger (ﷺ), and instead make their worship purely for Allaah, upon *tawheed*, and they establish the Prayer, and pay the *Zakaat*, then leave their way free.**"[249]

---

[248] Its sources have preceded.
[249] Soorah at-Tawbah (9):5.

"So this is what 'Alee, *radiyallaahu 'anhu,* proclaimed when he (ﷺ) sent him, and likewise the Prophet (ﷺ) used to come across the unbelievers, and he would safeguard their blood merely due to their repenting from *kufr*; he would never make any mention of the imaamate to them. And Allaah, the Most High, says after this:

$$\text{فَإِن تَابُوا۟ وَأَقَامُوا۟ ٱلصَّلَوٰةَ وَءَاتَوُا۟ ٱلزَّكَوٰةَ فَإِخْوَٰنُكُمْ فِى ٱلدِّينِ}$$

"So if they repent from their unbelief and their *shirk*, and they establish the Prayer, and pay the *Zakaat*, then they are your brothers in the religion (Islaam)."[250]

"So He made them brothers in the religion due to repentance. When the unbelievers in the time of Allaah's Messenger (ﷺ) became Muslims, then the rulings of Islaam became operative upon them. The imaamate was never mentioned to them. No one from the people of knowledge reports such a thing from Allaah's Messenger (ﷺ), neither through a report with limited sources, nor one widely reported. Rather we know by necessity that the Prophet (ﷺ) had not used to make any mention of the imaamate, neither generally nor specifically, so how can it be the most important matter from the rulings of the religion…

"**Secondly:** It should be said: *eemaan* in Allaah and His Messenger is more important than the question of imaamate in every time and place. Indeed the imaamate will neither be the more important, nor the more excellent at any time.

"**Thirdly:** It should be said: It would have then been obligatory upon the Prophet (ﷺ) to explain it to his *ummah* remaining after him, just as he explained to them the matters of the Prayer, the *zakaat*, fasting and *hajj*,

---

[250] Soorah at-Tawbah (9):11.

and just as he precisely explained the matters of *eemaan* in Allaah, and *tawheed* of Allaah and the Last Day. And as is known the question of the imaamate is not explained in the Book and the *Sunnah* with the explanation given to these fundamental matters." Then he said, "Also, as is known, the most excellent of the affairs of the Muslims, and the most important matter in the religion has the right that its mention in the Book of Allaah, the Most High, should be more frequent and prominent than other things, and that the Messenger's explanation of it should take precedence over other matters. So the Qur'aan is replete with the mention of the *tawheed* of Allaah, the Most High, and with mention of His Names, His Attributes, His angels, His Revealed Books, His Messengers, the Last Day, narratives, orders and prohibitions, prescribed punishments and laws of inheritance, contrary to the case with the imaamate. So how can the Qur'aan be replete with other than that which is most important and most excellent? Also, Allaah, the Most High, has made success dependent upon that wherein there is no mention at all of the imaamate. So He says:

$$\text{وَمَن يُطِعِ ٱللَّهَ وَٱلرَّسُولَ فَأُوْلَٰئِكَ مَعَ ٱلَّذِينَ أَنْعَمَ ٱللَّهُ عَلَيْهِم مِّنَ ٱلنَّبِيِّـۧنَ وَٱلصِّدِّيقِينَ وَٱلشُّهَدَآءِ وَٱلصَّٰلِحِينَ وَحَسُنَ أُوْلَٰئِكَ رَفِيقًا ۝}$$

"So whoever obeys Allaah and His Messenger - by submitting to their commands, and being pleased with their judgement, and withholding from what they forbid, then he is with those whom Allaah has blessed with guidance and obedience in this World and with Paradise in the Hereafter - with the Prophets, their sincere followers who were upon their way, the martyrs and the righteous. And what an excellent companionship in Paradise they are."[251]

---

[251] Soorah an-Nisaa (4):69.

"And He says:

$$\text{وَمَن يُطِعِ ٱللَّهَ وَرَسُولَهُ يُدْخِلْهُ جَنَّٰتٍ تَجْرِى مِن تَحْتِهَا ٱلْأَنْهَٰرُ خَٰلِدِينَ فِيهَا ۚ وَذَٰلِكَ ٱلْفَوْزُ ٱلْعَظِيمُ ۝ وَمَن يَعْصِ ٱللَّهَ وَرَسُولَهُ وَيَتَعَدَّ حُدُودَهُ يُدْخِلْهُ نَارًا خَٰلِدًا فِيهَا وَلَهُ عَذَابٌ مُّهِينٌ ۝}$$

"Whoever obeys Allaah and His Messenger, then Allaah will enter him into the Gardens of Paradise…, and whoever disobeys Allaah and His Messenger and transgresses the limits which He has laid down, then Allaah will enter him into the Fire in which he will remain forever and receive a humiliating punishment."[252]

"So Allaah explains in the Qur'aan that whoever obeys Him and His Messenger will be successful in the Hereafter, and that whoever disobeys Allaah and His Messenger and transgresses the limits He has laid down, then he will be punished, and this is the difference between the successful and the miserable, and the imaamate is not mentioned.

"So if someone were to say, 'But the imaamate is part of the obedience to Allaah and His Messenger!' Then it is to be said, 'Its status can at most be like some of the obligatory duties such as Prayer, *Zakaat*, Fasting and *Hajj*, and other duties which are a part of obedience to Allaah and His Messenger. So how can it alone be the most excellent of all the affairs in the religion?!'"[253]

---

[252] Soorah an-Nisaa (4):13-14.
[253] *Minhaajus-Sunnah* (1/28-29).

Shaykhul-Islaam says, "The fifth aspect is his saying, 'And it is one of the pillars of *eemaan* which produces the right to everlasting life in Paradise.' Then it is to be said: Who makes this a pillar of *eemaan* except for the people of ignorance and falsehood?! And we will speak, if Allaah wills, about what he mentioned concerning that. But Allaah, the Most High, has described the Believers and their condition, and the Prophet (ﷺ) explained *eemaan* and mentioned its branches. And Allaah did not mention the imaamate nor did His Messenger, amongst the pillars of *eemaan*. As occurs in the authentic *hadeeth*, the *hadeeth* of Jibreel when he came to the Prophet (ﷺ) in the form of a desert Arab and asked him about Islaam, *eemaan* and *ihsaan*. He (ﷺ) replied, "Islaam is that you testify that none has the right to be worshipped except Allaah, and that Muhammad is the Messenger of Allaah, and you establish the Prayer, pay the *Zakaat*, fast in *Ramadaan* and perform *Hajj* to the House." And he said, "*Eemaan* is that you have *eemaan* in Allaah, His Angels, His Books, His Messengers, the Last Day and the Resurrection after death, and that you have *eemaan* in Pre-Decree (*qadr*), the good and the bad of it." And he did not mention the imaamate. And he said, "*Ihsaan* is that you worship Allaah as if you were seeing Him, and even though you do not see Him, yet He certainly sees you." And the authenticity of this *hadeeth* is agreed upon, the scholars having knowledge of narrations are united in agreeing to its authenticity. It is also reported by the Compilers of the *Saheehs* through different chains, and it is agreed upon from the *hadeeth* of Aboo Hurayrah,[254] and it is reported by Muslim from the *hadeeth* of Ibn 'Umar.[255] And Allaah, the Most High, says:

---

[254] Reported by Reported by al-Bukhaaree (Eng. trans. 6/285 no.300), Muslim (Eng. trans. 1/3 no.4) and Ibn Maajah (no.64).
[255] Muslim (Eng. trans. 1/1 no.1), Aboo Daawood (Eng. trans. 3/1315 no.4678) and at-Tirmidhee (no.2610).

إِنَّمَا ٱلْمُؤْمِنُونَ ٱلَّذِينَ إِذَا ذُكِرَ ٱللَّهُ وَجِلَتْ قُلُوبُهُمْ وَإِذَا تُلِيَتْ عَلَيْهِمْ ءَايَٰتُهُۥ زَادَتْهُمْ إِيمَٰنًا وَعَلَىٰ رَبِّهِمْ يَتَوَكَّلُونَ ۝ ٱلَّذِينَ يُقِيمُونَ ٱلصَّلَوٰةَ وَمِمَّا رَزَقْنَٰهُمْ يُنفِقُونَ ۝ أُو۟لَٰٓئِكَ هُمُ ٱلْمُؤْمِنُونَ حَقًّا ۚ لَّهُمْ دَرَجَٰتٌ عِندَ رَبِّهِمْ وَمَغْفِرَةٌ وَرِزْقٌ كَرِيمٌ ۝

"The Believers are only those who when Allaah is mentioned then their hearts tremor with fear, those who comply with His orders and are humble and submissive when He is mentioned, and when the *Aayaat* of His Book are recited to them their *eemaan* increases, those who have certainty that His judgement and decree is operative upon them and they do not place their hope in other than Him, nor fear other than Him. Those who correctly establish the Prayer, and spend of the wealth which Allaah provided them with as He ordered and obligated upon them. They it is who are truly the Believers. For them are high ranks with their Lord and forgiveness and excellent provision in Paradise."[256]

"So He attested to the *eemaan* of these people without any mention of the imaamate. And Allaah, the Most High, says:

---

[256] Soorah al-Anfaal (8):2-4.

$$\text{إِنَّمَا ٱلْمُؤْمِنُونَ ٱلَّذِينَ ءَامَنُواْ بِٱللَّهِ وَرَسُولِهِۦ ثُمَّ لَمْ يَرْتَابُواْ وَجَٰهَدُواْ بِأَمْوَٰلِهِمْ وَأَنفُسِهِمْ فِى سَبِيلِ ٱللَّهِ أُوْلَٰٓئِكَ هُمُ ٱلصَّٰدِقُونَ ۝}$$

"The Believers are only those who truly believe in Allaah and His Messenger, and then do not doubt about that, and devote themselves to obedience to Allaah and His Messenger, not doubting about the duties made obligatory upon them by Allaah. Those who fight the *mushriks* with their wealth and their selves, fighting them as ordered by Allaah so that Allaah's Word should be uppermost. They are the ones who are truthful in their saying that they are Believers."[257]

"So He declared them truthful in their *eemaan* without any mention of the imaamate. And Allaah, the Most High, says:

$$\text{لَّيْسَ ٱلْبِرَّ أَن تُوَلُّواْ وُجُوهَكُمْ قِبَلَ ٱلْمَشْرِقِ وَٱلْمَغْرِبِ وَلَٰكِنَّ ٱلْبِرَّ مَنْ ءَامَنَ بِٱللَّهِ وَٱلْيَوْمِ ٱلْءَاخِرِ وَٱلْمَلَٰٓئِكَةِ وَٱلْكِتَٰبِ وَٱلنَّبِيِّـۧنَ وَءَاتَى ٱلْمَالَ عَلَىٰ حُبِّهِۦ ذَوِى ٱلْقُرْبَىٰ وَٱلْيَتَٰمَىٰ وَٱلْمَسَٰكِينَ وَٱبْنَ ٱلسَّبِيلِ وَٱلسَّآئِلِينَ وَفِى ٱلرِّقَابِ وَأَقَامَ ٱلصَّلَوٰةَ وَءَاتَى ٱلزَّكَوٰةَ وَٱلْمُوفُونَ بِعَهْدِهِمْ إِذَا عَٰهَدُواْ وَٱلصَّٰبِرِينَ فِى ٱلْبَأْسَآءِ وَٱلضَّرَّآءِ وَحِينَ ٱلْبَأْسِ أُوْلَٰٓئِكَ ٱلَّذِينَ صَدَقُواْ وَأُوْلَٰٓئِكَ هُمُ ٱلْمُتَّقُونَ ۝}$$

---

[257] Soorah al-Hujuraat (49):15.

"It is not righteousness that you (O Jews and Christians) turn your faces to the east or the west, but rather righteousness is the righteousness of those who truly believe in Allaah and the Last Day and the angels and the Books and the Prophets, and who give their wealth despite loving it to the near relatives, the orphans, the poor, the needy travellers, those who ask, and for freeing slaves. Those who correctly establish the Prayer and pay the *Zakaat*, and those who keep the Covenant which they have made. Those who patiently persevere upon obedience to Allaah and in avoiding disobedience to Him at times of need and times of illness. Those who remain firm at the time of fighting. They are those who are true in their *eemaan* and they are the ones who protect themselves from the punishment of Allaah, by doing what He has ordered and avoiding what He has forbidden."[258]

"And He did not mention the imaamate. Allaah, the Most High says:

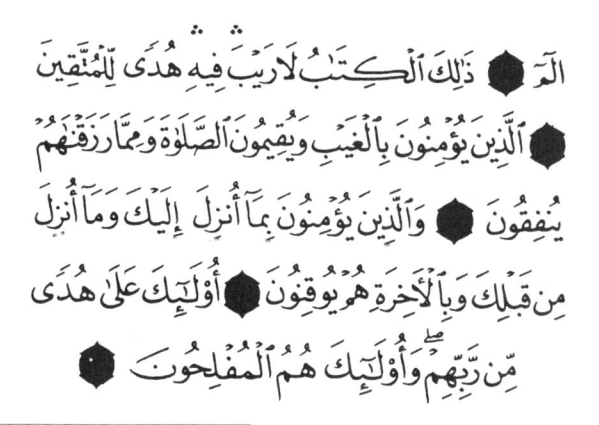

الٓمٓ ۞ ذَٰلِكَ ٱلْكِتَٰبُ لَا رَيْبَ ۛ فِيهِ ۛ هُدًى لِّلْمُتَّقِينَ ۞ ٱلَّذِينَ يُؤْمِنُونَ بِٱلْغَيْبِ وَيُقِيمُونَ ٱلصَّلَوٰةَ وَمِمَّا رَزَقْنَٰهُمْ يُنفِقُونَ ۞ وَٱلَّذِينَ يُؤْمِنُونَ بِمَآ أُنزِلَ إِلَيْكَ وَمَآ أُنزِلَ مِن قَبْلِكَ وَبِٱلْءَاخِرَةِ هُمْ يُوقِنُونَ ۞ أُوْلَٰٓئِكَ عَلَىٰ هُدًى مِّن رَّبِّهِمْ ۖ وَأُوْلَٰٓئِكَ هُمُ ٱلْمُفْلِحُونَ ۞

---

[258] Soorah al-Baqarah (2):177.

> "*Alif Laam Meem*. This Qur'aan is the Book containing no doubt. It is a guidance for those who seek to avoid Allaah's punishment - by avoiding disobedience to Him and doing what He has commanded. Those who believe truly in the 'Hidden and Unseen' (*al-Ghayb*, i.e. Belief in Allaah, His Angels, His Books, His Messengers, the Last Day, the Resurrection, Paradise and the Hell-Fire etc.) and who correctly establish the Prayer, and spend out of the wealth which Allaah has provided them with - as Allaah ordered. Those who truly believe in the Revelation sent down to you (the Qur'aan) and the Revelation sent down to the Messengers before you, and those who are certain of the Hereafter. They are the ones upon guidance from their Lord, and they are the successful ones who attain Paradise and avoid the Fire."[259]

"So He declared that they are the rightly guided and successful, and He did not mention the imaamate.

"Furthermore, we know necessarily from the religion of Muhammad ibn 'Abdillaah (ﷺ) that when the people used to enter into Islaam, their *eemaan* was not held dependent upon being aware of the imaamate. Nor did he make any mention of that to them. But as for whatever is a pillar of *eemaan*, then it is a duty upon the Messenger to explain it to the people of *eemaan*, so that they may have *eemaan* in it. So when it is known necessarily that this is something which the Messenger did not make a condition for *eemaan*, then we know that declaring it to be a condition for *eemaan* is one of the sayings of the people of falsehood. But if someone were to say, 'It enters within the general text, or it is

---

[259] Soorah al-Baqarah (2):1-5.

arrived at through the principle that it is something essential for the completion of an obligation, or something indicated by a further text.' Then it is to be said: Even if all of this were correct, then it would at most mean that it was one of the matters pertaining to the details of the religion, not that it is a pillar of *eemaan*. Since the pillars of *eemaan* are the things which are essential for the attainment of *eemaan*, such as the two testifications of faith, so a person cannot be a Believer unless he testifies that none has the right to be worshipped except Allaah and that Muhammad (ﷺ) is the Messenger of Allaah. So if the imaamate were a pillar of *eemaan*, and *eemaan* were not completed except with it, then it would have been binding upon the Messenger (ﷺ) to explain it openly to the people in such a manner so as to remove any excuse, in the way he explained the two testifications of Faith, and *eemaan* in the angels, the Books, the Messengers and the Last Day. So how about when we know necessarily from his religion that the huge throng of people who entered into his religion, did not have the imaamate made a condition for *eemaan* upon any of them, neither in general nor in particular."[260]

I have given a lengthy quote from Ibn Taymiyyah, *rahimahullaah*:

1 - Due to his being one of the foremost scholars of the religion, and his standing and the trust which the people have for the strength and depth of his understanding of Islaam, and their belief in his sincerity.

2 - Due to the similarity between the claims of Maududi and the claim of the *Raafidee Shee'ee*. Indeed it is very unfortunate that the reader will see that the claims of Maududi are even greater than the *Shee'ee* who said, "It is the most important of the rulings of the religion,'[261] and he said, "And it is one of the pillars of *eemaan*." Whereas Maududi declared

---

[260] *Minhaajus-Sunnah* (1/32-33).
[261] i.e. he did not say that it was the most important of the fundamentals of the Religion. [Translator's note]

it to be, "The most important question in human life and the most important principle," and, "The most important goal of the Prophets," as will follow.

3 - My intention is to give sincere advice to the Muslim youth so that they may cling to the way and guidance of their Prophet, and from my advice to them is that they should not merely seek to make a comparison between Rabee' and Maududi, but rather they must raise the importance they give to the Qur'aan, the Speech of their Lord, and raise the importance they give to the *Sunnah* of their Prophet. Then they should not equate the speech of any human with them, no matter what position and status they hold. This is what is demanded by *eemaan* and is a proof of a person's sincerity.

The View of the Scholars of Islaam with Regard to the Imaamate and their Proofs of its Obligation

Imaam Abul-Hasan al-Maawardee, *rahimahullaah,* said, "The imaamate is established to achieve *khilaafah* (caliphate) upon the Prophetic way in safeguarding the religion, and in running the worldly affairs and it is obligatory by consensus (*ijmaa'*) to place in that position one who will carry out that duty in the *ummah*. Even if al-Asamm was an exception, and people disagreed as to whether its obligation was due to the intellect or the *Sharee'ah*. So a group said, 'It is obligatory based upon the intellect due to the nature of intelligent people which causes them to accept a leader who will prevent them from mutual oppression. Al-Afwah al-Awdee said, 'The people will not be rectified by a state of anarchy, there being no leader for them, nor will there be leadership if the ignorant take control.''

"And a group say, 'Rather it is obligatory based upon the *Sharee'ah*, not the intellect, since the Imaam (ruler) establishes affairs of the *Sharee'ah* which may according to the intellect not have been meant as worship, therefore it could not be the intellect which caused its obligation. Then they agree upon its obligation due to the saying of Allaah, the Most High:

يَٰٓأَيُّهَا ٱلَّذِينَ ءَامَنُوٓا۟ أَطِيعُوا۟ ٱللَّهَ وَأَطِيعُوا۟ ٱلرَّسُولَ وَأُو۟لِى ٱلْأَمْرِ مِنكُمْ

"O you who believe, obey Allaah and obey the Messenger and those in authority over you."[262]

"So it is obligatory upon us to obey those in authority amongst us, and they are the leaders in authority over us.' Then he said: Hishaam ibn 'Urwah reported from Aboo Saalih from Aboo Hurayrah that Allaah's Messenger (ﷺ) said, *"After me rulers will take charge, so you will be*

---

[262] Soorah an-Nisaa (4):59.

ruled by righteous rulers, and by wicked rulers along with their wickedness. So hear and obey them in everything that is in accordance with the truth. So if they do good then that is for them and for you. And if they commit evil, then that is for you and against them." He said, 'So when the imaamate is established to be obligatory, then its obligation is binding upon some only (*Fard Kifaayah*), as with *Jihaad* and seeking knowledge.'"263

Al-Qaadee Aboo Ya'laa, *rahimahullaah*, said, "Establishment of the *Imaam* is obligatory." And Imaam Ahmad, *radiyallaahu 'anhu*, said in the narration of Muhammad ibn 'Awf ibn Sufyaan al-Himsee, "There will be discord if there is no *Imaam* in charge of the affairs of the people. This is because when the Companions differed in the enclosure (of Banoo Saqeefah), and the Ansaar said, 'There should be a ruler from us and a ruler from you.' So Aboo Bakr and 'Umar, *radiyallaahu 'anhumaa*, rebutted this and said, 'The Arabs will not submit except to this branch of Quraysh,' and they quoted some narrations in that regard. So if the imaamate were not obligatory then such a discussion and debate for it would not have been proper. Also someone could have said, 'It is not obligatory, neither that it is established with Quraysh nor with other than them.'"264

Imaamul-Haramayn said, "The matter of imaamate pertains to the details [of Islaam] (*al-Furoo'*)."265

So you see what they say with regard to the imaamate, that it is from the details (*al-Furoo'*), and is no more than a means. So it is there for the protection of the religion and for the running of the worldly affairs. Then there is disagreement about the proof for its obligation: is it the intellect

---

[263] *Al-Ahkaamus-Sultaaniyyah* pp.5-6.
[264] *Al-Ahkaamus-Sultaaniyyah* p.19.
[265] *Mugheethul-Khalq* p.9.

or the *Sharee'ah*? We indeed hold that it is an obligation, but the two proofs quoted by al-Maawardee are not direct texts with regard to the imaamate, since they are more general than the matter of the imaamate and they refer to the obligation of obedience to rulers already established in authority, and likewise with the *hadeeth*. So perhaps Aboo Ya'laa left them aside because he saw that they are not clear proofs for this matter. Anyway, how can it be said about a matter like this, where there is difference about the proofs for its obligation, that it is the true goal of the religion, and the most important role of the Prophets... and the rest of the exaggerations said about it? These sayings have over-inflated this matter and give to it a far greater importance than its true importance, and have at the same time reduced the importance of *'aqeedah* and of the religion itself.

Maududi said, "Therefore the goal aspired for in the Messengership of the Prophets, *'alayhimus-salaatu was-salaam*, in this world did not cease to be the establishment of the Islamic Government upon the earth. Through this they could establish the complete system for human life which they brought from Allaah."[266] I say:

Firstly: It is not possible to speak about the Messengers of Allaah and His Prophets based upon political conclusions and deductions. Rather the life stories of the Prophets and their histories are matters of the Hidden and Unseen which it is not possible to go into except when there is a text sent down as Revelation by Allaah to Muhammad (ﷺ). Allaah, the Most High, says at the beginning of the story of Yoosuf, *'alayhis-salaam*:

$$\text{نَحْنُ نَقُصُّ عَلَيْكَ أَحْسَنَ ٱلْقَصَصِ بِمَآ أَوْحَيْنَآ إِلَيْكَ هَٰذَا ٱلْقُرْءَانَ وَإِن كُنتَ مِن قَبْلِهِۦ لَمِنَ ٱلْغَٰفِلِينَ ﴿٣﴾}$$

---

[266] *Tajdeedud-Deen* p.34.

"We narrate to you, O Muhammad (ﷺ), the best of narratives about the past nations in this Qur'aan sent down, and before its revelation you did not know anything about that."[267]

Allaah, the Most High, says after the story of Nooh, *'alayhis-salaam*:

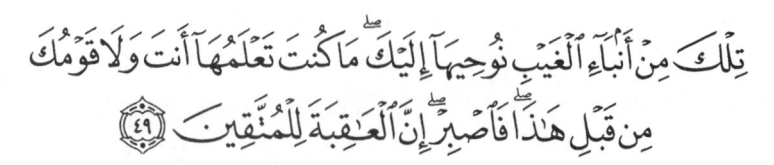

$$\text{تِلْكَ مِنْ أَنبَآءِ ٱلْغَيْبِ نُوحِيهَآ إِلَيْكَ مَا كُنتَ تَعْلَمُهَآ أَنتَ وَلَا قَوْمُكَ مِن قَبْلِ هَٰذَا فَٱصْبِرْ إِنَّ ٱلْعَٰقِبَةَ لِلْمُتَّقِينَ ﴿٤٩﴾}$$

"This story which We have informed you of is one of the affairs of the Unseen which you did not witness or know about, which We reveal to you. Neither you nor your people knew this previously. So patiently persevere in accomplishing the command of Allaah and conveying the message, just as Nooh patiently persevered. Indeed the good outcome is in favour of those who are obedient to Allah, doing what He has ordered and avoiding what He has forbidden."[268]

Then this prohibition is even more severe when these political conclusions are contrary to what Allaah has informed about them. So Allaah has explained what their goal was in summary, saying:

$$\text{وَلَقَدْ بَعَثْنَا فِى كُلِّ أُمَّةٍ رَّسُولًا أَنِ ٱعْبُدُواْ ٱللَّهَ وَٱجْتَنِبُواْ ٱلطَّٰغُوتَ}$$

"We sent a Messenger to every nation ordering them that they should worship Allaah alone, obey Him and

---

[267] Soorah Yoosuf (12):3.
[268] Soorah Hood (11):49.

make their worship purely for Him, and that they should avoid everything worshipped besides Allaah. So from them there were those whom Allaah guided to His religion, and there were those who were unbelievers for whom misguidance was ordained. So travel through the land and see the destruction that befell those who denied the Messengers and disbelieved."[269]

Allaah, the Most High, said:

وَمَآ أَرْسَلْنَا مِن قَبْلِكَ مِن رَّسُولٍ إِلَّا نُوحِىٓ إِلَيْهِ أَنَّهُۥ لَآ إِلَٰهَ إِلَّآ أَنَا۠ فَٱعْبُدُونِ ۝

"We did not send any Messenger before you, O Muhammad (ﷺ), except that We revealed to him that none has the right to be worshipped except Allaah, so make all of your worship purely for Him."[270]

He narrated to us in detail about some of them, such as Nooh, Ibraaheem, Hood and Saalih. We have already spoken about their methodology in what has preceded, and have quoted the *Aayaat* which make clear their methodology and their goal. This is in full accordance with what Allaah mentioned about them in general terms, with regard to the call to *tawheed*, fighting against *shirk* and its manifestations, whilst calling to all good. But there is nothing in the Qur'aan nor in the *Sunnah*, to support what Maududi claimed in his saying, "Because of this the goal aspired to in the Messengership of the Prophets, *'alayhimus-salaatu was-salaam*, in this world did not cease to be the establishment upon it of the Islamic Gov-

---

[269] Soorah an-Nahl (16):36.
[270] Soorah al-Ambiyaa (21):25.

ernment," or the "Divine Government," as reported by an-Nadawee from Maududi. So whoever has clear proofs for this very serious matter, from the Book and the *Sunnah* then let him produce them, and upon us is *eemaan* and compliance.

Secondly: Maududi lived in a time of party political struggle, and rivalry and the struggle for leadership which spread throughout the east and the west. Then because he was a political leader and head of a party he imagined that the Prophets must have given great importance to, and striven, and fought to attain authority and to achieve rulership. His words which follow emphasise what I have said. He said, "**The type of work carried out by the Prophet:** So to construct this civilisation and this society on the earth, Allaah sent His Messengers in succession. This is because every society in this world, except for the society of monks, whether societies of ignorance or Islamic societies, then if they have a comprehensive philosophy for human life and an all-encompassing methodology for the running of the affairs of the world, **then they must necessarily by their very nature take possession of authority and seize possession of the reins of the affairs**, and organise human life according to its particular view. So without **the desire for authority, there is no meaning for *da'wah* to a particular philosophy, and there is no meaning for what is lawful and what is forbidden, nor to the prescribed laws.** As for the monk in this life, then he does not wish to take charge of its affairs. Rather his preoccupation is to attain his imaginary goal of salvation, by following a particular way which leads him to avoid this world and what it contains. Therefore he has no need of rulership and authority and does not seek any of that. But one who comes as a caller to a particular way to take care of the affairs of this world, and he believes that by following this way a person will attain salvation and success, **then he must strive hard to attain the reins of rulership and authority**, since as long as he does not have the required power to enforce his particular way, then it can never be established in the real world."[271]

Maududi studied modern society and civilisation in all its branches and details, or most of them, and he believed that the Prophets had a society and civilisation comprising the same branches and details as those existing in present-day organised societies, except that they were different in their branches and details as those existing in their branches and details from the societies and civilisations of ignorance (*Jaahiliyyah*). Then upon this belief he built the idea that every society having a comprehensive theory for life and an all-embracing methodology for running the affairs of the world, that they must by their very nature take possession of authority and seize possession of the reins of control of the affairs. Then the Prophets came with a society and civilisation of this type, and their society and civilisation must therefore take possession of authority and seize the reins of control of the affairs. They must strive and work hard to attain the reins of rulership and therefore, "The goal aspired for in the Messengership of the Prophets, *'alayhimus-salaatu was-salaam*, in this world did not cease to be the establishment upon it of the Islamic Government, and to enforce upon it that complete system for human life which they brought from Allaah."

---

[271] *Tajdeedud-Deen* pp.32-33. He spoke at length about the civilisations and societies of the Prophets. So there is truth in part of what he said, and some of it is doubtful and in need of proofs, from the one who does not speak from his desires. So from these matters (i.e. which he attributes to them [transl.]) is his saying, "Organisation of the positions and offices in the branches of civil government, and the fundamentals of the laws, and derivation of detailed principles from these fundamentals, and organisation of the systems of justice, the policy and accounting, and levying taxes, and the section of economics and general works, and production, and business, and organisation of publications, information, education, organisation of civil-servants, training and organisation of armies, and the affairs of peace and war, and international relations and foreign affairs."

So hopefully it will have become clear to the reader that these conclusions are based upon intellectual and political analogies and deductions. They are not based upon proofs from the Qur'aan and the Prophetic *Sunnah*, and this is an area requiring Divine Revelation, not a place for intellectual and political discoveries.

Also he was under the false impression that people were of only two classes: Either a monk whose sole preoccupation is to reach his imaginary salvation...etc. and far removed are the Prophets from being of this type. However they may be similar, in the view of the people of politics, to the present-day scholars and callers: those who do not ride on the wave of politics, nor plunge into its hazards. Rather they follow the methodology of the Prophets in calling to Allaah, and of *tawheed* of Him, and that all worship should be made purely for Him, and warning against *shirk*, sins, innovation, with the wisdom of the *Sunnah* and with fine manners and preaching, and they are not infallible.

Then the other type of person is the one with political aspirations and cultural thinking who wishes to take the *ummah* to the highest levels of culture and society, and he wishes to establish the strongest state for his *ummah*.[272] Then the Prophets are the most eminent and highest ranking of the people so they must, in his view, be of this distinct class. But it escaped him that the Prophets were a special independent class, neither belonging to these nor those. Rather they are people distinct and free from the folly of the monks and their ignorance, and also from the aspirations of the people of politics and their sly tricks and devilish means which they use to attain authority. The Prophets are the people who have their souls purest and furthest removed from personal ambitions, and they are those with the highest intellects, and the best characters, and the purest in their descent and lineage. They were chosen and preferred by Allaah for the guidance of mankind, and to rescue them from misguidance. So

---

[272] Even if it is devoid of *tawheed* and established upon innovations and false beliefs.

they committed themselves fully to the field of calling to Allaah with full sincerity and selflessness. They did not desire any reward of wealth, status or sovereignty for that. Rather they only sought the Face of Allaah, and the Hereafter, and they bore patiently the various types of harm which would not be borne by other than them. Maududi however says, "Therefore every Prophet and every Messenger strove to cause a political revolution. So the efforts of some of them were limited to preparing the way and amassing the number of people required, such as Ibraaheem, *'alayhis-salaam*; others actually managed to start revolutionary movements, but their Messengership finished before the Divine Government could be established at their hand, such as 'Eesaa, *'alayhis-salaam*; and some of them managed with this movement to attain the level of success and victory, such as Moosaa, *'alayhis-salaam*, and our noble leader Muhammad (ﷺ)."

Firstly: The number of Prophets and Messengers is in excess of a hundred and twenty thousand[273] and Allaah only narrated to us the stories of about twenty-five of the Prophets and Messengers in the Qur'aan. Allaah, the Most High, says:

$$\text{وَرُسُلًا قَدْ قَصَصْنَاهُمْ عَلَيْكَ مِن قَبْلُ وَرُسُلًا لَّمْ نَقْصُصْهُمْ عَلَيْكَ وَكَلَّمَ ٱللَّهُ مُوسَىٰ تَكْلِيمًا ﴿١٦٤﴾}$$

"And Messengers about whom We have narrated to you previously, and Messengers about whom We have not narrated to you, and Allaah spoke directly to Moosaa."[274]

---

[273] As indicated in the *hadeeth* of Aboo Dharr, *radiyallaahu 'anhu*, which has preceded. [Translator's note]
[274] Soorah an-Nisaa (4):164.

Allaah, the Most High, says:

$$وَلَقَدْ أَرْسَلْنَا رُسُلًا مِّن قَبْلِكَ مِنْهُم مَّن قَصَصْنَا عَلَيْكَ وَمِنْهُم مَّن لَّمْ نَقْصُصْ عَلَيْكَ$$

> "And We sent, O Muhammad (ﷺ), Messengers before you. We have narrated to you the stories of some of them, and We did not narrate to you the stories of others of them."[275]

So what is obligatory upon us is that we believe in all of the Prophets and Messengers and their Books generally and comprehensively, and in those and their Books which Allaah mentioned in particular, then we believe in them as they were named to us. With regard to those whom we are not informed of, and those whose stories were not narrated to us by His Messenger Muhammad (ﷺ), then this is from the affairs of the Hidden and Unseen. Then I believe that the like of sayings such as, "Therefore every Prophet and every Messenger strove to cause a political revolution..."[276] is not from the knowledge inherited from the final Prophet (ﷺ), rather it is from the greatest affairs of the Hidden and Unseen which was kept hidden from Allaah's Mesenger (ﷺ) by Allaah. So how can anyone else know it? Indeed we say: How is it permissible for any Muslim to speak about this when Allaah, the Most High, has said:

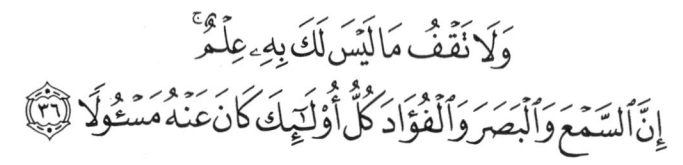

$$وَلَا تَقْفُ مَا لَيْسَ لَكَ بِهِ عِلْمٌ ۚ إِنَّ السَّمْعَ وَالْبَصَرَ وَالْفُؤَادَ كُلُّ أُولَٰئِكَ كَانَ عَنْهُ مَسْئُولًا ﴿٣٦﴾$$

> "Do not say that about which you do not have knowledge, for indeed Allaah will ask the servant concern-

---

[275] Soorah Ghaafir (40):78.
[276] *Tajdeedud-Deen* p.35.

ing the hearing, seeing and the heart on the Day of Resurrection."[277]

Allaah, the Most High, says:

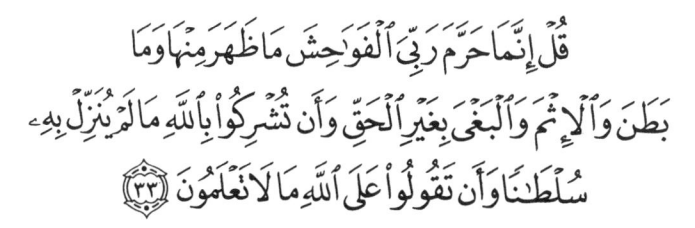

$$\text{قُلْ إِنَّمَا حَرَّمَ رَبِّيَ الْفَوَاحِشَ مَا ظَهَرَ مِنْهَا وَمَا بَطَنَ وَالْإِثْمَ وَالْبَغْيَ بِغَيْرِ الْحَقِّ وَأَن تُشْرِكُوا بِاللَّهِ مَا لَمْ يُنَزِّلْ بِهِ سُلْطَانًا وَأَن تَقُولُوا عَلَى اللَّهِ مَا لَا تَعْلَمُونَ ﴿٣٣﴾}$$

"Say, O Muhammad (ﷺ), rather my Lord has forbidden the foul and disgusting sins, whether done openly or secretly, and sin, and transgression against others, and that you associate with Allaah in worship that which He has sent down no proof for, and that you say about Allaah that which you do not know."[278]

Secondly: I believe that it is not permissible in the *Sharee'ah* with regard to the wise calls of the Prophets and their merciful guidance which comprised wisdom, knowledge, firmness, patient perseverance and full care and attention, to designate them as being attempts at political revolutions. Since political revolutions are brought about through plots, intrigues and conspiracies which are not undertaken except by people who are not concerned about spilling of blood, destruction of produce and offspring, and causing corruption upon the earth.

Thirdly: The interpretation of the duty and goal of the Prophets is extremely dangerous due to its serious effect upon the *ummah*, since they

---

[277] Soorah al-Israa (17):36.
[278] Soorah al-A'raaf (7):33.

will say, "If the Prophets were political leaders, and heads of revolutionary movements, then why should their followers not also be political revolutionaries and adopt the means necessary for their goal of political revolution, involving plots and whatever steps are necessary." Then they will be safe and preserved from error in causing political revolutions.

Fourthly: I do not know what Maududi intends by his saying, "The efforts of some of them were limited to preparing the way and amassing the number of people required." Also an-Nadawee reports from him the saying, "To preparation of the earth such as our noble leader Ibraaheem." Does he mean that they laid down political and revolutionary plans for the Prophets and political leaders who came after him, or does he mean something else? In any case this gives a very strange, and dreadful image of the Prophets, something not described in the Qur'aan or the *Sunnah*, nor known to the scholars of Islaam, and something which Allaah kept His Prophets far removed and free from.

Indeed the story of Ibraaheem, for example, is very clear in the Book and the *Sunnah*, and Allaah repeats it a number of times in the Qur'aan. All of it is a struggle for *tawheed*, and for the destruction of the idols with proof and guidance, and with the hand when he had to resort to that and after he had proclaimed the clear message, and established the strong and irrefutable proofs upon the stubborn *mushriks*, both the rulers and the people of the nation. He then physically destroyed their idols and false gods. So they became angry for their idols and seized him, and wished to give him the severest punishment. So they built a huge fire and threw him into it.

﴿قَالُواْ حَرِّقُوهُ وَٱنصُرُوٓاْ ءَالِهَتَكُمْ إِن كُنتُمْ فَـٰعِلِينَ ۝﴾

"They said, 'Burn him and aid your gods, if you do indeed wish to aid them and continue to worship them.'"[279]

---

[279] Soorah al-Ambiyaa (21):68.

$$\text{قُلْنَا يَا نَارُ كُونِي بَرْدًا وَسَلَامًا عَلَىٰ إِبْرَاهِيمَ ﴿٦٩﴾}$$

"We said, 'O fire, be cool and safe for Ibraaheem.'"[280]

Then when their haughty and stubborn rejection reached its limit and all hope of their responding to the call of Allaah was cut off he abandoned them and performed *Hijrah* for Allaah, and Loot believed along with him and he said:

$$\text{إِنِّي مُهَاجِرٌ إِلَىٰ رَبِّي إِنَّهُ هُوَ الْعَزِيزُ الْحَكِيمُ}$$

"I am leaving the land of my people and going to *Shaam* for my Lord, indeed He is the All-Mighty, the All-Wise."[281]

Allaah did not mention anything about him concerning political revolutions, nor preparing the required number of people, nor laying down the way for it. Then to complete the story of Ibraaheem he made *Hijrah* to *Shaam*, then after a while he went with his wife Haajar and his son Ismaa'eel to Makkah, which was at the time uninhabited and did not have any of the means to support life, not even water. Then he left his wife and his son with Allaah's permission and returned to *Shaam*. So he set off back to *Shaam* and when he reached the mountain pass where they could not see him, he turned towards the *Ka'bah* and supplicated with these words whilst raising his hands, saying:

$$\text{رَبَّنَا إِنِّي أَسْكَنتُ مِن ذُرِّيَّتِي بِوَادٍ غَيْرِ ذِي زَرْعٍ عِندَ بَيْتِكَ الْمُحَرَّمِ}$$

"O our Lord, I have settled my son in a valley without vegetation next to your Sacred House."[282]

---

[280] Soorah al-Ambiyaa (21):69.
[281] Soorah al-'Ankaaboot (29):26.
[282] Soorah Ibraaheem (14):37.

Then he made clear the purpose of that, saying:

> "O our Lord, so that they should establish the Obligatory Prayer therein, so cause the hearts of some of the people (i.e. the Muslims) to incline towards and yearn for them. And provide them with fruits of trees and plants as sustenance, so that they may give thanks to You."[283]

Ibraaheem, *'alayhis-salaam,* visited his son, Ismaa'eel, *'alayhis-salaam,* twice but did not find him as he had gone off in search of provision, so Ibraaheem returned from whence he had come. Then he visited him a third time, so when he saw him he stood to greet him and they welcomed each other as would be expected between father and son. Then Ibraaheem, *'alayhis-salaam,* said, "O Ismaa'eel! Allaah has given me a command." He said, "Then do as you Lord as ordered you." He said, "And you will help me?" He said, "I will help you." He said, "Then Allaah has commanded me to build a House here, and he pointed towards an area of ground raised above what surrounded it. So at that place they raised the foundations of the House. So Ismaa'eel would bring the stones whilst Ibraaheem built and Ismaa'eel passed the stones to him, and they were both saying:

$$رَبَّنَا تَقَبَّلْ مِنَّا إِنَّكَ أَنتَ ٱلسَّمِيعُ ٱلْعَلِيمُ ﴿١٢٧﴾$$

"O our Lord, accept this from us, indeed You are the All-Hearing, the All-Knowing.""[284, 285]

---

[283] *Ibid.*
[284] Soorah al-Baqarah (2):127.
[285] Abrdiged from a longer *hadeeth* reported by al-Bukhaaree (Eng. trans. 4/372-379 no.583).

So this is the story of Ibraaheem in the Book and the *Sunnah*. He called his people to Allaah and established proofs against them. Then he destroyed their idols, then he made *Hijrah*. Then these were his journeys from *Shaam* to visit his son Ismaa'eel in Makkah, in the valley devoid of vegetation. He had previously placed his son in this valley and had mentioned the purpose for which he had placed him there. Then when his son grew up they built the House together, and Allaah said to them both:

$$\text{أَن طَهِّرَا بَيْتِيَ لِلطَّآئِفِينَ وَٱلْعَاكِفِينَ وَٱلرُّكَّعِ ٱلسُّجُودِ}$$

"Purify My House from *shirk* and the worship of idols, for those who perform *tawaaf* around it, and those who stay there, and those performing *rukoo'* and *sujood* (in prayer)."[286]

So what can be taken from these actions: his *hijrah* from his land, the land of civilisation to the desert of *Shaam*, then his placing his son in a land devoid of vegetation and without inhabitants and the means to support life, and from his declared goal?

$$\text{رَّبَّنَآ إِنِّيٓ أَسْكَنتُ مِن ذُرِّيَّتِي بِوَادٍ غَيْرِ ذِي زَرْعٍ عِندَ بَيْتِكَ ٱلْمُحَرَّمِ رَبَّنَا لِيُقِيمُوا۟ ٱلصَّلَوٰةَ}$$

"O our Lord, I have settled my son in a valley without vegetation next to your Sacred House O our Lord, so that they should establish the Obligatory Prayer therein..."[287]

Can it be taken from these actions that he was preparing the way and the required number of people to cause a political revolution?! And when did

---

[286] Soorah al-Baqarah (2):125.
[287] Soorah Ibraaheem (14):37.

'Eesaa establish a revolutionary movement?! And when was it stopped, or when did this revolution collapse?!! And what is the proof for this very dangerous saying?! Then how is it that no-one except Moosaa and Muhammad (ﷺ) ever attained the level of success and triumph?! Even though every Prophet and every Messenger strove to achieve political revolution, as claimed by Maududi, then how is it they did not achieve triumph and success, when they numbered more than a hundred and twenty thousand?!

Can you not see, along with me, the bitter fruits of going to excesses, and the oppressive and dangerous results which shake the roots of *eemaan* and *'aqeedah*?! Since if only two of the huge number of Prophets managed to attain success and triumph, then will an unbeliever, or those weak in *eemaan* and the ignorant, will they not judge that the rest of the Prophets failed and were frustrated? Even with regard to the strong Believer, is it not to be feared that his *eemaan* would be shaken and troubled, if it were really the case that the unbelieving *Kisraas*, and Caesars, and Pharaohs should succeed in the past and the present and reach their desired goal of establishing great states and advanced civilisations, yet the efforts of the Prophets did not meet with success and victory?!

If we lay down these goals and make false and fanciful judgements about the calls, then the result will appear to be very bad, and the problems which this causes will be very difficult to overcome. However if in deciding what their goals were and describing their actions we depend upon the Book of Allaah and the *Sunnah* of His Messenger (ﷺ) who does not speak from his desires, then we will be following the correct methodology. And Allaah has laid down what their goals were, and explained their calls, saying:

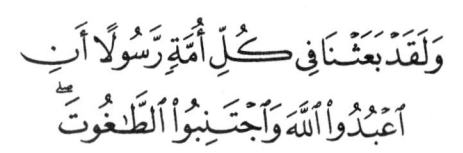

$$\text{وَلَقَدْ بَعَثْنَا فِى كُلِّ أُمَّةٍ رَّسُولًا أَنِ اعْبُدُوا اللَّهَ وَاجْتَنِبُوا الطَّاغُوتَ}$$

"We sent a Messenger to every nation, ordering them that they should worship Allaah alone, obey Him and make their worship purely for Him, and that they should avoid everything worshipped besides Allaah."[288]

Allaah, the Most High, said:

$$رُسُلًا مُّبَشِّرِينَ وَمُنذِرِينَ لِئَلَّا يَكُونَ لِلنَّاسِ عَلَى ٱللَّهِ حُجَّةٌ بَعْدَ ٱلرُّسُلِ$$

"Messengers who were sent with the good news of Allaah's reward for those who obey Allaah, do as he commands and believe in His Messengers; and warners of Allaah's punishment for those who disobey Allaah, contravene His commands and disbelieve in His Messengers, so that those who disbelieve in Allaah and worship others besides Him may have no excuse to avoid punishment after the sending of the Messengers."[289]

So this was their duty and this was their goal: the call to the *tawheed* of Allaah and to warn against *shirk* and sins, and to give good news of reward and Paradise to the Believers, and to warn the obstinate unbelievers of punishment in the Hell-Fire. So they carried out their duty and all reached the level of success and triumph, and Allaah aided them against their enemies in this world, and will aid them on the Day when the witnesses will stand forth, whereas the unbelievers in these correct standards will be the failures, the losers and the defeated in this world and the Hereafter. Allaah, the Most High, says:

---

[288] Soorah an-Nahl (16):36.
[289] Soorah an-Nisaa (4):165.

وَلَقَدْ سَبَقَتْ كَلِمَتُنَا لِعِبَادِنَا ٱلْمُرْسَلِينَ ﴿١٧١﴾ إِنَّهُمْ لَهُمُ ٱلْمَنصُورُونَ ﴿١٧٢﴾ وَإِنَّ جُندَنَا لَهُمُ ٱلْغَٰلِبُونَ ﴿١٧٣﴾

"And the saying has already preceded from Us to Our Messengers that they will be the triumphant ones, and that Our army will be victorious."[290]

Allaah, the Most High, says:

كَتَبَ ٱللَّهُ لَأَغْلِبَنَّ أَنَا۠ وَرُسُلِىٓ إِنَّ ٱللَّهَ قَوِىٌّ عَزِيزٌ ﴿٢١﴾

"Allaah has written and decreed: I and My Messengers shall be triumphant over those who rebel against Me. Indeed Allaah has full-power to destroy those who oppose Him and His Messenger, and is All-Mighty."[291]

Allaah explained how His Prophets were victorious over their enemies in many stories in the Qur'aan. Allaah, the Most High, says about Nooh, 'alayhis-salaam:

فَدَعَا رَبَّهُۥٓ أَنِّى مَغْلُوبٌ فَٱنتَصِرْ ﴿١٠﴾ فَفَتَحْنَآ أَبْوَٰبَ ٱلسَّمَآءِ بِمَآءٍ مُّنْهَمِرٍ ﴿١١﴾ وَفَجَّرْنَا ٱلْأَرْضَ عُيُونًا فَٱلْتَقَى ٱلْمَآءُ عَلَىٰٓ أَمْرٍ قَدْ قُدِرَ ﴿١٢﴾ وَحَمَلْنَٰهُ عَلَىٰ ذَاتِ أَلْوَٰحٍ وَدُسُرٍ ﴿١٣﴾ تَجْرِى بِأَعْيُنِنَا جَزَآءً لِّمَن كَانَ كُفِرَ ﴿١٤﴾ وَلَقَد تَّرَكْنَٰهَآ ءَايَةً فَهَلْ مِن مُّدَّكِرٍ ﴿١٥﴾

---

[290] Soorah as-Saaffaat (37):171-173.
[291] Soorah al-Mujaadilah (58):21.

"So Nooh called to his Lord, 'My people are overcoming me with their rebellion and rejection, so help and grant me victory against them.' So We opened the gates of the heavens pouring forth water in torrents, and caused all parts of the earth to gush forth with springs of water. So the water of the heavens joined with the water of the earth came together for a matter predecreed by Allaah. And We carried Nooh upon a ship made of planks and nails. Floating beneath Our Eyes, under Our observation, as a punishment for the peoples unbelief and a reward for Nooh who had been rejected. And We left the Ark as a sign and an admonition for those coming after them. So will anyone accept admonition?"[292]

Allaah, the Most High, says:

كَذَّبَتْ ثَمُودُ وَعَادٌ بِٱلْقَارِعَةِ ۝ فَأَمَّا ثَمُودُ فَأُهْلِكُوا بِٱلطَّاغِيَةِ ۝ وَأَمَّا عَادٌ فَأُهْلِكُوا بِرِيحٍ صَرْصَرٍ عَاتِيَةٍ ۝ سَخَّرَهَا عَلَيْهِمْ سَبْعَ لَيَالٍ وَثَمَانِيَةَ أَيَّامٍ حُسُومًا فَتَرَى ٱلْقَوْمَ فِيهَا صَرْعَىٰ كَأَنَّهُمْ أَعْجَازُ نَخْلٍ خَاوِيَةٍ ۝ فَهَلْ تَرَىٰ لَهُم مِّنْ بَاقِيَةٍ ۝ وَجَاءَ فِرْعَوْنُ وَمَن قَبْلَهُ وَٱلْمُؤْتَفِكَاتُ بِٱلْخَاطِئَةِ ۝ فَعَصَوْا رَسُولَ رَبِّهِمْ فَأَخَذَهُمْ أَخْذَةً رَّابِيَةً ۝

---

[292] Soorah al-Qamar (54):10-15.

"*Thamood* and *'Aad* disbelieved in the Last Hour. So as for *Thamood*, then Allaah destroyed them with the terrible thunderclap, and as for *'Aad*, then Allaah destroyed them with a violent and terrific wind which He set upon them for seven nights and eight days in succession. So that you could see the people cast down and destroyed as if they were the hollow trunks of felled palm-trees. So do you see anyone remaining or descended from them? And the Pharaoh and those before him, and the people of the towns which were overturned and destroyed (i.e. the people of Loot) came committing sins, and they disobeyed the Messenger of their Lord. So He punished them with a terrible punishment."[293]

Allaah, the Most High, says:

وَقَوْمَ نُوحٍ لَّمَّا كَذَّبُوا۟ ٱلرُّسُلَ أَغْرَقْنَٰهُمْ وَجَعَلْنَٰهُمْ لِلنَّاسِ ءَايَةً وَأَعْتَدْنَا لِلظَّٰلِمِينَ عَذَابًا أَلِيمًا ۝ وَعَادًا وَثَمُودَا۟ وَأَصْحَٰبَ ٱلرَّسِّ وَقُرُونًۢا بَيْنَ ذَٰلِكَ كَثِيرًا ۝ وَكُلًّا ضَرَبْنَا لَهُ ٱلْأَمْثَٰلَ وَكُلًّا تَبَّرْنَا تَتْبِيرًا ۝

"And the people of Nooh, when they denied the Messengers and rejected the truth they brought, We drowned them in the Flood and made that a sign and an admonition for the people coming after them. And We prepared for the unbelievers a painful punishment in the Hereafter. And We destroyed *'Aad*

---

[293] Soorah al-Haaqqah (69):4-10.

and *Thamood* and the *Rass* people and many nations between them. And We warned each of them by examples and by making the proof clear to them, and We utterly destroyed them all."[294]

So these were overwhelming and decisive victories granted to the Messengers, and clear triumphs and successes and also defeats, ruins, destruction and annihilation for the unbelievers. So by these correct and true Qur'aanic standards laid down by Allaah, all of the Prophets attained success and triumph, because they all fulfilled their duty with which they were obligated. They propagated the messages from their Lord which they were duty-bound to propagate, and the end of their enemies was as Allaah has described. Whereas by those political, or imaginary standards, or whatever you wish to call them, none of them succeeded except Muhammad and Moosaa, *'alayhimus-salaam*.

This is according to the theory of these people, but as for us, then we declare Moosaa and Muhammad, *'alayhimus-salaatu was-salaam*, free from having striven to cause political revolution, and we declare their success and victory above and far removed from having been based upon any such foundation.

Then we come to the story of Moosaa, *'alayhis-salaam*, and the story of his victory and success. Then Allaah certainly gave him a clear victory over the Pharaoh and his army. Allaah, the Most High, says:

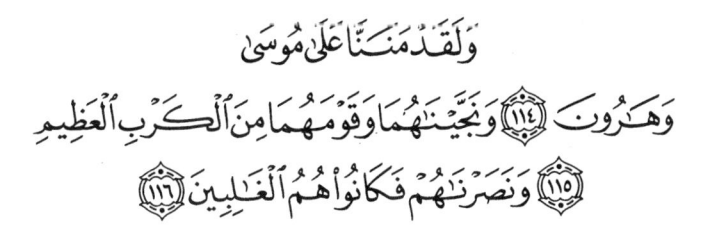

$$\text{وَلَقَدْ مَنَنَّا عَلَىٰ مُوسَىٰ وَهَٰرُونَ ۝ وَنَجَّيْنَٰهُمَا وَقَوْمَهُمَا مِنَ ٱلْكَرْبِ ٱلْعَظِيمِ ۝ وَنَصَرْنَٰهُمْ فَكَانُوا۟ هُمُ ٱلْغَٰلِبِينَ ۝}$$

---

[294] Soorah al-Furqaan (25):37-39.

> "And We indeed favoured Moosaa and Haaroon (with Prophethood), and We saved them and their people from the great suffering they underwent and We gave them victory over the Pharaoh and his people, whom We drowned, so they were the victors."[295]

So how did this great victory come about? Was it achieved by means of a political revolution through which Moosaa attained a throne of Egypt? The true answer is what Allaah informed us in the sublime Qur'aan. That Allaah chose and favoured Moosaa with Messengership and with His Speech to him directly. He placed upon him the duty of calling the Pharaoh to Allaah, and he carried out the command of his Lord, and he established the clear signs and proofs of the truthfulness of his message.

$$\text{فَأَرَاهُ ٱلْآيَةَ ٱلْكُبْرَىٰ ۝ فَكَذَّبَ وَعَصَىٰ ۝ ثُمَّ أَدْبَرَ يَسْعَىٰ ۝ فَحَشَرَ فَنَادَىٰ ۝ فَقَالَ أَنَا رَبُّكُمُ ٱلْأَعْلَىٰ ۝}$$

> "So Moosaa showed the Pharaoh the Great Sign (his hand shining and his rod which became a snake). But Pharaoh denied the signs which Moosaa came with and disobeyed his order for him to fear and obey his Lord. Then he turned away from what he ordered him (i.e. obedience to his Lord) and instead worked evil and corruption, and he gathered his people and his followers and said, 'I am your lord, the most high.'"[296]

---

[295] Soorah as-Saaffaat (37):114-116.
[296] Soorah an-Naazi'aat (79):20-24.

Allaah, the Most High, says:

$$\text{وَلَقَدْ أَرْسَلْنَا مُوسَىٰ بِآيَاتِنَا وَسُلْطَانٍ مُّبِينٍ ۝ إِلَىٰ فِرْعَوْنَ وَهَامَانَ وَقَارُونَ فَقَالُوا سَاحِرٌ كَذَّابٌ ۝ فَلَمَّا جَاءَهُم بِالْحَقِّ مِنْ عِندِنَا قَالُوا اقْتُلُوا أَبْنَاءَ الَّذِينَ آمَنُوا مَعَهُ وَاسْتَحْيُوا نِسَاءَهُمْ ۚ وَمَا كَيْدُ الْكَافِرِينَ إِلَّا فِي ضَلَالٍ ۝}$$

"And We indeed sent Moosaa with Our signs and manifest proof to the Pharaoh, and Haamaan, and Qaaroon. But they called him a sorcerer and a liar. So when he came to them with the truth, that they should worship Allaah alone and obey Him, and he established the proof upon them, they said, 'Kill the sons of those who believe along with him and take their women as slaves.' But the plots of the unbelievers are nothing but futile error."[297]

Then the people of the Pharaoh merely incited him further against Moosaa and his people. Allaah, the Most High, says:

$$\text{أَتَذَرُ مُوسَىٰ وَقَوْمَهُ لِيُفْسِدُوا فِي الْأَرْضِ وَيَذَرَكَ وَآلِهَتَكَ}$$

"Will you leave Moosaa and his people to cause mischief in the land when they have abandoned worship of you and worship of your gods?"[298]

---

[297] Soorah Ghaafir (40):23-25.
[298] Soorah al-A'raaf (7):127.

So Moosaa, *'alayhis-salaam,* stood firm in the face of this tyranny, and this contains a clear lesson for the callers to Allaah.

$$\text{قَالَ مُوسَىٰ لِقَوْمِهِ ٱسْتَعِينُوا۟ بِٱللَّهِ وَٱصْبِرُوٓا۟ ۖ إِنَّ ٱلْأَرْضَ لِلَّهِ يُورِثُهَا مَن يَشَآءُ مِنْ عِبَادِهِۦ ۖ وَٱلْعَـٰقِبَةُ لِلْمُتَّقِينَ ۝}$$

"Moosaa said to his people: Seek Allaah's help and be patient, the earth is Allaah's. He gives it as a heritage to whom He pleases from His servants. The final outcome is in favour of those who fear Allaah by avoiding disobedience of Him and doing what He orders."[299]

Then when the affair reached its peak and the Children of Israa'eel complained to Moosaa:

$$\text{قَالُوٓا۟ أُوذِينَا مِن قَبْلِ أَن تَأْتِيَنَا وَمِنۢ بَعْدِ مَا جِئْتَنَا ۚ قَالَ عَسَىٰ رَبُّكُمْ أَن يُهْلِكَ عَدُوَّكُمْ وَيَسْتَخْلِفَكُمْ فِى ٱلْأَرْضِ فَيَنظُرَ كَيْفَ تَعْمَلُونَ ۝}$$

"They said, 'We have suffered before you came to us with the message and after you came.' He said, 'Perhaps Allaah will destroy your enemy and make you the successors upon the earth, so that He may see how you act, obediently or disobediently.'"[300]

---

[299] Soorah al-A'raaf (7):128.
[300] Soorah al-A'raaf (7):129.

Look at the manners in which the Prophets cultivated the people, and their patience in facing the calamities and severe trials, then Allaah reprimanded them so that they may take heed.

$$وَلَقَدْ أَخَذْنَا آلَ فِرْعَوْنَ بِالسِّنِينَ وَنَقْصٍ مِّنَ الثَّمَرَاتِ لَعَلَّهُمْ يَذَّكَّرُونَ ﴿١٣٠﴾$$

"**And We tried the people of the Pharaoh with years of drought and failure of fruits and crops, as an admonition so that they might turn back from their error.**"[301]

Then Allaah wished to destroy and annihilate them and to save Moosaa and the Children of Israa'eel from their distress. So He laid down a wise plan for them which contained no revolution or political upheaval, since the laws laid down for the Prophets and their manners reject treachery and secret plots and the spilling of blood for the attainment of authority, no matter how lofty the goal is. Allaah, the Most High, says:

$$وَأَوْحَيْنَا إِلَىٰ مُوسَىٰ أَنْ أَسْرِ بِعِبَادِي إِنَّكُم مُّتَّبَعُونَ ﴿٥٢﴾ فَأَرْسَلَ فِرْعَوْنُ فِي الْمَدَائِنِ حَاشِرِينَ ﴿٥٣﴾ إِنَّ هَٰؤُلَاءِ لَشِرْذِمَةٌ قَلِيلُونَ ﴿٥٤﴾ وَإِنَّهُمْ لَنَا لَغَائِظُونَ ﴿٥٥﴾ وَإِنَّا لَجَمِيعٌ حَاذِرُونَ ﴿٥٦﴾ فَأَخْرَجْنَاهُم مِّن جَنَّاتٍ وَعُيُونٍ ﴿٥٧﴾ وَكُنُوزٍ وَمَقَامٍ كَرِيمٍ ﴿٥٨﴾ كَذَٰلِكَ وَأَوْرَثْنَاهَا بَنِي إِسْرَائِيلَ ﴿٥٩﴾ فَأَتْبَعُوهُم مُّشْرِقِينَ ﴿٦٠﴾ فَلَمَّا تَرَاءَى الْجَمْعَانِ قَالَ أَصْحَابُ مُوسَىٰ إِنَّا لَمُدْرَكُونَ ﴿٦١﴾ قَالَ$$

---

[301] Soorah al-A'raaf (7):130.

$$\text{كَلَّآ إِنَّ مَعِيَ رَبِّى سَيَهْدِينِ ۝ فَأَوْحَيْنَآ إِلَىٰ مُوسَىٰٓ أَنِ ٱضْرِب بِّعَصَاكَ ٱلْبَحْرَ ۖ فَٱنفَلَقَ فَكَانَ كُلُّ فِرْقٍ كَٱلطَّوْدِ ٱلْعَظِيمِ ۝ وَأَزْلَفْنَا ثَمَّ ٱلْءَاخَرِينَ ۝ وَأَنجَيْنَا مُوسَىٰ وَمَن مَّعَهُۥٓ أَجْمَعِينَ ۝ ثُمَّ أَغْرَقْنَا ٱلْءَاخَرِينَ ۝ إِنَّ فِى ذَٰلِكَ لَءَايَةً ۖ وَمَا كَانَ أَكْثَرُهُم مُّؤْمِنِينَ}$$

"And We inspired to Moosaa, 'Travel with the Children of Israa'eel by night and leave the land of Egypt, and you will be pursued by Pharaoh and his army.' So Pharaoh sent out his men to the cities to gather his army and said, 'They are only a small band and they have indeed angered us, and we are a host well prepared and armed.' So We expelled Pharaoh and his people from their gardens and springs, and their treasures and their stations of honour. Thus We expelled them and by destroying them made the Children of Israa'eel their inheritors. So Pharaoh and his army pursued them and reached them at sunrise. When the two hosts saw one another, the people of Moosaa said, 'We have been caught.' Moosaa said, 'That will not be so, indeed my Lord is with me, He will guide me to the way to deliverance.' So We inspired to Moosaa, 'Strike the sea with your staff.' So he did so and it parted. Each side was like a huge mountain. Then We brought the army of Pharaoh near to the sea. And We saved Moosaa and all those with him, and We drowned Pharaoh and those with him in the sea. Indeed in this is a clear sign, yet most of them are not Believers."[302]

---

[302] Soorah ash-Shu'araa (26):52-67.

So these are the means prescribed by the *Sharee'ah*, used by Moosaa and those who believed in him from his people. He patiently bore severe hardships and the slaughter of his people. That did not shake their *eemaan*, nor upset their *'aqeedah*, nor cause their patient perseverance to cease. So the way to their victory and the destruction of their enemy was the way laid down for them by their Lord, which is what we have just read, and it does not contain anything of politics or establishment of a political revolution. Then there is a further point: if it were the case that Moosaa strove to bring about a political revolution and earnestly sought to seize the reins of power and to establish the aspired goal of the messages of the Prophets of Allaah, i.e. the divinely inspired state, then he would have quickly turned back and returned to Egypt since the ideal opportunity had risen. Allaah had destroyed the Pharaoh and his army and none remained in Egypt except the women, children and servants. So why did Moosaa not seize this great opportunity and establish the divinely inspired state in the land which Allaah described in His saying:

$$\text{كَمْ تَرَكُواْ مِنْ جَنَّٰتٍ وَعُيُونٍ ۝ وَزُرُوعٍ وَمَقَامٍ كَرِيمٍ ۝ وَنَعْمَةٍ كَانُواْ فِيهَا فَٰكِهِينَ ۝ كَذَٰلِكَ وَأَوْرَثْنَٰهَا قَوْمًا ءَاخَرِينَ ۝}$$

"How many gardens and springs, crops and stations of honour, and bounties which they enjoyed did the Pharaoh and his people the Copts leave behind,"[303] and instead he went to reside in the Sinai desert without any state, any authority or any divinely-inspired government?! Therefore we have to say: Moosaa was indeed a noble and great Messenger, and from the strong and firmly resolute, and he carried out his Messengership in the most perfect and complete manner. At his hand, Allaah destroyed the despotic tyrant Pharaoh and his army, and with him Allaah saved the Children of Israa'eel, and this is sufficient honour and excellence for him, and sufficient for him is the victory he achieved over the Pharaoh and his people.

---

[303] Soorah ad-Dukhaan (44):25-27.

Then as for Muhammad (ﷺ), then he was a man of *'aqeedah* from the first instant and a Messenger of guidance. He patiently bore that which mountains could not bear, whilst conveying this *'aqeedah*. He was offered sovereignty at the beginning and he refused it and the victory and the establishment of the State of Islaam which Allaah gave him came only as a reward for his patient perseverance, his *taqwaa* and his forbearance. So it was a message and a call and then its resulting fruit, not a political revolution. Far from that, how far from that he was, and we have already explained his call in some detail so there is no need to repeat that.[304]

Then a further point of criticism of that orientation in general is that they lay down a principle which is that, "Islaam is a whole and cannot be divided up." And it is a great principle,[305] if only it were followed by the methodology of the Pious Predecessors (*as-Salafus-Saalih*) without committing excesses. But unfortunately you find that they seriously contradict it because their strong attachment to the establishment of the Islamic State (and they call it: The Call to the Sovereign Authority of Allaah (*al-Haakimiyyah*)) has preoccupied them from giving importance to the foundation of Islaam, which is *tawheed* with all its categories. And to this time they have not realised, due to that preoccupation, that the necessity of giving full importance to the call to *tawheed* is just as pressing and urgent as it was in the time of the Messengers, including Muhammad (ﷺ), if not more so. So can any intelligent and just person deny this?! Then can any alert and attentive Muslim say or believe that the Muslims today are like the Muslims in the time of the preferred and best generations, not taking their beliefs and their acts of worship except from the

---

[304] The fifth example from the examples of the Messengers: Muhammad (ﷺ). [Translator's Note]

[305] However, unfortunately, they give precedence over it to another principle, "We will co-operate in what we agree upon, and will excuse one another about those things where we disagree." This is a very broad statement which covers all differences whether in fundamental matters or points of detail, comprehending all the sects which claim attachment to Islaam.

Book and the *Sunnah*. Indeed the call to the sovereign authority (*al-Haakimiyyah*) of Allaah and its application is an important matter, and something important for every Muslim who understands Islaam (if its conditions are kept in mind), and everything which Allaah's Messenger (ﷺ) came with is important and serious.

But we need to ask the question, "Does the call to Allaah's sovereign authority (*al-Haakimiyyah*) necessitate neglect of or falling short with regard to the most fundamental principle of Islaam?" The answer is, "No!" The fact of Allaah's sovereign authority (*al-Haakimiyyah*) must be applied beginning with the greatest of the affairs of Islaam, which is correct Belief (*'aqeedah*) with regard to Allaah, and His Majestic Names and Perfect Attributes, with which Allaah has described Himself and made Himself known to us in His tremendous Book, and as was taught to us by our noble Prophet (ﷺ), so that our hearts may thereby be filled with light, *eemaan*, certain-Faith, awe and reverence.

Can it be permissible with regard to Allaah's sovereign authority (*al-Haakimiyyah*) and His religion that you deny or reject His Majestic Names and His Perfect Attributes or their meanings, when they are the highest, most exalted and greatest of what is comprised in the Book of Allaah and the *Sunnah* of His Prophet?!!

Why do we not earnestly demand from the scholars of the Muslims that they apply the judgement of the Book of Allaah and the *Sunnah* of His Prophet (ﷺ) in this extremely serious matter?!!

Can it be permissible with regard to Allaah's sovereign authority (*al-Haakimiyyah*) and His *Sharee'ah*, and the way He has laid down for the affairs, that many of the Muslims contradict the methodology of the Prophets with regard to *tawheed* of worship, and making worship purely for Allaah alone, and instead take rivals besides Allaah to whom they make supplication and call for their needs, calling out to them in times of distress? Then they sink so deeply into this that they even make them partners with regard to Allaah's Lordship (*Ruboobiyyah*), so they come to believe that they know the Hidden and the Unseen (*al-Ghayb*) and have control over creation?!!

Is this not a flagrant assault upon the greatest of Allaah's rights?! Is this not the worst and severest of all transgression and oppression? So where then are the callers to Allaah's sovereign authority (*al-Haakimiyyah*) and what has happened to justice?!!

Can it be permissible in the Judgement of Allaah and His revealed Law that we close our eyes to the *Sufis* whilst they play with the beliefs and minds of the Muslims, and so corrupt and destroy them with the belief that Allaah is incarnate and to be found within His creation (*Hulool*), and that everything in existence is in reality Allaah (*Wahdatul-Wujood*) and that all religions are in reality the truth... and the rest of the misguided deviance of *Sufism*?!

Can it be permissible with regard to the sovereign authority of Allaah and His religion that thousands of tombs are constructed in most of the lands of Islaam, for people to perform *tawaaf* around and devote themselves to, and travel to, and to consecrate huge amounts of money to, and to organise festivals for them, and for the Muslims to do such things around them and within them are a shocking disgrace and affront to Islaam, which only cause the Muslims and Islaam to be mocked and laughed at by their enemies from the idolaters, the Jews, the Christians and the Communists?

Can it be permissible with regard to the sovereign authority of Allaah that *sunnahs* be killed off and replaced by innovations, deviations and superstitious customs? Indeed these deviations and acts of *shirk* and innovations have wiped away the traces of *tawheed* and the traces of Islaam in general.

So I hope that the intellectuals from this orientation will try, after bearing in mind that Allaah observes them, with regard to themselves and the *ummah*, to give the due importance to the methodology of the Prophets, and to give each aspect of Islaam the importance it deserves, and that they keep in their minds the saying of Allaah's Messenger (ﷺ), *"That Allaah should guide through you a single man is better for you than red camels."*306

It also used to be said to me, "These matters (the innovations and the acts of *shirk*) are things which have come to an end and been buried." But we see that they are still alive and still remain as secure as ever, and there are schools and governments which support them and protect them. They also have their own 'priests,' 'rabbis' and custodians. **So why is it that we do not explain to the Muslims that these actions of *jaahiliyyah* contradict the sovereign authority of Allaah?! And why do we not call those guilty of such actions to submit to the Judgement of Allaah, and to submit to the sovereign authority of Allaah in all these spheres?!**

So if our brothers who give such importance to the sovereign authority of Allaah realise and are certain that those who do these actions and hold such beliefs are contradicting the sovereign authority of Allaah and are not submitting to it in these things, then let them set to work earnestly and apply their full efforts to this area, and let them lay down plans of action, found schools, write books, and let the supports of the *minbars* quake with forceful speeches and correct guidance for correction of this. And I believe that if Ibraaheem, Nooh, Moosaa, Muhammad and all their brothers from the Prophets and Messengers, *salawaatullaahi wa salaamuhu 'alayhim*, were to come, along with all of the Companions, that they would not follow except their methodology which is reported

---

306 Reported by al-Bukhaaree (Eng. trans. 5/43 no.51) and Muslim (Eng. trans. 4/1285 no.5918).

from them in the Qur'aan; and they would obliterate the presence of these elevated tombs and every manifestation of *shirk* and misguidance. Muhammad (ﷺ) would order the companions of theological rhetoric[307] and the Philosophers and all the sects who have deviated from the Qur'aan and the *Sunnah* to return to the Qur'aan and the *Sunnah* and, *"By Allaah, if Moosaa were to come it would not be correct except for him to follow me."*

Do you think that these are unimportant and insignificant matters?

$$\text{وَتَحْسَبُونَهُ هَيِّنًا وَهُوَ عِندَ ٱللَّهِ عَظِيمٌ}$$

"And you think that it is a harmless matter but it is something very serious with Allaah."[308]

But the matter is not as they suppose or as they are told, **indeed the corruption caused by the evil scholars, the priests and the rabbis, and the leaders of innovation is worse and more dangerous than the corruption caused by the rulers and others, since the people are deceived and taken in by them, so that they love them and trust their words and the way which they are upon. So they follow them and because of them stray from the way laid down by Allaah.**

Look at the Qur'aan which guides to what is right and proper and cures diseases and dangers with full knowledge, since it is Revelation sent down by One who is All-Knowing, All-Wise, Worthy of All-Praise. The Prophet (ﷺ) lived in the same time as the Jews who had no state and were cov-

---

[307] *'Ilmul-Kalaam:* Establishment of matters of belief (*'aqeedah*) by means of argument and debate, which they call 'intellect', instead of by means of textual proof, this being the way of the *Mu'tazilah, Ash'arees, Maatureedees* and others who stray from the way of the followers of the *Sunnah*. [Translator's Note]

[308] Soorah an-Noor (24):15.

ered with humiliation and misery. So how many are the *Aayaat* that were sent down concerning them, and how many are the places where they are censured, and where their evil deeds, corrupt actions, and filthy beliefs are exposed. Allaah, the Most High, says:

قُلْ يَٰٓأَهْلَ ٱلْكِتَٰبِ هَلْ تَنقِمُونَ مِنَّآ إِلَّآ أَنْ ءَامَنَّا بِٱللَّهِ وَمَآ أُنزِلَ إِلَيْنَا وَمَآ أُنزِلَ مِن قَبْلُ وَأَنَّ أَكْثَرَكُمْ فَٰسِقُونَ ۝ قُلْ هَلْ أُنَبِّئُكُم بِشَرٍّ مِّن ذَٰلِكَ مَثُوبَةً عِندَ ٱللَّهِ مَن لَّعَنَهُ ٱللَّهُ وَغَضِبَ عَلَيْهِ وَجَعَلَ مِنْهُمُ ٱلْقِرَدَةَ وَٱلْخَنَازِيرَ وَعَبَدَ ٱلطَّٰغُوتَ أُو۟لَٰٓئِكَ شَرٌّ مَّكَانًا وَأَضَلُّ عَن سَوَآءِ ٱلسَّبِيلِ ۝ وَإِذَا جَآءُوكُمْ قَالُوٓا۟ ءَامَنَّا وَقَد دَّخَلُوا۟ بِٱلْكُفْرِ وَهُمْ قَدْ خَرَجُوا۟ بِهِۦ وَٱللَّهُ أَعْلَمُ بِمَا كَانُوا۟ يَكْتُمُونَ ۝ وَتَرَىٰ كَثِيرًا مِّنْهُمْ يُسَٰرِعُونَ فِى ٱلْإِثْمِ وَٱلْعُدْوَٰنِ وَأَكْلِهِمُ ٱلسُّحْتَ لَبِئْسَ مَا كَانُوا۟ يَعْمَلُونَ ۝ لَوْلَا يَنْهَىٰهُمُ ٱلرَّبَّٰنِيُّونَ وَٱلْأَحْبَارُ عَن قَوْلِهِمُ ٱلْإِثْمَ وَأَكْلِهِمُ ٱلسُّحْتَ لَبِئْسَ مَا كَانُوا۟ يَصْنَعُونَ ۝ وَقَالَتِ ٱلْيَهُودُ يَدُ ٱللَّهِ مَغْلُولَةٌ غُلَّتْ أَيْدِيهِمْ وَلُعِنُوا۟ بِمَا قَالُوا۟ بَلْ يَدَاهُ مَبْسُوطَتَانِ يُنفِقُ كَيْفَ يَشَآءُ وَلَيَزِيدَنَّ كَثِيرًا مِّنْهُم مَّآ أُنزِلَ إِلَيْكَ مِن رَّبِّكَ طُغْيَٰنًا وَكُفْرًا وَأَلْقَيْنَا بَيْنَهُمُ ٱلْعَدَٰوَةَ وَٱلْبَغْضَآءَ إِلَىٰ يَوْمِ ٱلْقِيَٰمَةِ كُلَّمَآ أَوْقَدُوا۟ نَارًا لِّلْحَرْبِ أَطْفَأَهَا ٱللَّهُ وَيَسْعَوْنَ فِى ٱلْأَرْضِ فَسَادًا وَٱللَّهُ لَا يُحِبُّ ٱلْمُفْسِدِينَ ۝

"Say, O Muhammad, to the People of the Book, the Jews and Christians, 'Do you hate from us, or find anything against us, that carries you to mock our Religion, since when we are called to the prayer you poke fun at the call, except that we believe in the Book sent down to us by Allaah and in the Revealed Books sent down before to the Prophets, and most of you are rebellious and disobedient to Allaah.' Say to them, O Muhammad, 'Shall I tell you of what is worse in its recompense with Allaah, than what you think of us, the Jews whom Allaah has cursed and removed from His Mercy, and upon whom is His Anger, and from them were those whom He transformed into apes and swines, and those who worshipped idols. These are the ones who are worse in their plight in this world and the Hereafter, and are far astray from the right path.' When the hypocrites from the Jews come to you they say, 'We believe,' but they enter as unbelievers and leave as unbelievers, and Allaah knows best what they conceal. And you see many of them hastening for sin and transgression and devouring bribes. Evil indeed is that which they do. Why do not the Rabbis and the learned men forbid them from their falsehood and from devouring bribes. Evil indeed is what they practice. And the Jews say, 'Allaah's Hand is tied (He does not give of His Bounty).' Rather their hands be tied up from good and from giving, and they are accursed for what they say. Rather both His Hands are outstretched, He spends plentifully of His bounty, as He wills. And that which We reveal to you with regard to the affairs which the rabbis and learned of the Jews hide only increases many of them in obstinate rejection and disbelief. And We have placed enmity and hatred between the Jews and the Christians until the Day of Resurrection. Whenever they kindle the fire of war against you, Allaah extinguishes it, and they (the Jews and Christians) always strive to cause corruption upon the earth through sins and unbelief and disobedience to Allaah and His Messenger, and Allaah does not love those who cause corruption."[309]

He says concerning them:

$$\text{فَبِمَا نَقْضِهِم مِّيثَاقَهُمْ لَعَنَّاهُمْ وَجَعَلْنَا قُلُوبَهُمْ قَاسِيَةً يُحَرِّفُونَ ٱلْكَلِمَ عَن مَّوَاضِعِهِۦ وَنَسُوا۟ حَظًّا مِّمَّا ذُكِّرُوا۟ بِهِۦ وَلَا تَزَالُ تَطَّلِعُ عَلَىٰ خَآئِنَةٍ مِّنْهُمْ إِلَّا قَلِيلًا مِّنْهُمْ فَٱعْفُ عَنْهُمْ وَٱصْفَحْ إِنَّ ٱللَّهَ يُحِبُّ ٱلْمُحْسِنِينَ}$$ ﴿١٣﴾

"So because they broke their covenant We cursed them (the Jews) and caused their hearts to be hard. They change and alter the Words of their Lord and have abandoned a good part of what Allaah commanded them, and you will not cease to discover their treachery and breaking of covenants, except for a few of them. But forgive them and overlook their misdeeds. Indeed Allaah loves those who do good by forgiving and pardoning those who treat them badly."[310]

---

[309] Soorah al-Maa'idah (5):59-64.
[310] Soorah al-Maa'idah (5):13.

And the Messenger (ﷺ) lived in the time of the Christians who had empires and kings. The Roman Empire covered Europe, Greater Syria and Egypt. The Abyssinian Empire covered Abyssinia and Africa. So did the Qur'aan confront their rulers and kings, or did it confront the Christians themselves and their deviations, and at the head of them their monks and priests?!

Come, let us look to the Qur'aan to see who was more deserving of being confronted, and who actually was confronted. Allaah, the Most High, says:

$$\text{وَمِنَ ٱلَّذِينَ قَالُوٓاْ إِنَّا نَصَٰرَىٰٓ أَخَذْنَا مِيثَٰقَهُمْ فَنَسُواْ حَظًّا مِّمَّا ذُكِّرُواْ بِهِۦ فَأَغْرَيْنَا بَيْنَهُمُ ٱلْعَدَاوَةَ وَٱلْبَغْضَآءَ إِلَىٰ يَوْمِ ٱلْقِيَٰمَةِ وَسَوْفَ يُنَبِّئُهُمُ ٱللَّهُ بِمَا كَانُواْ يَصْنَعُونَ ۝}$$

"And We took a covenant from the Christians that they would obey Me, fulfil the obligatory duties, follow and believe in My Messengers. But they abandoned a good part of the covenant they were commanded with. So We planted enmity and hatred between them till the Day of Resurrection. And Allaah will soon inform them, when they return to Him, of their breaking their covenant, their altering His Book and His Commandments, and will punish them as they deserve."[311]

---

[311] Soorah al-Maa'idah (5):14.

He said concerning the Jews and the Christians:

وَقَالَتِ ٱلْيَهُودُ وَٱلنَّصَٰرَىٰ نَحْنُ أَبْنَٰٓؤُا۟ ٱللَّهِ وَأَحِبَّٰٓؤُهُۥ قُلْ فَلِمَ يُعَذِّبُكُم بِذُنُوبِكُم بَلْ أَنتُم بَشَرٌ مِّمَّنْ خَلَقَ يَغْفِرُ لِمَن يَشَآءُ وَيُعَذِّبُ مَن يَشَآءُ وَلِلَّهِ مُلْكُ ٱلسَّمَٰوَٰتِ وَٱلْأَرْضِ وَمَا بَيْنَهُمَا وَإِلَيْهِ ٱلْمَصِيرُ ۝

"And the Jews and the Christians said, 'We are the sons of Allaah and His beloved.' Say to those liars, 'Then why does your Lord punish you for your sins?' Rather you are human beings from those whom He created. He pardons whomever He wills by His grace and He justly punishes whomever He wills. And to Allaah belongs the dominion and control of the heavens and the earth and everything between them, and everything will return to Him."[312]

Allaah, the Most High, said:

ٱتَّخَذُوٓا۟ أَحْبَارَهُمْ وَرُهْبَٰنَهُمْ أَرْبَابًا مِّن دُونِ ٱللَّهِ وَٱلْمَسِيحَ ٱبْنَ مَرْيَمَ وَمَآ أُمِرُوٓا۟ إِلَّا لِيَعْبُدُوٓا۟ إِلَٰهًا وَٰحِدًا لَّآ إِلَٰهَ إِلَّا هُوَ سُبْحَٰنَهُۥ عَمَّا يُشْرِكُونَ ۝

---

[312] Soorah al-Maa'idah (5):18.

"They have taken their learned men and their Rabbis as lords besides Allaah, and also the Messiah, the son of Mary. But they were not ordered except to worship Allaah alone. None has the right to be worshipped except Him. How free and far removed is Allaah from the partners they associate with Him."[313]

'Adiyy ibn Haatim entered upon Allaah's Messenger (ﷺ) when he was reciting this *Aayah*, so he said, *"By Allaah, O Messenger of Allaah, we do not worship them (i.e. the priests and rabbis)'* So he said to him, *"Do they not declare forbidden things to be lawful, and so you declare them to be lawful; and they declare lawful things to be forbidden, and so you declare them to be forbidden?"* He said, *"Yes."* He said, *"That is worship of them."*[314]

He said with regard to the Jews and the Christians:

$$\text{يَٰٓأَيُّهَا ٱلَّذِينَ ءَامَنُوٓا۟ إِنَّ كَثِيرًا مِّنَ ٱلْأَحْبَارِ وَٱلرُّهْبَانِ لَيَأْكُلُونَ أَمْوَٰلَ ٱلنَّاسِ بِٱلْبَٰطِلِ وَيَصُدُّونَ عَن سَبِيلِ ٱللَّهِ ۗ وَٱلَّذِينَ يَكْنِزُونَ ٱلذَّهَبَ وَٱلْفِضَّةَ وَلَا يُنفِقُونَهَا فِى سَبِيلِ ٱللَّهِ فَبَشِّرْهُم بِعَذَابٍ أَلِيمٍ ۝٣٤}$$

"O you who believe in Allaah and His Messenger and affirm *tawheed* of your Lord: Many of the learned men and the Rabbis, from the Jews and the Chris-

---

[313] Soorah at-Tawbah (9):31.
[314] Reported by Ahmad and at-Tirmidhee. [Translator's Note]

tians, devour the wealth of men whilst changing the Book of Allaah, writing books with their own hands and claiming it to be from Allaah and then taking a small price for that; and they hinder people from entering into Islaam. And those who hoard up gold and silver and do not spend in the way of Allaah, then give them the tidings of a painful punishment on the Day of Resurrection."[315]

Allaah's Messenger (ﷺ) died whilst cursing the Jews and the Christians for their deviance in belief, so he said, *"Allaah's curse is upon the Jews and the Christians, they took the graves of their Prophets as places of Prayer.'"*[316]

The *Aayaat* and *ahaadeeth* rebuking them for their deviations in beliefs and manners are many, and there is not a single *Aayah* mentioning a rebuke of the Christian kings and rulers present in the time of the Prophet, despite their evil and corruption.

So why does the Islamic *da'wah* have this orientation?

It is because this is the true and correct methodology of *da'wah*, **and because the deviant leadership in religious matters is far more dangerous than corrupt leadership in political affairs, since religious leaders earn the trust and love of the people and their friendship. The people submit to them out of choice and lovingly. So if this religious leadership is misguided and deviant, then the people will deviate away from the methodology and way laid down by Allaah. They will lead them to Allaah's Anger and to the Fire, and even the rulers themselves may submit to these religious**

---
[315] Soorah at-Tawbah (9):34.
[316] Reported by al-Bukhaaree.

leaders and heads. So the Jew submits to religious leadership, the Christian does the same, and amongst those who claim attachment to Islaam, the *Shee'ee*, the *Mu'tazilee*, the *Ash'aree*, the *Khaarijee*, the *Soofee* and so on, are likewise.

So the deviant leaders and heads of religion are the ones who have corrupted the beliefs of this *ummah*, and their manners, their worship and their civilisation. They have ripped all this to shreds. So why do we flatter them and treat them and their danger lightly, when they are the source of every affliction?!! So over there we see the *Shee'ah* and the *Raafidees* and their various sects, and the evil heretics and apostates who are hidden amongst them. And over there are the leaders of *Sufism* and the heads of their many orders (*tareeqahs*) and their misguided beliefs, Unity of everything, the Creator and the created being one, the equality of all religions, that Allaah is incarnate within the creation, their acts of *shirk* and their innovations, and their deviations which do not stop at any limit. And over there are the heads of the *Khawaarij*, and the *Mu'tazilah*, the *Murjiah* and the *Jabariyyah*. All of these leaderships have crowned the *ummah* with trials and misfortunes whose extent is known only to Allaah. Then most of the Muslims are only puppets moved by these ideas just like the froth carried along by the torrent. So whoever sincerely and earnestly wishes to rectify the situation of the Muslims, then let him follow the way of the Prophets and their methodology, and at the head of them the final Prophet, and we have repeatedly made it clear.

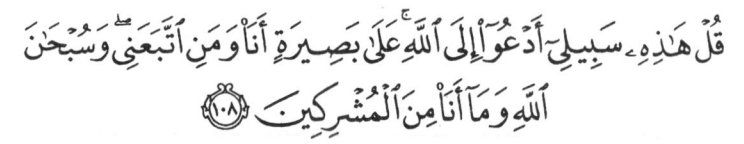

قُلْ هَٰذِهِۦ سَبِيلِىٓ أَدْعُوٓاْ إِلَى ٱللَّهِ عَلَىٰ بَصِيرَةٍ أَنَا۠ وَمَنِ ٱتَّبَعَنِى وَسُبْحَٰنَ ٱللَّهِ وَمَآ أَنَا۠ مِنَ ٱلْمُشْرِكِينَ ۝

"Say, O Muhammad (ﷺ), this is my way, I call to Allaah (i.e. to the testification that none has the right to be worshipped except Allaah, alone, with no partner) upon certain knowledge - I, and those who follow me. I declare Allaah free and far removed from all that they associate as partners with Him, and I am free of those who worship anything else along with Him."[317]

I believe that those who lead the youth and the callers to deviate from this methodology do not know the methodology and the call of the Prophets which is the best that can be said in their regard, whether the political calls, the *Soofee* calls or whatever else, since Allaah's Messenger (ﷺ) left us upon clear white guidance from which no one strays except that he is destroyed. **And whoever gives the impression to the people that the sole source of corruption is the rulers, then he is contradicting what is affirmed by the Noble Qur'aan, the Prophetic *Sunnah*, human and Islamic history, and he is seeking to better the methodology of the Prophets, particularly when the callers restrict all their efforts and apply them solely to the political field.** Rather the fundamental and primary source of corruption and danger are for those affirmed by Allaah upon the tongues of all His Messengers, and He laid down a methodology for them to block and rectify them. Then all other causes of corruption follow on from them. So let the caller to Allaah understand that, and let them cling to the Rope of Allaah, and let them adhere to the way of the Prophets, *'alayhimus-salaatu was-salaam*.

So these were some examples from the thoughts of Maududi, and the thought of this orientation which is followed by many people in the east and the west and has become, in their minds, the essence of Islaam, and their final goal for which they struggle and sacrifice. Then this view produced from the thinking of Maududi and others like him was given added support by some Islamic authors such as 'Abdul-Qaadir 'Awdah who said,

---

[317] Soorah Yoosuf (12):108.

"The rulings of Islaam were prescribed for this worldly life and for the Religion, and the rulings which Islaam came with are of two types:

"(i) Rulings meant for the establishment of the religion, and this covers the rulings of matters of beliefs (*'aqeedah*) and worship.

"(ii) Rulings meant for organisation of the State and the organised body of Believers, and establishment of relations between individuals and organised groups. This covers the rulings and mutual dealings, punishments, and personal, constitutional and state affairs... So Islaam combines the religion and the worldly affairs, and the mosque and the state. So it is a religion and a State, worship and leadership, and just as the religion is a part of Islaam, then the government is its second part, indeed the more important part of it."!318

So he believes that Islaam has two parts: religion (worship) being one part, and the State (leadership) being the other part. Then he declares the more important part to be the second (government), and this is a slight to the importance of the religion, of belief (*'aqeedah*) and worship (*'ibaadah*)...!

Then the intellectual Muslims in general, and some of the leaders of this orientation have realised that this orientation has led the youth into going beyond bounds in the importance they give to politics to the extent that it damages *'aqeedah* (belief) and the Call to Allaah and harms the youth themselves. They therefore put forward advice for them, and from these writers are:

---

318 *Al-Islaam Baina Jahl Abnaaihi Wa Ajz 'Ulamaa'ihi* p.80 and it was printed by the *Idaaraatul-Buhoothil-'Ilmiyyah wal-Iftaa wad-Da'wah wal-Irshaad*, and they did not caution against the error in these words.

1 - Sayyid Qutb[319], *rahimahullaah*, who said, "After long research and study of the movement of the *Ikhwaanul-Muslimoon*, and by comparing it with the first Islamic movement in Islaam, it becomes clear to my mind that the movement today faces a situation similar to that which human societies were upon when Islaam first came, with regard to ignorance of the reality of the Islamic *'aqeedah*, and their being far from the straight way and Islamic manners. It is not just a case of being far from the Islamic system and the Islamic *Sharee'ah*. Then at the same time we find strong colonialist armies of the Zionists and the Christians who wage war upon every attempt at Islamic *da'wah* and they work to demolish it using localised organisations and systems to establish and realise their plots and enforce their instructions for the attainment of this goal. **Therefore whilst Islamic movements occupy themselves much of the time with localised and limited political movements, such as fighting a treaty or agreement, or fighting against a party, or an opposition coalition in elections, and likewise preoccupy themselves with demanding from the governments that they follow and apply the Islamic system and *Sharee'ah*, then at the same time the societies themselves as a whole have become far removed from understanding the Islamic *'aqeedah* and from concern and respect for it,** and from Islamic manners, **therefore the Islamic movements must begin with the fundamental matter,** and that is to revive the meaning of the Islamic *'aqeedah* in the hearts and minds, and to educate and cultivate those who accept this call and the correct understanding with correct Islamic education and cultivation (*tarbiyah*), **and not to waste time in current political events, and not attempting to bring about the obligatory Islamic system by seizing power before the Islamic basis is found in the societies, then they will themselves seek the Islamic order because they comprehend its reality and**

---

[319] *Al-Muslimoon* magazine (1st year, no.3, 4/61405H, p.7) part of a series entitled, "Why did they execute me?" and it has been printed as a book with the same title, and this is found in it on p.28.

wish to judge by it... So attainment of application of the system of Islaam and rule by Allaah's *Sharee'ah* is not a goal that can be attained in the short term, since it cannot be achieved until the societies themselves, or a good proportion of them, carrying weight and importance in the life of the common people, are conveyed to **a correct understanding of the Islamic *'aqeedah*.** Then to the Islamic system, and correct Islamic cultivation upon the manners of Islaam. No matter how long and how many slow stages it takes." "This situation makes it a duty upon me that I begin with each youth and proceed slowly and carefully with the necessity of understanding the Islamic *'aqeedah* correctly before discussing the details of the Islamic system and laws, **and the necessity of avoidance of exerting efforts in present day domestic political movements in the Islamic lands**, in order to bring about correct Islamic cultivation (*tarbiyyah*) with the largest number of people possible. Then after this the following steps come naturally, following on from acceptance of and cultivation upon the principle in the society itself. This is because human societies today, including the societies in the Islamic lands, have come to closely resemble or be just like the societies of the days of ignorance (*Jaahiliyyah*) on the day when Islaam first came.[320] So it began with them from *'aqeedah* and manners, not with the Islamic laws and system. So today it is binding that the movement and the *da'wah* begins from the same point which Islaam first began with, and that it proceeds with similar steps whilst observing some changed circumstances."[321]

---

[320] It appears from this that Sayyid Qutb persisted in what he affirmed in his books such as *al-Dhilaal* and *Ma'aalim fit-Tareeq* (Milestones) and *al-'Adaalatul-Ijtimaa'iyyah* (Social Justice), that present-day Islamic societies are societies of ignorance (*jaahiliyyah*), and that Islaam refuses to recognise their correctness and their Islaam. But our witness of the Islamic nature of this is due to examining the results that come about, which is that being totally preoccupied with politics harms the Islamic youth and does not benefit them.

[321] *Limaadhaa A'damoonee* pp.6-7 in the magazine, and pp.28-30 and 34 of the book.

So these words from Sayyid and others is something good and correct which is a withdrawal from preoccupation with politics. However, unfortunately, Sayyid and others did not withdraw from mistakes in 'aqeedah and thinking which are still read and studied... so this has made it necessary that we should warn against Sayyid's mistakes in thinking and 'aqeedah in a special treatise, may Allaah facilitate its printing.[322]

2 - 'Umar at-Tilmisaanee, *rahimahullaah*, having been dismayed by the total preoccupation of the youth with the political side and lack of attention and importance for the other aspects of Islaam said, "However, unfortunately, whilst I am writing this at the beginning of the eighties, the work of the youth in the field of Islaam is restricted to the political aspect which takes up the greatest share of their efforts, and has caused them great strain and has caused them to lose a great deal. **It is as if nothing is counted as being from the Call of Allaah except the political aspect!....**" Then he said, indicating the reasons which led them to preoccupation with politics, "And there is no doubt that continual political events and the means through which successive governments sought to solve them, imposed themselves upon Egypt to the extent that they forced the Muslim youth to give their view about them and to suggest the solution. And whoever prevents the University students from thinking and giving their view about what affects their country internally and externally, then he is preventing them from a natural right of theirs..." Then he said, "However, at the same time, I criticise the University students for the fact that they almost entirely restrict their efforts and attention to the political side, and to using means which are not to be approved of. They do not establish a conference in the University or in al-Azhar or in any other place except for the political goals. Then would that they were ob-

---

[322] The first Arabic edition of *Adwaa Islaamiyyah 'alaa 'Aqeedah Sayyid Qutb wa fikrihi* was printed in 1414H and is a book of 238 printed pages, printed by *Maktabatul-Ghurabaa* in al-Madeenah. [Translator's Note]

jective in these conferences. This is something which they must understand and keep to..."[323]

So at-Tilmisaanee was correct in his criticism of this going overboard with regard to the political aspect, but he fell short in appraisal of its causes. Indeed, there is no doubt that what he mentioned is from the causes, but there are more important reasons producing a stronger effect upon the minds and emotions of the youth. These are the political thoughts which they grow up on, like the thoughts of al-Maududi which we have discussed in what has preceded in this treatise, and that was only a small part of a great deal from his writings and the writings of others from the leaders of this orientation.

So if it is the case that even some of the leaders of this orientation have realised the craving of the youth for politics and their excessiveness in it to the point that, "They almost entirely restrict their efforts and attention to the political side, and to using means which are not to be approved of," as at-Tilmisaanee said, then why do they not re-examine, out of mercy upon this youth, their training (*tarbiyyah*) systems and those dangerous political thoughts which must be studied carefully in the light of the Book and the *Sunnah*, and whatever agrees with the Book and the *Sunnah* is to be confirmed, and whatever does not agree with them is to be abandoned?

It is essential that the *ummah* is cultivated upon the correct *'aqeedah*, and this must be the foundation and starting point. And we ask Allaah that He grants the Islamic *ummah* and its callers that they accept and adhere to the methodology of the Prophets, wherein lies their well-being, success and ascendancy.

---

[323] *Al-Mawhoob Ustaadhul-Jeel* p.90.

Conclusion

In conclusion I say: Indeed I believe in the sovereign authority (*Haakimiyyah*) of Allaah and that judgement is for Allaah alone, and I believe in the comprehensiveness of this sovereign authority, and that all individuals, groups, rulers and callers must submit to it. And that whoever does not judge by what Allaah sent down in his call, and his *'aqeedah*, and his state, then they are the transgressors, the ones guilty of infidelity, and the wicked, as Allaah said and as understood by the Pious Predecessors (*as-Salafus-Saalih*), not as understood by those who go beyond bounds or those who fall short of what is correct. I reproach those who restrict it to one particular aspect or oppose the wise and clear methodology of the Prophets and begin with matters of detail before the fundamental principles, and with the means to an end which they turn into goals themselves and cause delay or fall short with regard to the true goals which were followed by all of the Prophets.

I hold out my hands, humbly beseeching Allaah that He guide all of the Muslims, their common folk, their rulers and their callers, that they should judge by and apply the Book of Allaah and the *Sunnah* of His Messenger, in all of their affairs - affairs of *'aqeedah*, manners and behaviour, economic affairs, social affairs and political affairs - and that He unites their ranks upon the Truth, and that He save them from all desires and sectarian beliefs and sicknesses of the souls which have split their ranks and shattered their unity.

Indeed my Lord hears and responds to the supplication, and may Allaah send His praises and blessings of peace upon our Prophet Muhammad and upon his family and true followers, and upon his Companions.

Appendix[324]

All praise is for Allaah alone, and may He send praises and blessings of peace upon the Messenger of Allaah, upon his family, true followers, his Companions and those who follow his way.

To proceed, I praise Allaah, with abundant, pure and blessed praise for every blessing which He has bestowed on me, and I give thanks to Him, the Most High, and praise and extol Him, and I cannot praise and extol Him as truly befits Him, and no-one can do so.

Then from the blessings which Allaah has bestowed on me is that He has enabled me, despite my weakness, to speak the truth openly according to my capability, whether in writing or face to face encounters, so I thank Him and praise Him with praise such as would fill the heavens and the earth and whatever is between them. I also ask that He grants me firmness upon that until I meet Him and that He is pleased with me. I further ask that He grants me increase in guidance to what is correct, and protection, and I do not forget, and all praise is for Allaah, that when my book, 'The Methodology of the Prophets in Calling to Allaah - That is the Way of Wisdom and Intellect,' was published it was accepted by the true Muslim youth in every place with joy and was greatly welcomed. This was because it made the call of the Prophets clear to them, until it became as clear as the sun in the middle of the day, and it removed confusion, distortions and the deception of some writers whose hearts were like those of devils in the form of humans those whose only concern is to gather the people around them and around their fraudulent slogans. It does not worry such people that this gathering of people should include the

---

[324] In the orignal Arabic print this was the "Introduction to the Second Edition" by the author. [Publisher's Note]

Raafidees (extreme *Shee'ah*), the hypocrites, the heretical *Khawaarij*,[325] the extreme Sufis who are guilty of apostasy, the ignorant and their like from the worshippers of the graves, or whichever of the wretched and unfortunate groups.

It does not worry them that this type of people rally together with them and rally to their slogans, despite the evil consequences of this in this world and the Hereafter. This is because they are as they were described by Allaah's Messenger (ﷺ), *"Callers to the gates of Hell, whoever answers their call will be thrown into it,"* and because they are as the sincere, truthful and trustworthy Messenger (ﷺ) described them, *"Devils in the bodies of humans."* If this is not the case then what is it that causes them, and those who follow their lead, to flee from and separate themselves from the clear and radiant way and methodology of the Prophets, which is made clear by the Qur'aan and shown to be their way and their methodology?

Tawheed of Allaah with regard to this His Names and Attributes, *tawheed* of Allaah in His Lordship, and *tawheed* of Allaah in His worship, and to disbelieve and reject everything that is worshipped besides Him - that is the pure religion. Allaah the Most High, says:

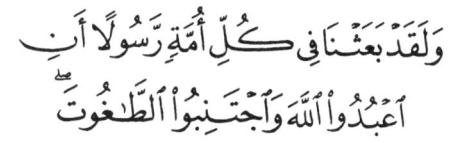

$$\text{وَلَقَدْ بَعَثْنَا فِي كُلِّ أُمَّةٍ رَسُولًا أَنِ اعْبُدُوا اللَّهَ وَاجْتَنِبُوا الطَّاغُوتَ}$$

"We sent a Messenger to every nation, ordering them that they should worship Allaah alone, obey Him and make their worship purely for Him, and that they

---

[325] For more details on the *Shee'ah* and the *Khawaarij* refer to "The Devils Deception", edited by Abu Ameenah Bilal Philips (Al-Hidaayah Publishing and Distribution, U.K., 1996).

should avoid everything worshipped besides Allaah."[326]

He said:

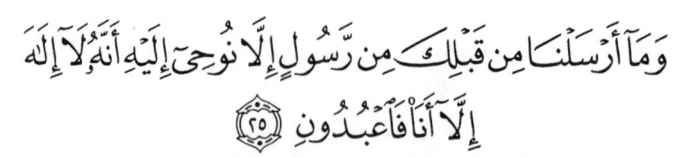

$$وَمَآ أَرْسَلْنَا مِن قَبْلِكَ مِن رَّسُولٍ إِلَّا نُوحِىٓ إِلَيْهِ أَنَّهُۥ لَآ إِلَٰهَ إِلَّآ أَنَا۠ فَٱعْبُدُونِ ۝$$

"We did not send any Messenger before you, O Muhammad (ﷺ), except that We revealed to Him that none has the right to be worshipped except Allaah - so make all of your worship purely for Allaah."[327]

Study any of the other *da'wah*s of the sects and parties - other than the *Salafee*[328] *da'wah* - do you see this methodology or any trace of it in their schooling, their persons, or their *jamaa'aat*? Then show it to me if you are truthful. As for myself I do not find in these sects and parties except that they wage a fierce war against this methodology and its people. I do not see except belittlement and mockery of this methodology and its people. I do not see except hatred and enmity for this methodology and its people, and I do not see except warm greetings and respect from them for the deviant and misguided calls and their people. Indeed you will frequently see and hear the last of these from those who disguise themselves as *Salafees* but are in reality closer in relation to their enemies, and

---

[326] Soorah an-Nahl (16):36.
[327] Soorah al-Ambiyaa (21):25.
[328] Publisher's note: One who attributes himself to the *salaf*. The *salaf* being primarily the Companions of the Prophet (ﷺ), and the two generations that came after them (*taabi'een* and the *atbaa at-taabi'een*). Therefore a *Salafee* will always refer to the Qur'aan and *Sunnah*, relying on the understanding of the *salaf*.

there are ties and relationships between them which are such as they are known only to Allaah.

Then there are some who are passionately in love with the state of superstitions, innovations and misguidance who think - and evil are their thoughts, and evil is the lie which they invent - that I make a separation between the religion and the State, and that I dispute about the importance of the subject of authority of sovereignty.

$$كَبُرَتْ كَلِمَةً تَخْرُجُ مِنْ أَفْوَاهِهِمْ إِن يَقُولُونَ إِلَّا كَذِبًا$$

"What a serious word it is that comes out of their mouths! What they say is nothing but a lie"[329]

So this book displeased them and it made clear the falsity of their calls and their misrepresentation and distortion of Islaam and of the text concerning *tawheed* - particularly with regard to the *da'wah* of the Messengers, may Allaah's praise and blessings of peace be upon them. The book did not join them in welcoming the state of the *Raafidee Shee'ahs*. Nor did it support them in seeking establishment of statelets founded upon the building of the tombs and upon the belief that the pious who have died know the Hidden and Unseen and have some control over the creation. Nor did it support them in seeking establishment of statelets based upon any such things as have preceded, nor in accepting the misguidance and *shirk* of secularism which seeks to disguise itself in the guise of Islaam.

Rather the book, and all praise is for Allaah, made clear that the true and trustworthy *da'wah* is that which follows the methodology of the Prophets in calling to Allaah, and the state which is established upon this correct methodology - that is the Islamic state. Then despite the fact that the

---

[329] Soorah al-Kahf (18):5.

book was dealing with a particular topic - which was to explain the methodology of the Prophets in calling to Allaah - it still gave attention to mentioning the Islamic state which it mentioned repeatedly and emphasised a number of times. It even had a chapter headed: "The View of the Scholars of Islaam with Regard to the Imaamate and their Proofs of its Obligation". Then the scholars sayings about that were quoted and their proofs mentioned. However what angered the people of innovations and desires, and the callers to falsehood, is that I placed leadership and the state in the place given to them by Allaah and which was accepted by the scholars of Islaam. I did not support the people of innovation and desires in their abandonment of the methodology of the Prophets in calling to *tawheed*, and fighting *shirk*, innovations and the rest of the types of misguidance and deviation, and fighting idolatry and grave-worship.

Nor did I support them in making leadership (*imaamate*) the most important matter, and the most fundamental principle - which is something which has led people to rejection of the methodology of the Prophets and has lead them to fight against it. It has also led them to fling themselves into the arms of the *Raafidee Shee'ah*, and to having affection for them, and to allying themselves with them, defending them and to falsley adorning their ideology which is at war with Islaam, in opposition to the Book and the *Sunnah* and waging war against the Companions of Allaah's Messenger (ﷺ) and his pure wives and the rest of the Muslims and their scholars. Indeed it goes beyond that to the point that they declare these great people to be disbelievers and make the foulest attacks against them.

I did not support them in this misguidance and this loathsome excess, so they disliked the book and thought evil about its author. they said the falsehood which they said in order to turn the youth who thirst for the truth away from the irrefutable and clear truth in this book. This book which openly spoke the truth and placed both correct creed and belief (*'aqeedah*) and the State in the place given to them by Allaah - without going beyond the bounds or falling short, and without distortion and deception. Then it is essential that I explain to the youth the distinction between the state (*ad-Dawlah*) and the dominion and sovereignty of Allaah (*al-Haakimiyyah*). As for the state, then it is a gathering of people who may be disbelievers, may be misguided deviants, or may be Believers. The people may be gathered under a rightly-guided *khilaafah*, or restricted kingships - which has been the case with the Islamic states after the rightly-guided *khilaafah*. So these individuals who form the Believing state are no more than the means to implement the *Sharee'ah* of Allaah - the establishment of *jihaad*, the ordering of good and forbidding of evil, establishment of the Prescribed Punishments and retribution, and the protection of the *ummah* from the plots and aggression of the enemies against the lands of the Muslims and against their souls, their wealth and their honour. So the Muslims must establish a state to accomplish these great obligations - either: by giving the pledge of allegiance to a *khaleefah* whom all of the Muslims are united upon; or by the fact that an individual from the *ummah* gains ascendancy and has power, an army and authority - which means that the benefit of the *ummah* lies in accepting him as long as he proclaims Islaam, establishes the laws and the creed (*'aqeedah*) and protects the *ummah* from its enemies and does whatever is required, the details of which are known and mentioned in the source works of Islaam; or by the fact that some individuals gain ascendancy over some areas as happened in the lands of Islaam after the weakening of the *khilaafah*, so overall benefit necessitated submitting to this situation.

As for dominion and sovereignty then these are attributes of Allaah and qualities particular to Him alone, as He, the Most High, says:

إِنِ ٱلْحُكْمُ إِلَّا لِلَّهِ

أَمَرَ أَلَّا تَعْبُدُوٓا۟ إِلَّآ إِيَّاهُ ذَٰلِكَ ٱلدِّينُ ٱلْقَيِّمُ

"Judgement and command is for Allaah alone, He ordered that you should worship none but Him. That is the true and straight religion."[330]

This authority and sovereignty is not denied except by one who is a disbeliever in Allaah and is severe in his enmity to Allaah, His Messenger (ﷺ) and His Books. Indeed one who even denies Allaah's authority in the slightest matter, not to mention with regard to fundamental matters, then he is a disbeliever in Allaah, outside the fold of Islaam if he knowingly denies that. As for the ignorant person, then he has excuse until the proof is established against him.

What I have said applies to the rulers, the ruled and to indivduals and groups (*Jamaa'aat*). This has been affirmed by the trustworthy scholars of Islaam, and from them Shaykhul-Islaam Ibn Taymiyyah, *rahimahullaah,*[331] and his student Ibnul-Qayyim.[332] So whoever accepts and abides by this rule and authority in the fundamentals of the religion and its details, and in matters of creed and belief, and matters of worship, and dealings and political affairs, and economic affairs, and manners, and social affairs - then he is a Believer. But he who does not abide by it all or some of these then he is a disbeliever, whether he is an individual or a group, a ruler or one ruled, a caller or one called. Indeed I fear, by Allaah, for many of the sects, parties and individuals that they may fall into disbelief due to their not abiding by the rule and authority of Allaah with regard to the fundamentals of the religion, indeed with regard also to its details. I fear for many of them, against whom the proof has been established and to whom the truth has been made clear, yet still they persist in

---

[330] Soorah Yoosuf (12):40.
[331] *Minhaajus-Sunnah an-Nabawiyyah* (3/32) where he clearly explains that one not accepting the rule and authority of Allaah is a disbeliever, and he explains how that applies in matters of knowledge and action.
[332] *Madaarijus-Saalikeen* (91/336).

opposing the call to *tawheed* and oppose waging war against *shirk* and innovation, aswell as opposing its people and to cutting off from them. Instead these people incite others against and warn against those who call with the call of the Prophets, and those who seek truly and sincerely to amend the affairs. After establishment of the proof against such a person he would fall into the abyss of disbelief.

I call all of the *ummah* - its rulers and its ruled, its individuals, sects, and parties, to all have true belief in the all-encompassing authority and sovereignty of Allaah which covers the fundamental matters of the religion and its details, and that they should fully abide by it with regard to the fundamental matters of the religion and its details. I also call the heads of the states, from those who abide generally by the rule and authority of Allaah, and yet are negligent in some areas of practice, I call them to abide by it totally and unrestrictedly in every field, in the matter of *'aqeedah*, worship, dealings, economics, politics, with regard to ordering good and forbidding evil, that they should strive to fight against *shirk* and innovations, and against sins and against evil - particularly usury and the rest of the major sins which harm the *ummah* and its manners. Indeed Allaah prevents by means of the rulers those who are not prevented by the Qur'aan. They should be fully aware that Allaah will question them about every small and large matter which they are responsible for. *"Each of you is a guardian and is responsible for those whom he is in charge of."* I also remind them of the saying of the Prophet, *"There is no ruler having authority over Muslim subjects who dies while he is deceiving them except that Allaah has forbidden Paradise for him."*[333] and his saying, *"There is no servant whom Allaah places in authority over some people, and he does not deal with them sincerely and honestly, except that he will not find the fragrance of Paradise."*[334]

---

[333] Reported by al- Bukhaaree (Eng. trans. 9/197/no.265).
[334] Al-Bukhaaree (Eng. trans. 9/197/264).

From sincerity to the *ummah* is that you encourage them to abide by the rule of Allaah and His *Sharee'ah*, by teaching them, directing them, encouraging and warning them, by ordering the good and forbidding the evil, by establishing prescribed punishment and using every means which will cause them to respect the *Sharee'ah* of Allaah in *'aqeedah*, worship, political affairs and manners.

I also call the heads of state in Islamic lands who do not abide by the *Sharee'ah* of Allaah that they should turn back to Allaah and respect His religion which is found in the Book and the *Sunnah*, and that they should cling to the creed and beliefs of this religion and its rulings, and to be proud of that - since therein lies honour and nobility. However total disgrace and humiliation comes from submission to laws laid down by the most despicable humans, the enemies of this *ummah* whether they are Jews, Christians, Magians or atheists. So I call such leaders to respect the feelings of the *ummah* of Islaam which has striven and fought and sacrificed millions of its sons for the achievement of a noble and lofty goal - which is that it should be ruled by Islaam, and Islaam alone is the religion of Allaah, the Creator of this creation, the Creator of mankind and *jinn* so that they should worship Him alone and submit to His revealed laws alone. They should abide by the *Sharee'ah* of Allaah and impose it upon the *ummah* in creed and beliefs, in manners, in teaching and in Islamic curriculae which education and training are to be based upon.

I also enjoin the scholars of the *ummah*, its callers, parties and groups that they should sincerely advise all of the *ummah*, its elders and its youth, its males and its females, and unite them upon the Book of Allaah, the *Sunnah* of his Messenger, and upon the methodology and understanding of the *Salafus-Saalih* (the Pious Predecessors), the Companions, the *Taabi'een* and those who followed them upon good, the *imaams* of guidance, the scholars of *fiqh*, the scholars of *hadeeth* and of *tafseer*, in creed and beliefs, in worship, in manners, in dealings, in economic affairs, and all the other affairs of Islaam and *eemaan*. Then they should fully comprehend the Sayings of Allaah, the Most High,

﴿وَمَن لَّمْ يَحْكُم بِمَآ أَنزَلَ ٱللَّهُ فَأُو۟لَٰٓئِكَ هُمُ ٱلْكَٰفِرُونَ ۝﴾

"And whoever does not judge by what Allaah has revealed then they are the ones guilty of infidelity."[335]

﴿وَمَن لَّمْ يَحْكُم بِمَآ أَنزَلَ ٱللَّهُ فَأُو۟لَٰٓئِكَ هُمُ ٱلظَّٰلِمُونَ ۝﴾

"And whoever does not judge by what Allaah has revealed then they are the transgressors."[336]

﴿وَمَن لَّمْ يَحْكُم بِمَآ أَنزَلَ ٱللَّهُ فَأُو۟لَٰٓئِكَ هُمُ ٱلْفَٰسِقُونَ ۝﴾

"And whoever does not judge by what Allaah has revealed then they are the disobedient."[337]

They should understand that these Sayings of Allaah apply to all individuals, groups, rulers and subjects. So to restrict it to refer to the rulers alone and not to the people of deviant sects and misguidance, those who do not judge by the *Sharee'ah* of Allaah in their creed and beliefs, nor in their worship and their behaviour, then this is from ignorance, misguidance and foolishness, since Allaah sent these *Aayaat* down concerning the Jews at a time when they had not had any state or authority for centuries. He sent these *Aayaat* down concerning them at a time when He had imposed humiliation and lowliness upon them. I have explained the authority and sovereignty of Allaah in this broad and all-embracing sense in the book itself. I should also not fail to draw attention to an error made by the author of '*Meezaanul-I'tidaal litaqyeem Kitaabil-Mawridiz-Zallaal fir-Tanbeeh 'alaa Akhtaa'iz Zilaal,*' who is 'Isaam ibn

---

[335] Soorah al-Maa'idah (5):44.
[336] Soorah al-Maa'idah (5):45.
[337] Soorah al-Maa'idah (5):47.

Muhammad ibn Taahir al-Barqaawee, who attributed to me something which my tongue has never uttered and which I never believed, nor have I ever written such a thing. Furthermore I seek Allaah's refuge from what he said, and I declare myself free before Allaah from it, and I ask Allaah to save me and all the Muslims from it. Al-Barqaawee said in a footnote (p.15) to his aforementioned book: "This also reminds me of what Shaykh Rabee' ibn Haadee al-Madkhalee, *hafidhahullaahu ta'aalaa*, did in his book, '*Manhajul-Ambiyaa fid-Da'wah illallaah...*' when he criticised the view of al-Maududi, *rahimahullaah ta'aalaa*, about the importance of leadership (*imaamah*), *khilaafah*, and judging by that which Allaah sent down, since he also sought to use as evidence the saying of Shaykhul-Islaam Ibn Taymiyyah about the position of the *imaamah* with the Raafidee (*Shee'ahs*). So he took up six pages in quoting the discussion of Shaykhul-Islaam with those *Raafidee (Shee'ahs)*. However the numerous and great differences between the beliefs of the *Raafidees* concerning the *imaamah* and the infallibility of the *Imaams*, and the twelve *imaams* and so on, and between what al-Maududi and others call to, i.e. the necessity and importance of striving to return to judging by the *Sharee'ah*, through the *khilaafah*, and to establish a single ruler for the people of Islaam; the differences between these two are well known. Even if the words of Shaykhul-Islaam Ibn Taymiyyah contain something which is fitting in this regard, yet most of it, if a just person were to examine it, is not fitting to this discussion, rather it applies to the matter of *imaamah* with the *Raafidee (Shee'ah)* with its well known details... so he should not have quoted it all... for fear of deception."

Al-Barqaawee's scales are unbalanced and he has not judged between myself and al-Maududi with justice, and perhaps he has forgotten the saying of Allaah:

$$\text{وَزِنُوا۟ بِٱلْقِسْطَاسِ ٱلْمُسْتَقِيمِ}$$

"And weigh justly with the true balance."[338]

---

[338] Soorah al-Israa (17):35.

And His saying,

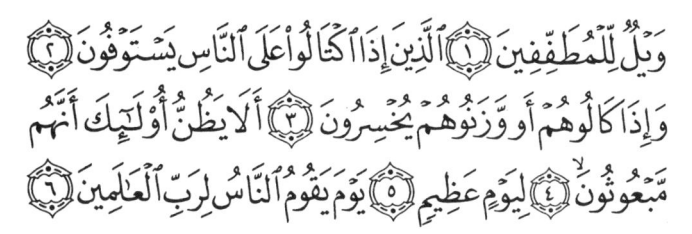

$$\bismillah \; وَيْلٌ لِّلْمُطَفِّفِينَ ۝ ٱلَّذِينَ إِذَا ٱكْتَالُواْ عَلَى ٱلنَّاسِ يَسْتَوْفُونَ ۝ وَإِذَا كَالُوهُمْ أَو وَّزَنُوهُمْ يُخْسِرُونَ ۝ أَلَا يَظُنُّ أُوْلَٰٓئِكَ أَنَّهُم مَّبْعُوثُونَ ۝ لِيَوْمٍ عَظِيمٍ ۝ يَوْمَ يَقُومُ ٱلنَّاسُ لِرَبِّ ٱلْعَٰلَمِينَ ۝$$

"Woe to those who give short measure to others. Those who demand full measure from others, but when they give them in measure or weight then they give them less than their due. Do these people not think that they will be resurrected for reckoning on a formidable Day. The Day when all mankind will stand before the Lord of the Worlds."[339]

O brother al-Barqaawee, I was debating the view of al-Maududi about the importance of the matter of leadership (*imaamah*), the *khilaafah* and judging by that which Allaah has sent down!

As regards the fact of their importance, then no Believer having a trace of *eemaan* would dispute that. But O brother you have failed to note the point of disagreement between myself and al-Maududi. I debated with the view of al-Maududi with regard to his going beyond the due limits about leadership to such an extent that no Muslim who has respect for Islaam could remain silent about this excess, and it was of such a level that even the misguided would not accept it, not to mention the people of *hadeeth* and the *Salafees*. Indeed very many scholars from his own land, from the *Salafees* and others have replied to him. Then this excess of his has travelled and has reached many Arab and Islamic lands, and it has fooled an overwhelming majority of authors and youth, which has

---

[339] Soorah al-Mutaffifeen (83):1-6.

led to great neglect of the *'aqeedah* of *tawheed*, and even comtempt of it and of its people. It has also led people to treat *shirk* and innovation lightly and has caused al-Maududi and his like to ally themselves with and to befriend the devotees of the graves and even the *Raafidees (Shee'ah)*, and to gather these people under their banner, to treat them as brothers, to love and defend them and their beliefs and creed, and this is something which is a reality and is clear to everyone possessing intellect and religion. So since the matter has reached this frightful state, I replied to al-Maududi with regard to some of his excess in order to make the people in general aware, and also the people of the Arabian Peninsula, to which the followers of al-Maududi and their helpers direct their attention. So they seek to wipe away the *'aqeedah* of *tawheed*, and the *'aqeedah* of true and correct alliance and enmity (*al-Walaa wal-Baraa*). Do you think that my reply to al-Maududi was so unreasonable that you seek to defend his view with falsehood, and by forgetting to judge justly, to the point that you take my words to mean something which I did not say, and which they did not mean?! Listen to what al-Maududi says:

"The question of leadership is the most important matter in human life and its most fundamental principle." Then try to defend this saying with clear and unequivocal texts from the Book of Allaah and the *Sunnah* of His Messenger, and the words of the Companions and the scholars of Islaam. If you have not seen this, then you must adjust your scales in order to establish justice, equity and fairness, and to abandon the excess which has led al-Maududi and his followers to scorn the call of the Prophets and the goal of their *da'wah*, and to turn the affairs upside down. Listen to his saying: "The true goal of the religion is to establish the system of the rightly guided and righteous leadership (*imaamah*)." So to him this is the true goal of the religion. So *tawheed*, and the Prayer, and *Zakaat*, and *jihaad* and other matters from the religion become only means to reach this goal in the view of al-Maududi. So produce the clear proofs from the Book of Allaah and the *Sunnah* of His Messenger (ﷺ),

in place of al-Maududi, to support this and if you are unable then do not be too embarrassed to say, 'This poor weak servant, Rabee' ibn Haadee, has spoken the truth and has been sincere towards Islaam and the Muslims, and has put matters in their due place.' Then listen to the saying of al-Maududi: "This is the purpose for which the Prayer, Fasting, the *Zakaat* and the *Hajj* have been made obligatory in Islaam. Then the fact that they are called acts of worship does not mean that they are themselves worship, rather its meaning is that they prepare mankind for the true and fundamental worship, and these are a training course which are essential for that.' He also says, 'You think that standing facing the *Qiblah*, placing the right hand upon the left, and *rukoo'* with your hands upon your knees, and prostration upon the ground, and reciting particular words, and these actions and movements are themselves worship; and you think that fasting from the start of *Ramadaan* until the start of *Shawwaal*, and going hungry and thirsty from morning until evening, you think that this is worship; and you think that reciting a number of *Aayaat* from the Qur'aan is worship; and you think that performing *Tawaaf* around the *Ka'bah* is worship. In summary you have called the manifestation of certain actions worship, and when a person performs these actions with their form and manners you think that he has worshipped Allaah... but the truth is that the worship which Allaah created you for, and which he ordered you to perform is something else."[340]

Are you pleased by this derisive manner about speaking about the great pillars of Islaam and those who worship in this way? These are not, in the view of al-Maududi, forms of worship for which man was created, rather the worship for which man was created and which they were ordered to fulfil is something else. O Barqaawee, do you take this as your religion before Allaah? That the forms of worship are only a training course which

---

[340] Quoted from the book, "The book of al-Maududi, what is for it and what is against it," of Muhammad Zakariyyaa al-Kandahlaawee (pp.45-46), 2nd Edn.

if applied will... etc. Is this something stated textually in the Qur'aan and the *Sunnah*, and which the Prophets came with and which was accepted by the best of the people of this *ummah*? If you agree with al-Maududi then bring the proofs to support his saying. Otherwise bite upon your knuckles in regret and grief for having deserted the truth and offended its people and helped falsehood. This, O my brother, was the subject of my debate with al-Maududi, and about which I quoted the words of Shaykhul-Islaam concerning the exceeding of the bounds by the *Raafidees* about leadership (imaamate). What I quoted from him was all relevant, not just a part of it as al-Barqaawee claimed. Then if you were correct, O Barqaawee, then why did you not explain what was relevant from the words of Shaykhul-Islaam and what was not? As for the claim of 'infallibility' for the 'twelve imaams,' then I did not attribute it to al-Maududi, nor did I debate about it with him, nor did I quote Shaykhul-Islaam's words about it. So your words are totally opposed to justice! As for your equity and justice which you set up for yourself in judging between Sayyid Qutb and ad-Duwaysh, then I do not know what you have done. Indeed you have totally failed to be just between myself and al-Maududi, and how would it have harmed you to speak the truth? Then as for the *khilaafah*, I do not know if you read what I wrote and quoted from the scholars of Islaam, or if you merely took the subject with the tips of your fingers with your eyes closed, thinking that justice and equity would be achieved that easily. So read this and that anew and speak the truth, supporting it with proof, not alarmism and agitation!

As for judging by that which Allaah sent down, then how can you imagine that I would dispute about it with al-Maududi or anyone else, when it is something known necessarily in the religion, and not even the deviant and deviated sects dispute about it?! So I seek Allaah's refuge from what the author of *'al-Meezaan,'* attributed to me. Rather read again what I wrote concerning the authority and sovereignty of Allaah, and that it comprehends every part of the religion, and you will see the extent of the mistake of al-Barqaawee, may Allah guide him. Then finally the points of criticism of al-Maududi and his like are so many that this introduction is not the place for them. But in summary, he is one of those furthest from abiding by the authority and sovereignty of Allaah with regard to his *'aqeedah* and his *fiqh*, and with regard to his stance on the *Sunnah* of Allaah's Messenger (ﷺ), and his stance with regard to the Companions of Allaah's Messenger (إِنِ ٱلْحُكْمُ إِلَّا لِلَّهِ), and with regard to their enemies the *Raafidee Shee'ah*. Indeed he and his followers have alliance and friendship with those *Raafidees*, they support them and they praise their *Taaghoot*, al-Khomeini and his students, the *Aayatur-Raafidiyyah*. So noble reader be aware of this, and judge the people according to the truth, and do not judge the truth according to its people, and beware of falling into the abyss of over-exaggerated respect for personalities so that it leads you to reject the truth, and to argue against its people.

May Allaah guide and grant the *ummah* to loving the truth and its people. Indeed my Lord hears and responds to supplications.

Written by:
Rabee' ibn Haadee al-Madkhalee,
13/6/1413H.

Glossary

Aayah (pl. Aayaat): the Words or a Sign of Allaah; a verse of the Qur'aan.
Aayaat: See *Aayah.*
Aboo (Abee, Abaa): father of; used as a means of identification.
'Alayhis-salaam: "may Allaah protect and preserve him." It is said after the name of a Prophet of Allaah or after the name of an angel.
Ahaadeeth: See *Hadeeth.*
Ansaar: "Helpers"; theMuslims of Madeenah who supported the Muslims who migrated from Makkah.
Ash'aree: the name of one who attributes himself to the *Ash'ariyyah* which is the name of a creed attributed to Abul-Hasan al-Ash'aree (d.324H)-*rahimahullaah* -He initially advocated the belief of the *Mu'tazilah*. After learning from Ibn Kullaab, al-Ash'aree gave up the beliefs of the *Mu'tazilah* and formulated a new doctrine by piecing together (*talfeeq*) doctrines from different Muslim sects. This belief then became known as *'Aqeedah Ash'ariyyah*. Towards the end of his life Abul-Hasan-Ash'aree rejected this belief too and accepted the beliefs of *Ahl us-Sunnah wal-Jama'ah*. He realised that success lies only in following the way of the *Salaf,* in the way they understood the *Deen.* For the *Deen* was not revealed, so that the people may develop their own ideas of what to believe. For Allaah sent a Messenger with the Book to explain it, so that the people would have no excuse to dispute regarding its meaning. It is simply a case of affirming what Allaah had revealed be it in His Book or upon the tongue of His Messenger. So, Abul-Hasan al-Ash'aree said in his book *al-Ibaanah 'an Usool id-Diyaanah,* "We have faith in the Qur'aan and the traditions and therefore hold the opinion that these have to be followed ungrudgingly. What has been handed down by the Companions, their Successors and the traditionists has to be accepted completely and with unquestioning submission, for this was the way of Ahmad ibn Hanbal." In this book he also affirmed the attributes of Allaah which the *Jahmiyyah* and the *Mu'tazilah* rejected, saying that these have to be accepted as

stated in the texts, believing in them and without asking how they are. This is totally opposite to the belief of those who call themselves Ash'arees, for they, instead of affirming Allaah's attributes as stated in the Book and the *Sunnah*, explain them away by means of ta'weel (interpretation)-assigning false meanings to them such as their saying that Allaah's Hand (*Yad*) means His Power (*Quwwah*) and similar futile sayings.

He also affirmed those things which the *Jahmiyyah* and *Mu'tazilah* rejected, such as the Believers seeing Allaah in the Hereafter and the Punishment in the grave.

Awliyaa:

Badr: The first decisive battle between three hundred and thirteen Muslims and one thousand *Mushriks* fought in the second year after Hijrah, in Ramadaan.

Companions (Ar. *Sahaabah*): the Muslims who saw the Prophet (ﷺ) and died upon Islaam.

Da'ee: one engaged in *Da'wah*; caller.

Da'wah: invitation; call to Allaah.

Deen: way of life prescribed by Allaah i.e. Islaam.

Dhikr: remembrance of Allaah with the heart and tongue, and remembrance of what He has ordered and prohibited.

Eemaan: faith; to affirm all that was revealed to the Messenger (ﷺ), affirming with the heart, testifying with the tongue and acting with the limbs. The actions of the limbs are from the completeness of *Eemaan*. Faith increases with obedience to Allaah and decreases with disobedience.

Fard: An action which Allaah and His Messenger have made obligatory; one who does the action is rewarded and one who fails to do it is punished (unless Allaah chooses to forgive him). There are two types: *fard-'ayn*- an action which is obligatory on every sane, mature individual (eg. the prayer), and *fard kifaayah*- an act obligatory on Muslims: if fulfilled by one or more of them, it absolves the others of the responsibility, otherwise all are sinful (eg. the funeral prayer).

Ghayb: Matters relating to Allaah, His Angels, Predecree, Paradise and the Fire aand so on, which we can only know about through the Revelation brought by the Messenger of Allaah (ﷺ).

Haakimiyyah: The sovereign authority of Allaah.

Hadeeth (pl. **Ahaadeeth**): narration concerning the utterances of the Prophet (ﷺ), his actions or an attribute of his.

Hajj: Pilgrimage to Makkah.

Hijrah: the migration of the Prophet (ﷺ) from Makkah to al-Madeenah; migration of the Muslims from the land of the disbelievers to the lands of the Muslims.

Hulool: The belief that Allaah is incarnate and to be found within His creation, a deviant Soofee belief.

'Ibaadah: worship; worship of Allaah.

Ibn: son of; used as a means of identification.

Ijmaa': "consensus"; a unified opinion of scholars regarding a certain issue.

Imaam: leader; leader in *Salaah*, knowledge or *fiqh*; leader of a state.

Jaahiliyyah: ignorance; the period before the advent of the Prophet (ﷺ).

Jamaa'ah: the united body of the Muslims, together upon the truth, i.e. the Companions and those who remain upon their way.

Jihaad: striving and fighting to make the Word of Allaah supreme.

Jinn: a creation of Allaah created from smokeless fire.

Jizya: a tax levied on the non-Muslims living under the authority of the Muslims [see Soorah at-Tawbah (9:29)].

Kaafir (pl. **Kuffaar**): a rejector of Islaam i.e. a disbeliever.

Khaleefah (pl. Khulafaa'): the head of the Islamic government (the *khilaafah*) to whom the oath of allegiance is given.

Khaarijee (pl. **Khawaarij**): Those who declare that a Muslim becomes a *Kaafir* due to committing a major sin alone. The first *Khawaarij* split away from the army of 'Alee-*radiallaahu 'anhu*- and declared him and other prominent Companions to be Disbelievers.

Khilaafah: the Islamic state.

Khulafaa': see *khaleefah*.
Khutbah: sermon.
Kufr: Disbelief.
Manhaj: Way; method; methodology.
Muhaajir: One who migrates from the lands of the disbelievers to the land of the Muslims for the sake of Allaah.
Muhaddith: scholar of the science of *hadeeth*.
Murji'ah: They are the extreme opponents of the *Khawaarij*. They believe that *Eemaan* (faith) is mere knowledge, that one does not lose it through sin no matter how grave. Whether or not he will be punished in the Hereafter is left to the Will and Mercy of Allaah; hopefully he will be forgiven. The extremists amongst them believe that given faith, sin will cause no harm in the Hereafter. However what is correct is that actions are part of *Eemaan* (faith), and *Eemaan* increases with good actions and decreases with evil actions. The claim of the Murji'ah that *Eemaan* is constant, and that the *Eemaan* of all the Muslims (including the Prophet (ﷺ), the Companions etc.) is the same is far from the truth. In fact this misbelief has been a major cause for the Muslims to leave doing the acts of worship thinking that their mere utterance of the *shahaadah* (declaration of faith) is enough to save them on the Last Day.
Mushrik: one who worships others along with Allaah or ascribes one or more of Allaah's attributes to other than Him; one who commits *shirk*.
Mu'tazilah: The name which was given to Waasil ibn Ataa and his friends and their followers when he left his teacher Hasan al-basree (d.110/728) on the issue regarding the position of one who commits a major sin (*kabeerah*). Waasil (d.131/748) said that he is neither a Muslim nor a Kaafir; he has a position between belief and disbelief.
Qiblah: the direction the Muslims face during prayer (i.e. towards Makkah).
Qiyaas: analogical deduction of Islamic laws. New laws are deduced from old laws based on a similarity between their causes.

Raafidee: The correct title for the extreme *Shee'ah*. Those who bear malice and grudge against the noble Companions, to the extent that they declare them to be apostates. They also hold that the Qur'aan which the Muslims have is neither complete nor preserved from corruption.

Radiyallaahu 'anhu/'anhaa/'anhum/'anhumaa: may Allaah be pleased with him/her/them/both of them.

Rahimahullaah/Rahimahumullaah: may Allaah bestow His mercy upon him/them.

Rak'ah: one cycle of the Prayer, consisting of standing, bowing and prostrating.

Ramadaan: the ninth month of the Islamic calendar, in which the Muslims fast.

Ruboobiyyah: See *Tawheed*.

Rukoo': "bowing," a part of the prayer.

Sahaabah: the companions of the Prophet (ﷺ). See Companions.

Saheeh: correct; an authentic narration.

Salaat: prescribed prayer (e.g. the five obligatory prayers); prayers upon the Prophet (ﷺ).

Salaf: predecessors; the early Muslims; the Muslims of the first three generations: the *Companions*, the *Successors* and their successors.

Salafee: one who ascribes himself to the *salaf* and follows in their way.

Salafus-Saaliheen: pious predecessors; the Muslims of the first three generations: the *Companions*, the *Successors* and their successors.

Seerah: The life story of the Prophet (ﷺ).

Shaykh: scholar.

Sharee'ah: the Divine code of Law.

Shawaal: the tenth month of the Islamic calendar. It is the month after Ramadaan.

Shee'ah: A collective name for various sects claiming love for Ahl ul-Bait. See *Raafidee*.

Shirk: assocciating partners with Allaah; compromising any aspect of *tawheed*.

Soorah: a Chapter of the Qur'aan.

Successor(Ar. Taabi'i pl. *Taabi'een*):a Muslim (other than another Companion) who met a Companion.

Sujood: "prostration," a part of the prayer.

Sunnah: in its broadest sense, the entire *Deen* which the Prophet (ﷺ) came with and taught, i.e. all matters of belief, rulings, manners and actions which were conveyed by the *Companions*. It also includes those matters which the Prophet (ﷺ) established by his sayings, actions and tacit approval - as opposed to *bid'ah* (innovation).

sunnah: an action of the Prophet (ﷺ).

Soorah: a chapter of the Qur'aan.

Taabi'ee (pl. Taabi'een): a Muslim (other than another *Companion*) who met a *Companion*.

Taabi'een: see *taabi'ee*.

Taaghoot: one who goes beyond the limits (set by Allaah); one who is worshipped besides Allaah and is pleased with it.

Tafseer: explanation of the Qur'aan.

Takbeer: "Allaahu akbar."

Taqwa: "*taqwa* is acting in obedience to Allaah, hoping for His mercy upon light from Him and *Taqwa* is leaving acts of disobedience, out of fear of Him, upon light from Him."

Tashahud: From *shahaadah* (to witness); the sitting in Prayer in which one bears witness that there is no true god except Allaah, and that Muhammad (ﷺ) is His Messenger.

Tawaaf: circling the Ka'bah seven times as an act of worship (many ignorant people have begun to circle graves and other such places, this is completely forbidden, being a flagrant violation of the Qur'aan and the Sunnah).

Tawheed: Allaah is the only Lord of creation, He alone, is their provider and sustainer, Allaah has Names and Attributes that none of the creation share and Allaah is to be singled out for worship, alone. Tawheed is maintaining the Oneness of Allaah in all the above mentioned categories. Islaam makes a clear distinction between the Creator and the created.

Ummah: "nation"; the Muslims as a group.

Wahdatul-Wujood: The belief that everything in existence is infact Allaah. This deviant belief is one held by many Soofees.

Zakaat: charity that is obligatory on anyone who has wealth over and above a certain limit over which a year has passed.